# ANCIENT NOMADS

## of the Eurasian and North American Grasslands

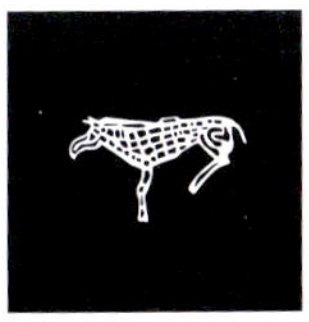
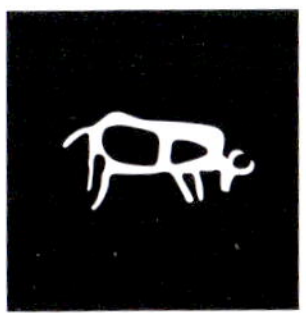

**Elena Ponomarenko and Ian Dyck**
with contributions by Anna Kochkina, Ludmila Kuznetsova,
Dmitry Stashenkov, Mikhael Turetzky and Edward Dubman

Canadian Museum of Civilization Corporation
Samara Museum of History and Regional Studies

Published by the Samara Museum of History and Regional Studies, Russia, with the participation of the Canadian Museum of Civilization, Canada.

Printed in Samara, with funding from the Samara Regional Government.



**Library and Archives Canada Cataloguing in Publication data can be found at the end of this book.**

**ISBN 978-0-660-19771-5**

**Front cover images**
Prairie grasslands near the Missouri River, North Dakota (I. Dyck). The crossed iron and chipped stone projectile points symbolize a comparison of nomadic peoples in the North American and Eurasian grasslands. The horse and bison pictographs are used throughout the book to mark steppe and prairie sections, respectively.

# CONTENTS

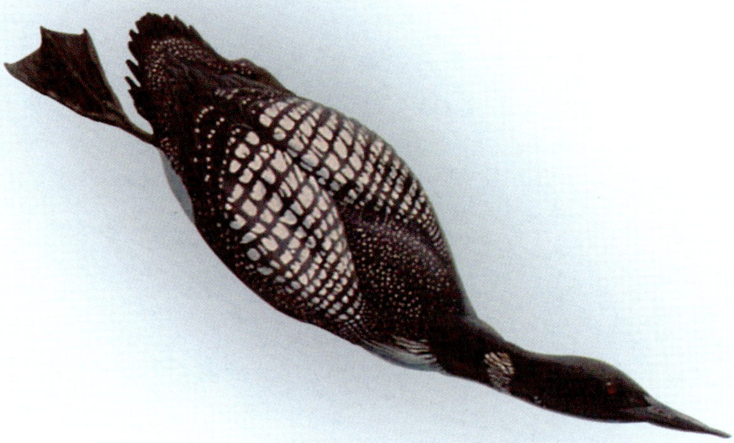

*A very long time ago, the whole surface of the earth was covered by water. And then, once upon a time, two ducks appeared over that immense and vast expanse of water with no end or shore. For a long time they swam around the boundless waters trying to find a place where they could lay their eggs, but they could not find even a patch of land a hand's breadth in size. Not knowing what to do, they started to dive. Perhaps it was from the bottom, or from somewhere else, but they started bringing pieces of mud onto the surface. One would hold the mud under her wing, hugging it close to her body, while the other would keep bringing more and more pieces up to her. And that is how ducks created land, by bringing clumps of mud to the surface and gluing them together until they formed a large area of dry land.*

**Origin myth of Bashkirs, Western Steppes**

*In the beginning there was water everywhere; nothing else was to be seen. There was something floating on the water, and on this raft were Old Man and all the animals. Old Man wished to make land, and he told the beaver to dive down to the bottom of the water and to try to bring up a little mud. The beaver dived and was under water for a long time, but he could not reach the bottom. Then the loon tried, and after him the otter, but the water was too deep for them. At last the muskrat was sent down, and he was gone for a long time, so long that they thought he must be drowned. But at last he came up and floated almost dead on the water, and when they pulled him onto the raft and looked at his paws, they found a little mud in them. When Old Man had dried this mud, he scattered it over the water and land was formed...*

**Origin myth of Blackfeet, Western Prairies**

# INTRODUCTION

In a world that is increasingly sedentary and dominated by densely populated cities, nomads are an anachronism. They are peoples with a lifestyle that belongs to a different time—pastoral wanderers, who attune their lives to the habits and needs of herd animals. Today, nomadic peoples exist only on the margins of certain regions—for example, in eastern portions of the Eurasian Steppes. Yet, in many respects, nomads hold a favoured place in our historical memories. In North America, images of Plains Native peoples with feathered headdresses invoke notions of wide-open spaces, self-sufficiency and fierce independence. Once both feared and admired, they were the last to be conquered by modern North American civilizations. In Eurasia, memories are somewhat similar. People recall the Scythian warriors of Greek history, the Huns that sacked Rome, and the hordes of Genghis Khan that swept into thirteenth-century Europe and the Middle East creating the largest empire the world has ever known. All were steppe nomads and their political, cultural and genetic impact is still evident throughout temperate portions of the Eurasian landmass.

This book is a companion piece for an exhibition entitled "Masters of the Plains: Ancient Nomads of Russia and Canada." Both book and exhibition are products of a comparative project, undertaken by the Canadian Museum of Civilization (Canada) and the Samara Museum of History and Regional Studies (Russia). The project focuses on the nomads who dominated the temperate grasslands of Eurasia (the Steppes) and the North American Great Plains (specifically, the northern Prairies) from about 5,000 years ago until about 300 years ago. In the Eurasian Steppes, nomads lived by herding domestic sheep, goats, horses and cattle. In the North American Great Plains, they lived by following and harvesting wild herds of bison.

**Opposite** Diving loon (Ruth King)

For people who have seen both the northern Prairies and the western Steppes, the usual initial reaction is amazement at the similarities. The landscapes as a whole, and many of their components—relief, plants, birds and animals—look so much alike that one can hardly see much difference between the two regions at first glance. Indeed, the northern Prairies and the western Steppes are the most similar temperate grasslands in the world. One might, therefore, assume that these strongly similar environments shaped the lives of their inhabitants in similar ways. People were subject to an open landscape, scarcity of water and fuel, long cold winters, hot dry summers, strong winds and dazzling sunshine year-round. However, as soon as one looks closely at the vestiges of human occupation, the impression of similarity fades. The history of nomadic occupations in the two regions and the adaptations, themselves, are similar in some ways but quite different in others. What are these similarities and differences?

To date, there have been no systematic comparisons of the ancient histories of steppe and prairie nomads. Many factors may have inhibited such studies, including political differences, linguistic differences, differences in archaeological approach and terminology, and differences in the actual paths of the respective histories. We decided, therefore, to focus our comparisons on the way people solved the same general problems and satisfied the same general needs. What were the nomadic means of subsistence, transportation, and shelter? What did people use for food and clothing? How did they satisfy their spiritual needs? Finally, how did they interact with other peoples? Our comparisons showed that despite many differences, there was one fundamental similarity—the nomadic lifestyle itself. How this lifestyle was implemented in each of the two regions is the subject of this book.

Creating this comparison has presented some challenges. For one thing, approaches to archaeology in the Russian Steppes and the Northern American Prairies have tended to deal with different parts of the archaeological record. In Russia, knowledge of ancient nomadic cultures is based largely on the excavation of human burials. In North America, excavations of human burials are relatively rare. Instead, most attention has been placed on bison-harvesting and camp sites. There is, of course, a certain degree of overlap in the kinds of remains found in nomadic burials, campsites and animal processing sites. However, special attention to any particular kind or combination of sites skews the record in certain ways. For example, artifacts found in graves tend to be finely made, whole and sometimes rare examples of their kind; whereas artifacts found in camp and processing sites tend to be common, well worn or broken discards. One has to keep these tendencies in mind when making comparisons. Our approach uses a range of objects representing various facets of nomadic life.

**Opposite** Grasslands of the World with blocked areas indicating: (1) Canadian Prairies and (2) Russian Steppes (Oleksiy Vasilenko, Canadian Museum of Civilization)

We have also drawn on historical and ethnohistorical records as an aide to our interpretation. Historical descriptions of the Russian steppes go back about 2,500 years. Made mostly by foreign travellers, these are to some extent parallel to the results of historical descriptions and ethnological observations made in the northern Prairies from the late 1600s to the early twentieth century. We are aware of the perils of interpreting archaeological evidence from one age by analogy with historical records of similar evidence from a later age. It might be argued that the historically recorded objects or events, although similar in form, were different in significance. Yet, there are huge improvements to be gained in understanding if an analogy is apt and carefully applied. Keeping that in mind, we present historical and ethnological data in this book along with archaeological results, in the hope that the combination will be illuminating.

Finally, it should be noted that, in doing this comparison, we have compressed the long and varied records of nomadic occupation into one generalized account for each region. Inevitably, this approach overlooks much detail, variation and nuance. In this short book, we simply want to present a broad overview of how the cultural traditions and environments in the two regions compare.

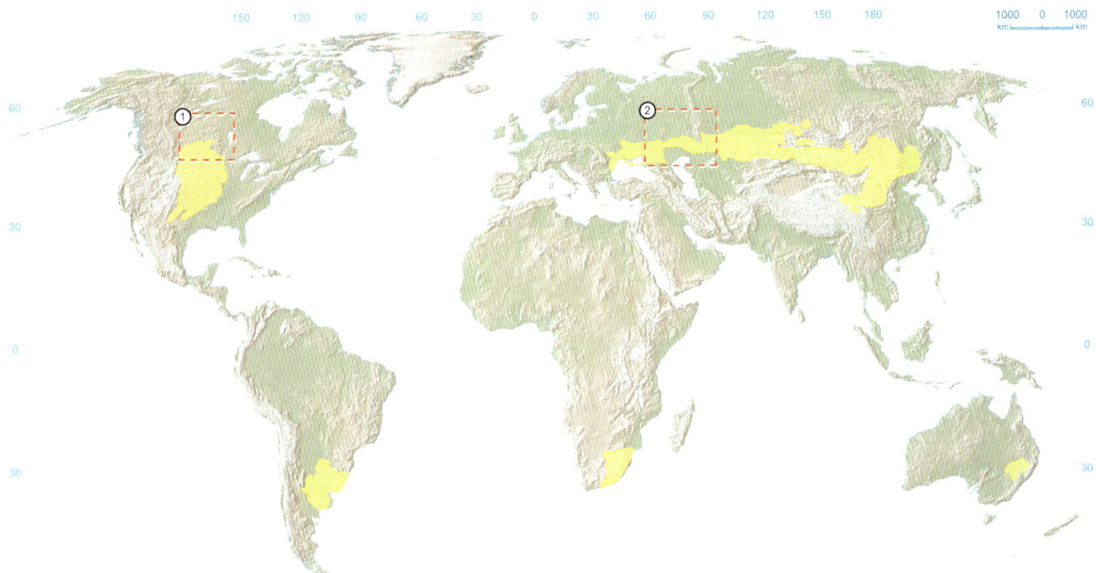

1000 0 1000
km km
1
2


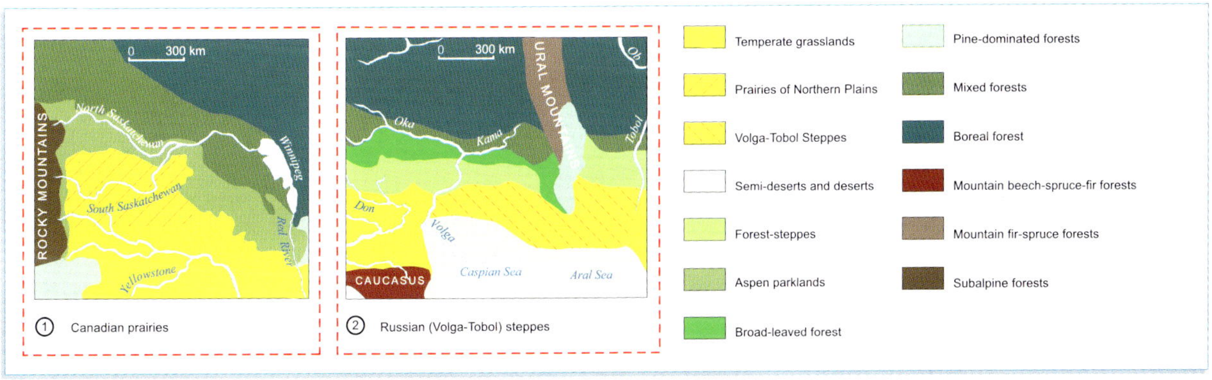

0 300 km
ROCKY MOUNTAINS
North Saskatchewan
South Saskatchewan
Winnipeg
Red River
Yellowstone
① Canadian prairies
0 300 km
URAL MOUNT
Ob
Tobol
Oka
Kama
Don
Volga
CAUCASUS
Caspian Sea
Aral Sea
② Russian (Volga-Tobol) steppes
Temperate grasslands
Prairies of Northern Plains
Volga-Tobol Steppes
Semi-deserts and deserts
Forest-steppes
Aspen parklands
Broad-leaved forest
Pine-dominated forests
Mixed forests
Boreal forest
Mountain beech-spruce-fir forests
Mountain fir-spruce forests
Subalpine forests

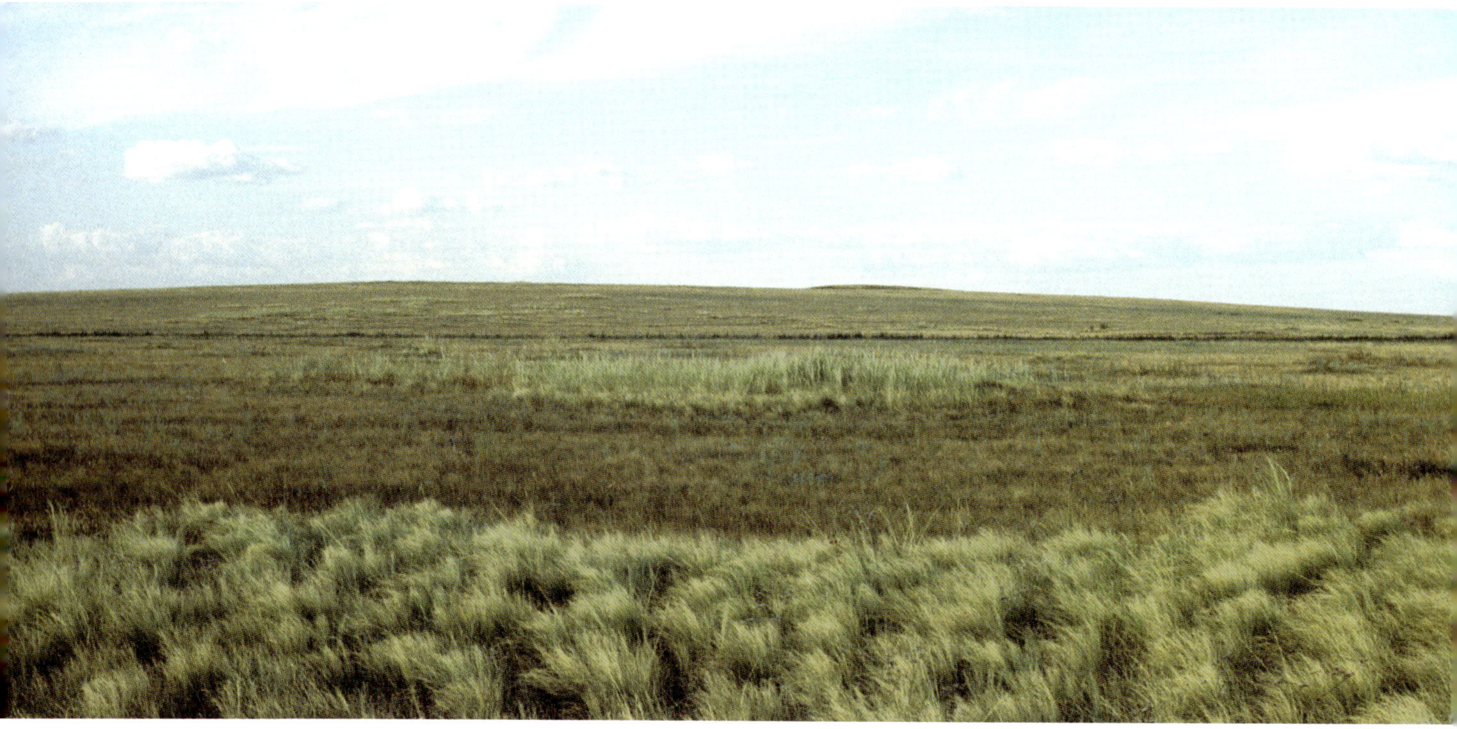

**Above** Steppe landscape (E. Ponomarenko)
**Below** Prairie landscape (I. Dyck)

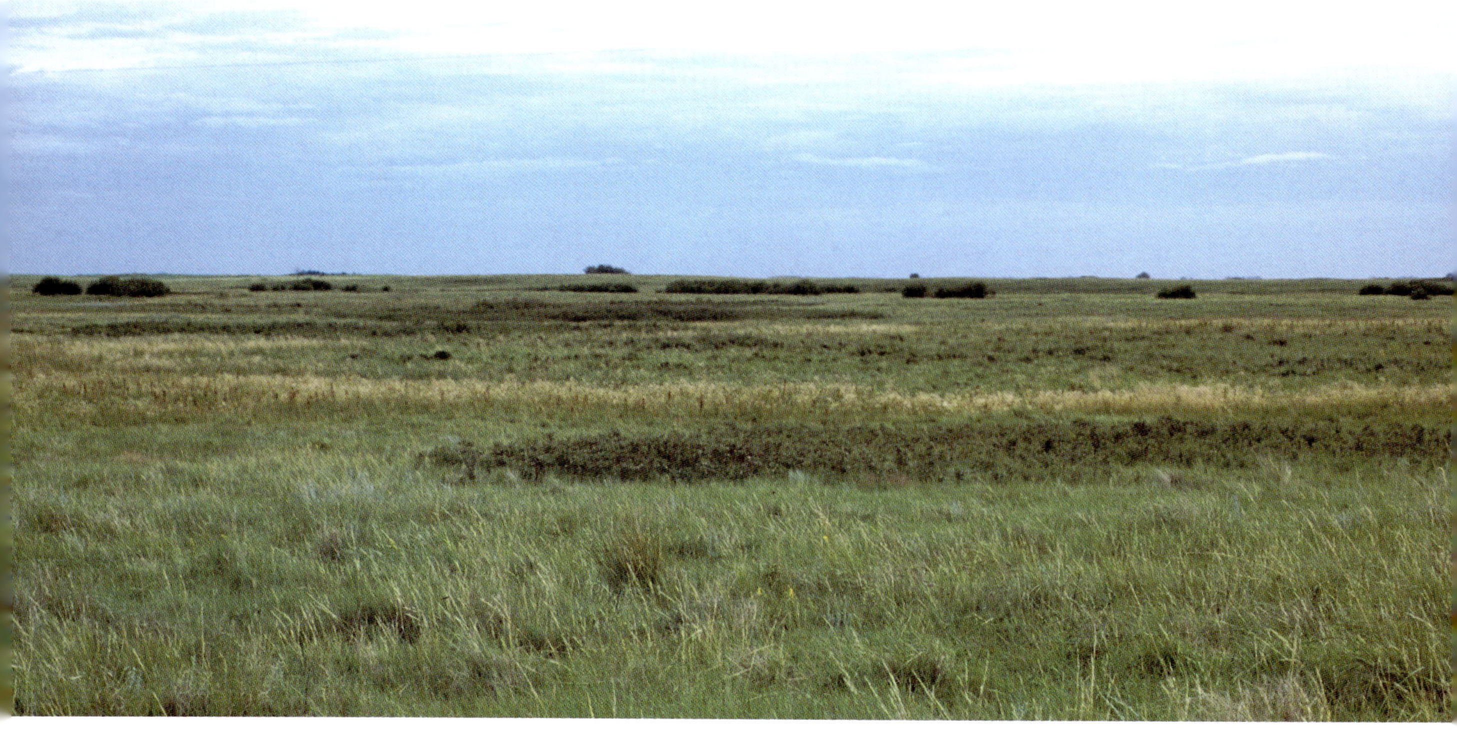

# GRASSLANDS

Grasslands are biomes that occupy the hearts of continents where rainfall is low. They are dominated by wind, grass, rodents and ungulates. These youngest landscapes of the temperate zone were formed as a result of tectonic activity during the Miocene geological epoch, about 18 million years ago. At that time, mountain ranges were thrust up, blocking the passage of humid oceanic air masses to the interiors of continents.

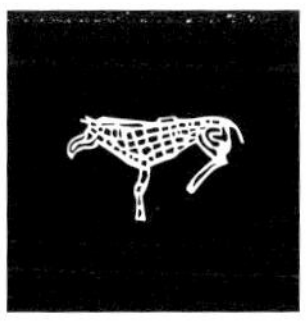

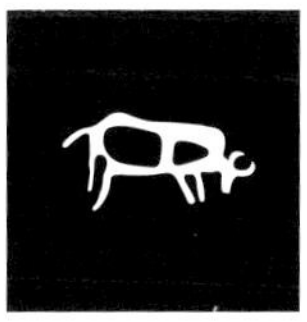

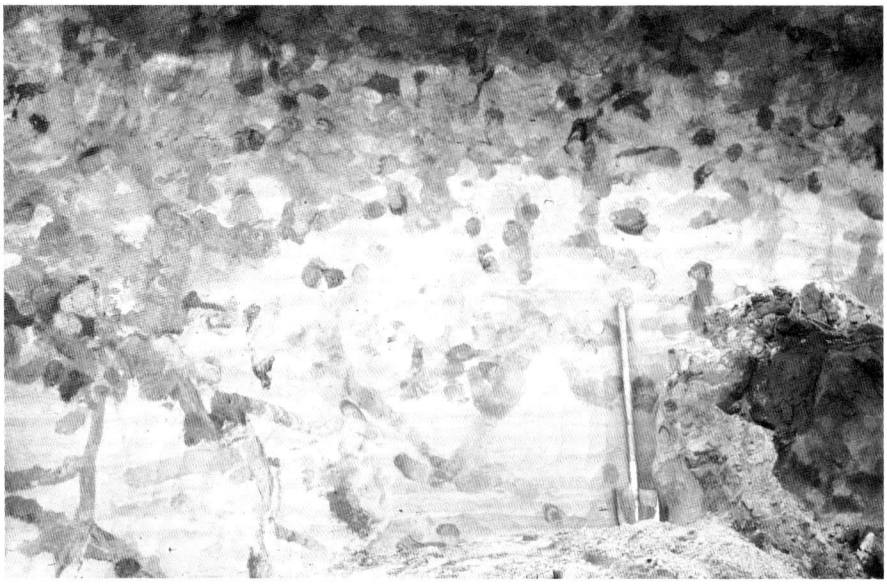

Steppe soil with numerous traces of soil-digging animals (E. Ponomarenko)

These changes in atmospheric circulation created the so-called continental climate. It is a climate of alternating extremes: the temperature drops as much as 80° C from summer to winter, and long droughts are followed by heavy rains. Strong winds carry silt and sand for many kilometres from disturbances on the soil surface. The terrain in grasslands is commonly flat, with only small patches of tree vegetation growing in dissected, sheltered areas of relief. As a result, grasslands are regions with open horizons, where sky and land appear in equal proportion to the human eye. The flowers of grasslands saturate the air with pleasant aromas, and countless insects and birds make the space vibrant with sounds.

Temperate grasslands—called "pampas" in South America, "veld" in South Africa, "steppes" in Russia and "prairies" in North America—developed on the world's most fertile soils, the chernozems. Since the rise of industrial agriculture, most of these areas have been converted to ploughed lands. About 70% of food for humans comes from these grassland zones, and less than 5% of the native grasslands remain unploughed. These ecosystems are the most altered in the world, almost lost in their natural state. And so are the lifestyles of the peoples who occupied them before the intrusion of modern agriculture.

Although separated by thousands of kilometres, the Northern North American Great Plains (Prairies) and the East-European Steppes (Steppes) are the two most similar temperate grasslands. Both are vast, open, grass-covered plains that are subject to seasonal extremes of climate. In both, the key components of fauna are rodents and gregarious ungulates. Both are located in the Northern Hemisphere, at the same latitudes, have similar levels of annual precipitation and solar radiation, and a similar number of growing days. Both areas are rich in mineral resources such as coal, gas, and oil, but poor in water and wood. In both areas, soils and climate allow very high yields of grass, but agriculture is risky because severe droughts recur at ten-year, hundred-year and thousand-year intervals. Nevertheless, over the last two centuries, grasslands have been converted into the main agricultural areas in both Russia and Canada. Over 98% of the territories once covered by grasslands in these countries is now farmed.

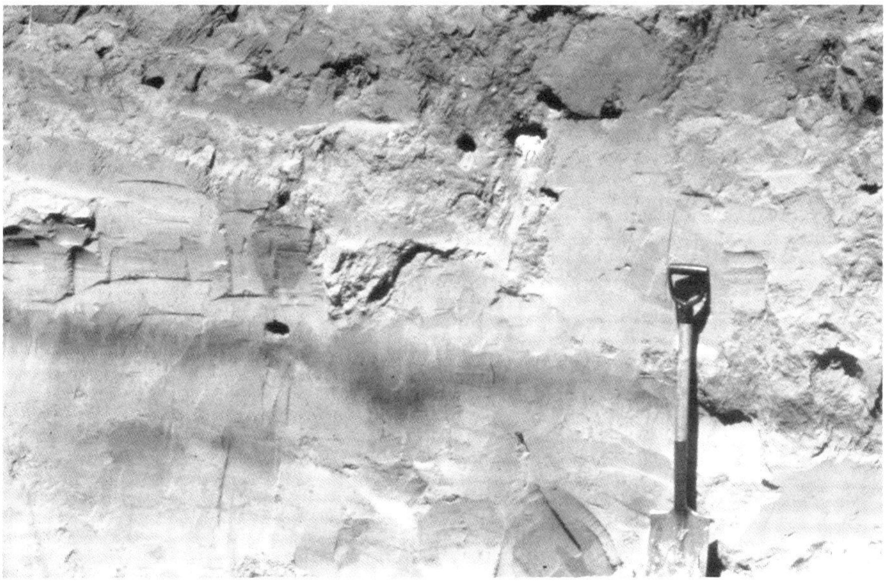

Black prairie soil with a band of older soil buried under aeolian sand deposits (E. Ponomarenko)

Under conditions of modern agriculture, the density of population in both areas remains low, less than five people per square kilometre. During nomadic times, populations were even lower, as little as one person per two square kilometres in the Steppes and one person per 20 square kilometres in the Northern Great Plains. These figures fluctuated through time in accordance with long-term climatic cycles that turned the grasslands into rich pastures during humid periods, and hostile "deserts" during periods of drought that sometimes lasted for centuries. As a result, there was a constant flow of human populations—individuals, ethnic groups, and even entire states—into the grasslands when conditions were good and out when conditions worsened.

## The Steppes

The Eurasian Steppes are a 400- to 900-kilometre-wide belt, oriented latitudinally, that spans a distance of about 7,000 kilometres from the Danube River in the west to the Irtysh River in the east. Isolated fragments of intermountain steppes are found even further east and southeast, extending into Inner Mongolia and China. To the north, the Steppes are bordered by oak-linden parklands in their European part and by aspen-birch parklands in their Asian (Siberian) part. To the south, they are limited by the Black Sea, the Caspian Sea and the Caucasus in their European part, and by the mountains of Central Asia in their Asian part.

The Steppes are commonly divided on a formal basis into European and Asian Steppes, separated by the Ural Mountain range. A better division, taking climate and relief into account, distinguishes Western Steppes (from the Danube River to the Altai Mountains) and Eastern Steppes (from the Altai Mountains to the Khingan Mountains). The Western Steppes lie at lower elevations (200 to

300 metres above sea level), whereas the Eastern Steppes are generally higher (300 to 400 metres above sea level). The portion of the Steppes that most closely resembles the American Prairies is the eastern portion of the Western Steppes. Although we will draw on materials from all of the Steppes, our focus will be on the area bordered by the Volga River in the west and the Tobol River in the east.

Spatial and seasonal changes in precipitation within the Steppes are governed by the varying influences of moist warm Atlantic air masses, dry cold Arctic air masses, and warm continental air masses. Prevailing winds are from the south in winter and from the north in summer.

The western parts of the European Steppes, influenced by Atlantic air masses, have a more humid climate with mild winters, long summers, and precipitation evenly spread throughout the year. At the western edge, in modern Hungary and Romania, the mild climate favours production of the greatest grass biomass, providing the best pastures for ungulates and the highest crop yields on ploughed lands. In this part of the Steppes, agriculture was possible for most of the Holocene Epoch. In the middle of the Western Steppes, the climate becomes more continental with sporadic and reduced precipitation. East of the Volga River, Atlantic air masses do not play any role in precipitation.

Most of the Western Steppes receive 250 to 500 millimetres of precipitation annually. Much of it occurs in summer, while the winters are dry and cold. Summer lasts 150 days, from the last frosts in mid-May to the first frosts of early October. The first snow cover appears in the Western Steppes at the end of October, and by the end of November, the winter snow cover is established. In the northern part of the Steppes, snow depth can reach 40 centimetres; however, the snow cover is rather unstable due to strong winds. Winter temperatures vary greatly within the steppe zone. In the western and southern parts, for instance in the Black Sea Lowlands, winter temperatures do not drop below 5° C. In the continental part of the Western Steppes, winter lasts 140 to 150 days, with temperatures below 5° C. Here temperatures range from an average of +20° in the summer to an average of –10° in the winter. East of the Volga River, temperatures range from the maximum of +41° in the summer to the minimum of –40° in the winter.

The Eastern Steppes have a continental climate with lower precipitation, hot summers and harsh winters. Most precipitation falls in the summer (up to 200 millimetres can fall in 24 hours), while winter precipitation is minimal. Summer lasts about 70 to 80 days, about half as long as in the Western Steppes. Most plants start growing at the beginning of May in the Western Steppes, but only by the end of May in the Eastern Steppes. However, the eastern edge of the Eastern Steppes (the modern territories of Tuva and Manchuria) has higher precipitation due to the higher elevation of the region and the influence of moist Pacific air masses. Pastures here were better than anywhere else in the Eastern Steppes, and (irrigated) agriculture was possible at some oases for most of the Holocene.

Such differences in climate and seasonality within the steppe zone prompted wild herd animals and, later, pastoralists with herds of domestic ungulates, to move seasonally into areas where grass and water were optimal. Seasonal migrations were directed mainly longitudinally, to richer northern pastures in the spring and summer and to warmer (but poorer) southern pastures in the fall. Major human migrations, on the contrary, were directed either westward or toward the eastern margins of the Steppes—whenever the political situation allowed it—to areas with a milder climate and a longer growing season.

The major relief on the Steppes is caused by erosion, which has produced deeply incised river valleys fed by networks of ravines and gullies. During the last ice age, the Steppes were south of the ice sheet, in the so-called periglacial zone, an area that served as a repository for silts transported by wind from the glaciated area. Up to 400 metres of silty deposits, called "loess," accumulated in the Steppes during that period. Loess covers the Steppes as an almost uninterrupted blanket of varying thickness. It does not contain any rock fragments large enough to be made into tools. All sources of useable stone are associated with deeply incised river valleys and gullies, where calcareous pre-Quaternary (Cretaceous) deposits are exposed by erosion. In several areas there are chalk hills above the level of the surrounding plain. Samara Luka is another unique area in the mid-Volga River region. Here, the Volga bends in a large loop around the Zhiguli Mountains, which were formed by tectonic uplift. This area is an island of forest vegetation within the Steppes. Dunes are rather uncommon in the Western Steppes, but may be found on terraces of large rivers and at the junctions of large rivers.

The major steppe rivers are the Dnieper (Black Sea catchment), the Don (Azov Sea catchment), the Volga and the Ural (Caspian Sea catchment), and in the Siberian part, the Tobol and Ishim Rivers, which flow to Irtysh and empty into the Arctic Ocean. All rivers flow in a longitudinal direction, southward in the western part and northward in the eastern part of the Steppes, dividing the region into large longitudinal segments that connect parklands to the north with semi-deserts to the south. Migrations of plants, animals, and humans are easiest within the longitudinal direction of these segments. Most small rivers that feed the large rivers east of the Volga dry up in summer, although small temporary creeks remain in some gullies (bairaks). Short-lived sloughs can be found in depressions on the landscape after spring thaw and during the summer following periods

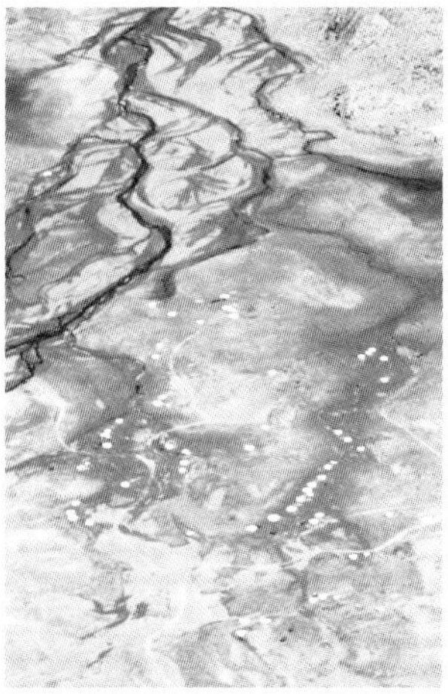

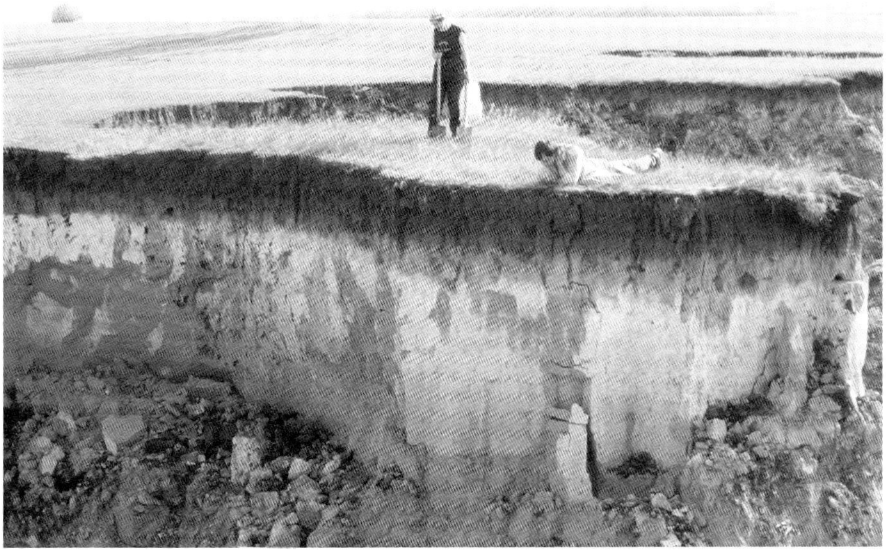

**Above** Oblique view of modern steppe–nomad camps along seasonal streams (courtesy of Matt Reichel)
**Below** Ravine cutting through silt (loess) deposits, Samara region (E. Ponomarenko)

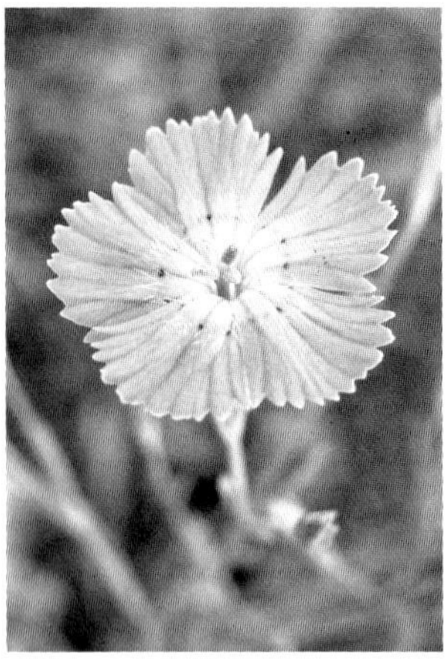

**Above** Wild carnation (*Dianthus versicolor*) (courtesy of Ilya Smeljanski)
**Below** Marmot (*Marmota bobak*) (courtesy of Tatjana Bolonina)

of rain. In the eastern portion of the European Steppes, snow is an additional source of summer water. Wind-blown snow accumulates in depressions, where, on north-facing slopes, it does not melt until July. The immense area of the Caspian lowlands was periodically flooded by the sea in the past. Numerous lakes can be found in this area, but they are mainly saline. Generally, lakes, both saline and brackish, are much more common in the Siberian Steppes than in the European Steppes.

Vegetation cover changes latitudinally and longitudinally within the steppe zone, following trends in precipitation. From north to south and from west to east, vegetation becomes shorter, sparser and less diverse. In the northern part of the Western Steppes, grasses, such as needle grasses, fescue grasses and brome grass, grow along with many species of flowering plants, such as dropwort, clary, carnations and milk-vetch. The southern part of the Western Steppes is dominated by grasses, mainly by shorter species of needle grass. In spring, flowering plants such as onions, primroses, prairie anemones and tulips come into bloom. By the beginning of June, the Steppes become green with grasses, highlighted by the many flowering plants that continue to bloom from early to midsummer. By the beginning of September, grasses start to turn dry and flowers are no longer seen. Tangles of tumbleweed roll before the wind across the surface of the land, covered by pale, dry, sparse grass. In the forest-steppe transition zone, aspen and birch grow in some depressions, whereas in the Steppes proper, trees (oak, elm, poplar and willow) grow only in river valleys and deep ravines. Dissected slopes/bairaks typically have a dense cover of shrubs (including caragana, steppe cherry, tern, golden chain and dwarf almond), especially in the northern part of the Steppes.

The Steppes are inhabited by over 90 species of mammals, and several hundred species of birds. Carnivores include wolf, fox, dog fox, ferret, badger and ermine. Rodents include marmot, mole rat, ground squirrels, and various species of small rodents. As to larger animals, domesticated ungulates (sheep,

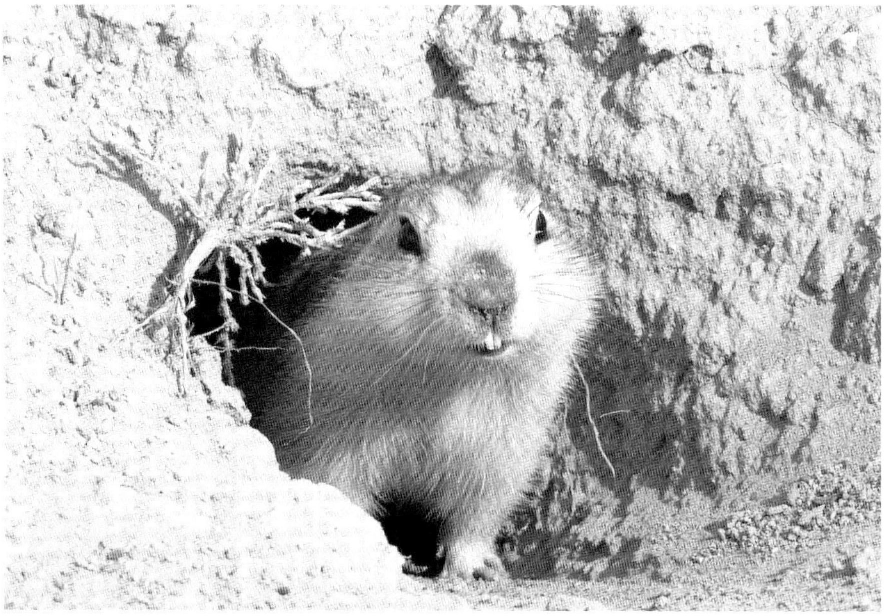

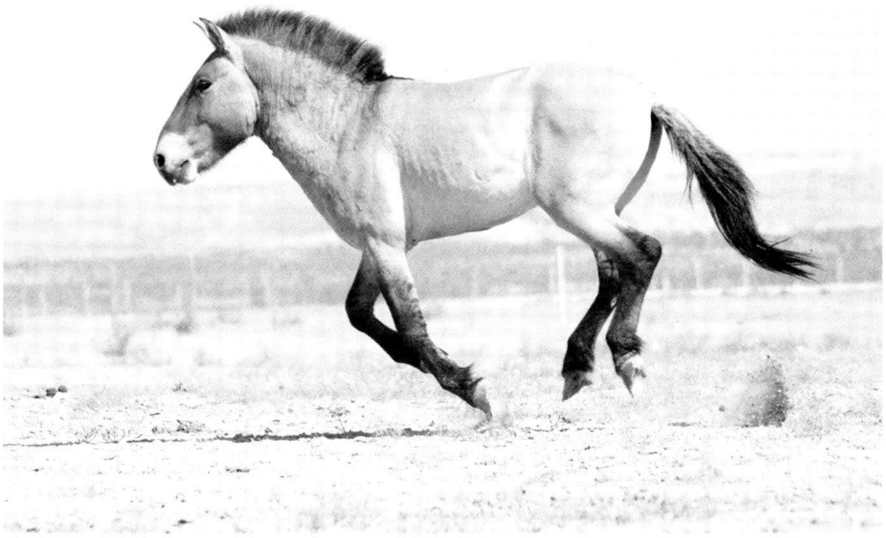

Przhevalski horse
(courtesy of Danila Mukhin)

goats, horses and cattle) dominate most of the Steppes. Only in the southern part of the Western Steppes do small populations of saiga antelope and dzeren survive in protected areas. Formerly the steppe fauna included wisent (*Bison bonasus*) and tarpan (wild horse). The meadowlark is the most common songbird of the Steppes and is often used as a symbol of the area, as are birds of prey such as the steppe eagle, bustard, buzzard and kestrel.

## The Prairies

The grasslands of the Great Plains of North America are oriented longitudinally, stretching about 3,000 kilometres from Saskatchewan in the north to Texas in the south, with a width of about 500 to 800 kilometres from the Rocky Mountains to the Eastern Woodlands. The portion of the Great Plains that is in the same latitude as the Russian Steppes is the northern half, roughly from 47° to 54° North latitude. This is the area that contains the richest pasturelands, and it is the zone with which we will be chiefly concerned in this comparative project. The grassland part of the Northern Great Plains (known in Canada as "the Prairies") is bordered by the Rocky Mountains to the west, aspen parklands to the north, aspen-oak woodlands to the east, and dry plains to the south. Lands in the eastern part of this area lie at about 500 metres above sea level; those in the western part from 600 to 1,200 metres above sea level.

The continental climate of the Prairies is characterized by cold winters and hot summers. Variability in climate is controlled by the changing influences of several air masses: warm dry air from the Pacific, cold dry air from the Arctic, and moist tropical air from the Gulf of Mexico. The input of each of these masses varies through time and causes seasonal change. The chinook, a warm winter wind, occurs when air from the Pacific Coast crosses the Rocky Mountains and descends onto the Prairies. This results in a dramatic short-term temperature rise in the western part of the region several times during a winter. Elsewhere on the Prairies, occasional bursts of warm air from the south can have the same effect. The fluctuation of the temperature produces a hard ice crust on the surface of snow, which causes massive mortality among mammals and birds. Penetration of cold Arctic air masses into the grasslands during winter produces intensely cold weather, sometimes accompanied by such phenomena as northern lights and sundogs (the appearance of multiple sun-like sources of light in cold, crystalline air), both of which are unusual in the Steppes. Prevailing winds are northwesterly throughout the year. During the summer, in addition to regular strong winds, tornadoes appear from time to time, developing speeds of over 350 kilometres per hour. Precipitation, usually in the form of heavy rains during late spring and early summer, decreases from east to west across the Prairies, with an annual average of about 500 millimetres in the eastern part and about 250 millimetres in the west. During winter, precipitation is low.

Temperatures span a large range during the course of a year. Summer temperatures can be well over 38° C, while winter temperatures can be as low as –45° C, but the average is from –15° C in winter to +18° C in summer. The frost-free period is 100 to 120 days (140 days in southern portions). On average, the last frosts in the spring occur in late May, and the first frosts in fall occur in mid-October.

The prairie landscape is generally level to moderately rolling and displays many glacial features resulting from its coverage by land glaciers during the last Ice Age. Glacial till plains and glacial lakebeds have produced vast flat lands. In areas near these flat features, low rolling hills are common, often the result of moraines left by the glaciers. Many of the river and creek valleys are much bigger than one would expect on the basis of modern water flows, their size being due to the discharge of immense amounts of water from former glacial lakes. Some ancient runoff channels are now almost completely dry and are known

Rocks scattered on the prairie surface, southern Saskatchewan (E. Ponomarenko)

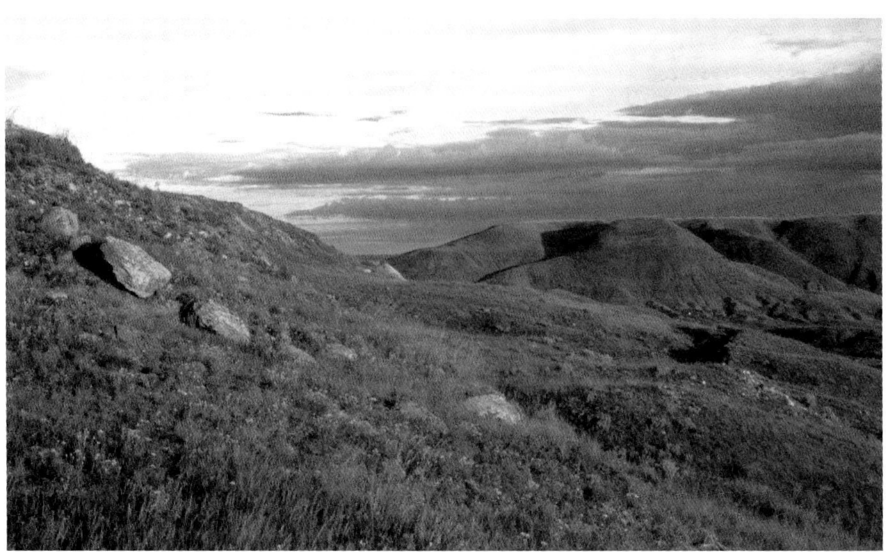

as coulees. Dune fields occur throughout the Prairies and are deltaic deposits of former glacial lakes. The dunes are mostly covered by aspen woods now, but many were active in the past. Relics of pre-Quaternary uplands remain scattered across the Prairies, in features such as the Cypress Hills, Hand Hills, Moose Mountain and Neutral Hills.

Surface deposits in the Prairies are mainly Quaternary in age and of glacial or fluvioglacial origin. In areas outside sand dune complexes and silty glacial lakebeds, the surface is generally sandier and much stonier than that in the Steppes. These glacial deposits are rich in cobbles and rock fragments of materials such as quartzite, chert, siltstone, petrified peat and wood, sandstone, granite, gneiss, and basalt—most redeposited by glaciers, and all useful for the manufacture of tools. The sandy deposits are more prone to lateral movement under mechanical disturbances (trampling, wind erosion, etc.) than are the silts of the Steppes. Therefore, objects in low areas get buried quite quickly. As a result, deeply stratified archaeological sites are more common here than in the Steppes.

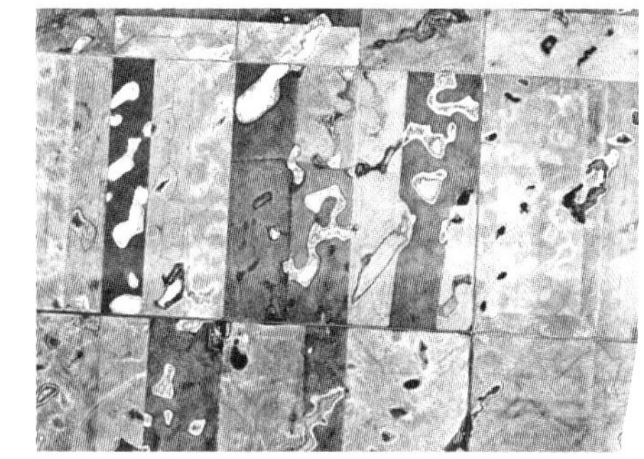

Satellite image of modern Prairies: numerous dots are potholes left by the melting ice of the last glaciation © 2007. Reproduced with the permission of the Minister of Public Works and Government Services Canada, 2007; courtesy of the National Air Photo Library of Natural Resources Canada.

The unglaciated southwestern part is much more dissected, but only along larger streams has erosion created substantial relief. In the western part of the Prairies, isolated mountains form part of the grassland landscape, including such features as the Little Belt (2,207 metres) and Black Hills (2,207 metres), which are of pre-Quaternary origin. In the southern part of the Prairies, badlands are common. Badlands are elevated areas where outcrops of soft pre-Quaternary sediments, mostly volcanic ash, have been deeply eroded. Due to the continuing erosion and the nature of the deposits, the badlands remain heavily dissected and barren, with little or no vegetation.

Prairie drainage is divided between two huge basins. Rivers in the northern half of the region all flow northeast into Hudson Bay. These include the North Saskatchewan, South Saskatchewan, Assiniboine and Red. Rivers in the southern half, including the Missouri and its tributaries, all flow into the Gulf of Mexico. Rivers in the Hudson Bay basin facilitate the movement of plants and animals in a latitudinal direction and pose a barrier for the northward migration of some species, such as soil-digging animals. The northeast orientation of rivers also made those waters subject to frequent ice jams and flash flooding. In the other basin, the north-south orientation of rivers and the lower latitude offered greater opportunities for north-south exchange. For pedestrian people and the game they followed, however, the divide between the two basins was almost imperceptible and posed little problem to movement.

The Prairies are dotted with small lakes and seasonal sloughs. Sloughs occupy almost every depression during the spring months. Most of them disappear later in the summer, but until mid-July, water is still abundant throughout the Prairies. Some areas within the northern Prairies have only internal drainage and saline lakes.

Prairie vegetation changes from east to west and from north to south according to the trends in precipitation: from tall grass prairies in the east to mid-grass or mixed-grass prairies in the centre, and short-grass prairies to the west and south. In the eastern part, the dominant plants are wheat grass, prairie June grass, prairie dropseed, and purple needle grass, along with several hundred species of flowering plants, such as sunflowers, asters, blazing stars, coneflowers,

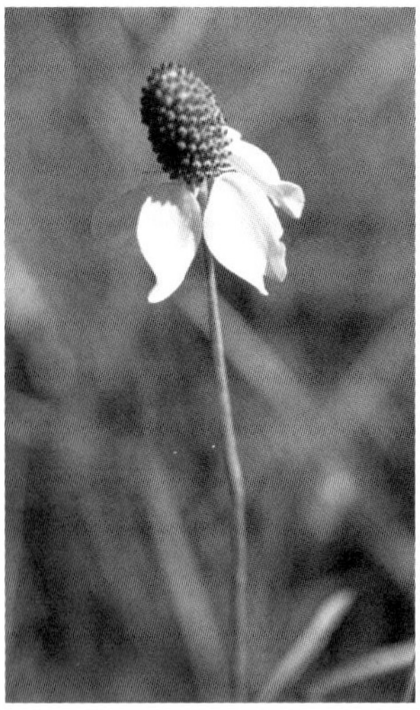

**Above** Rudbeckia (I. Dyck)
**Below** Buffalo berries (*Shepherdia canadensis*) (I. Dyck)

psoraleas and wild indigos. Further west, short grasses, such as buffalo grass and blue grama, become increasingly dominant along with sedges and sages. The flora includes four species of cacti that are adapted to cold winters.

The Prairies change seasonally: in the early spring, they bloom with anemones, primroses and sedges, while the overall colour of the grasslands is brown to buff. By the end of May, the Prairies turn green when grasses dominate the vegetation cover. Most of the plants flower in June; by the beginning of July most plants produce seeds; and by the end of August their colour changes to golden buff as they mature and dry out.

Under natural conditions, trees do not grow in the open prairies. However, parts of the river and creek valleys—more so in the eastern part of the region—are forested with aspen, cottonwood, willows, ash and oaks. Other dissected areas in the foothills, on bedrock escarpments and dune fields, are also often forested. In the southwestern parts of the Prairies, forests are made up of aspen and juniper, in the eastern part, of aspen and oak. A dense cover of shrubs is also typical for areas of dissected relief. The Prairies are rich in berry shrubs, such as service berry, buffalo berry, chokecherries, red haw, wild grapes, currants, gooseberries and red plums.

Prairie fauna contains over 80 species of mammals and over 300 species of birds. Ungulates include bison, elk, mule deer, Virginia white-tailed deer and pronghorn antelope. During nomadic times, bison were by far the most numerous of the large mammals. Rodents include pocket gopher, ground squirrels, prairie dog, beaver and numerous kinds of mice and voles. Among the carnivores (before the twentieth century) were grizzly bears, cougars, wolves, coyotes, badgers, swift foxes, weasels and the black-footed ferret. Many songbirds, such as the western meadowlark, horned larks and grasshopper sparrows, inhabit the Prairies along with several species of grouse (hen-like birds), such as the prairie chicken, common partridge and sage grouse. Prairie birds of prey are

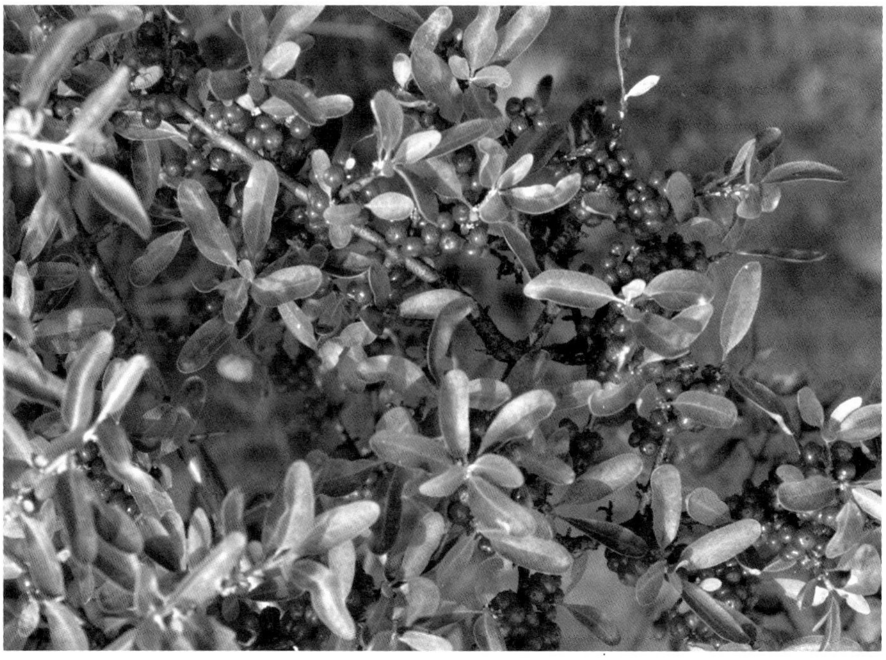

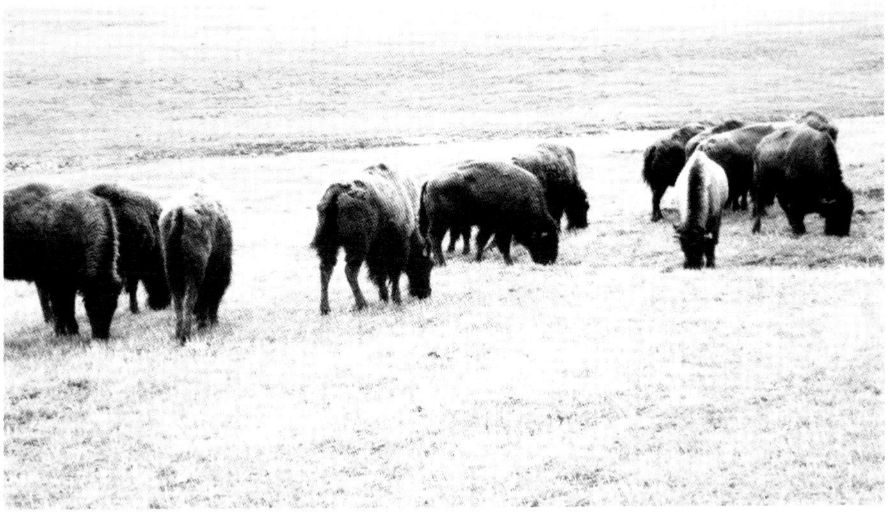

Prairie bison, southern Alberta (I. Dyck)

golden eagle and bald eagle, several species of hawks, prairie falcon, horned owl and burrowing owl. Besides a few truly prairie species, such as magpie, many birds stop in the Prairies during their migrations in spring and fall. Among them are various waterfowl, such as Canada and snow geese, cranes, ducks, pelicans, shorebirds, etc. Several species of snakes are common in the Prairies, including the poisonous rattlesnake.

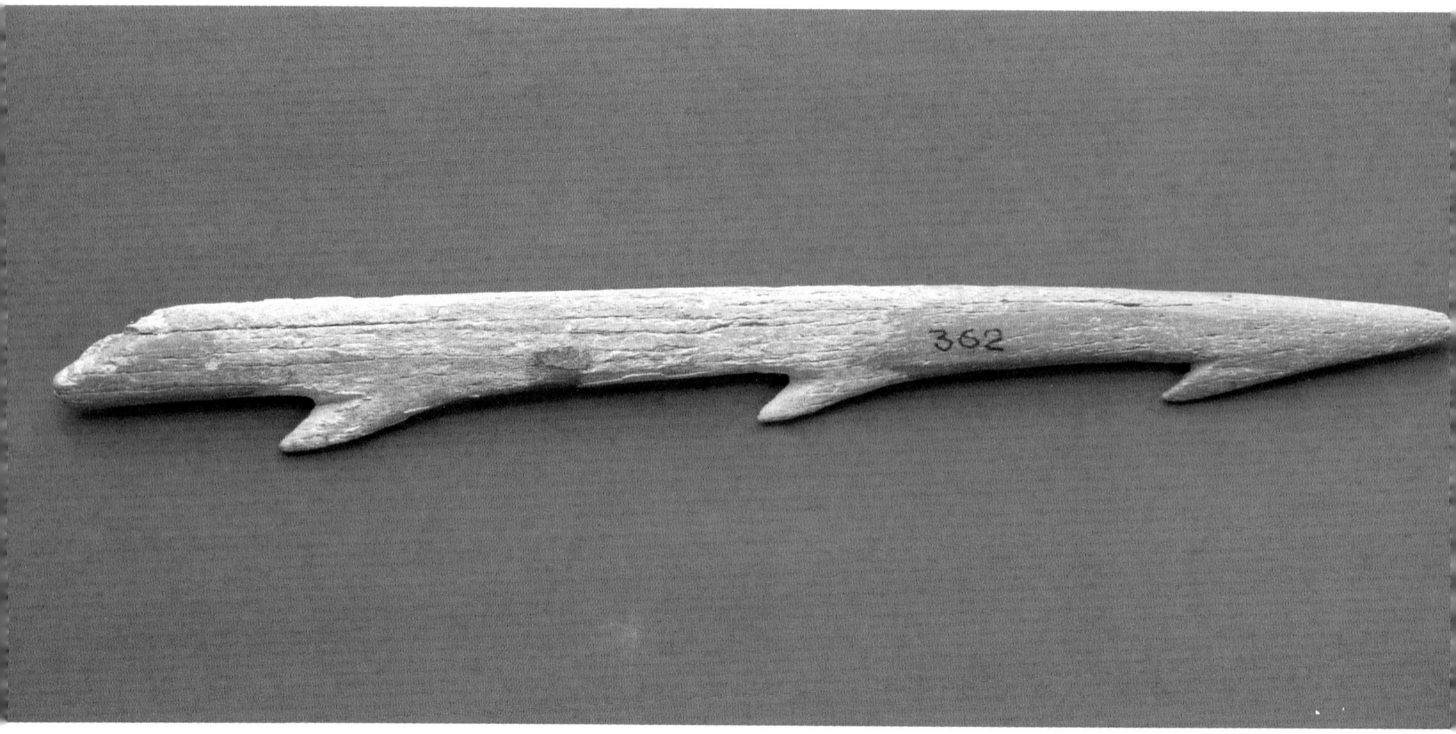


**Above** Bone harpoon, 15,000–12,000 years old (Upper Palaeolithic–Mesolithic transition) (P. V. Alabin Museum of History and Regional Studies, Samara, KP-22674)
**Below** Clovis culture bone point, ca. 11,000 years old (Canadian Museum of Civilization, X-B-2)

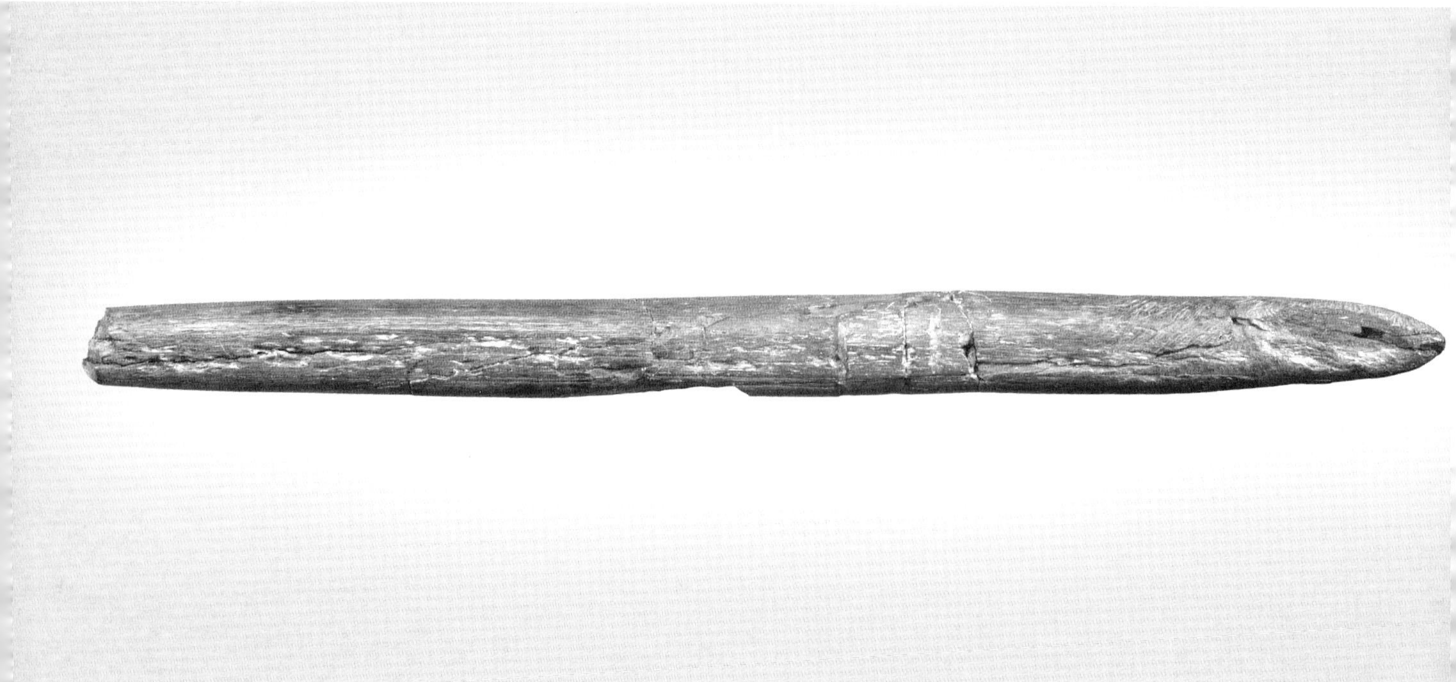

# Archaeological Cultures Before the Nomads

The grasslands of North America and Northern Eurasia first appeared around 18 million years ago in the mid-Miocene epoch and assumed approximately their modern form by about 5 to 7 million years ago. The time of their formation is close to the age of the earliest known hominids in Africa (3 to 4 million years ago). However, the first signs of human occupation in grasslands of the northern hemisphere appeared much later.

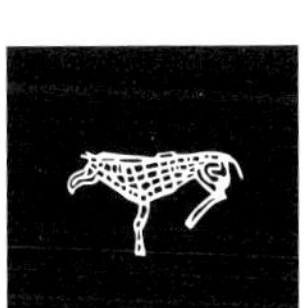
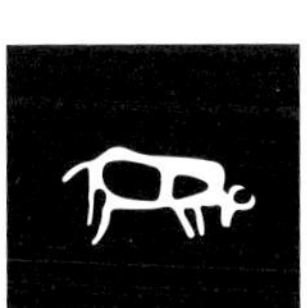

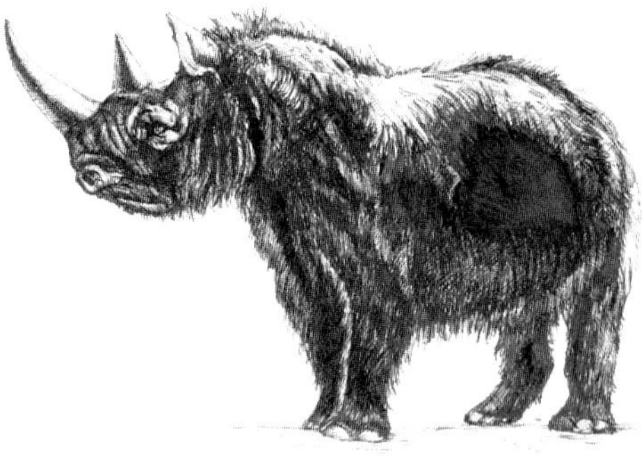

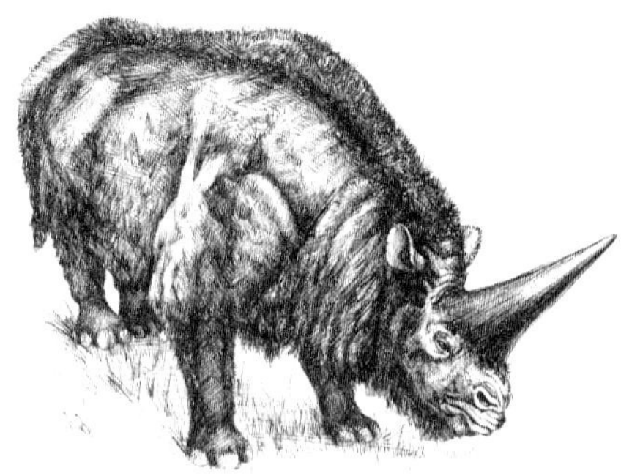

**Above/Left** Woolly rhinoceros (*Coelodonta antiquitatis*) (Larisa Nikolaeva, P. V. Alabin Museum of History and Regional Studies, Samara)
**Above/Right** Giant unicorn (*Elasmotherium*) (Larisa Nikolaeva, P. V. Alabin Museum of History and Regional Studies, Samara)
**Below** Mousterian flint biface (chopping tool), ca. 120,000 years old (Middle Palaeolithic) (P. V. Alabin Museum of History and Regional Studies, Samara, KP-23991/9)

For most of the last two million years, during the Pleistocene geological era, the northern hemisphere was affected by a series of glaciations, which alternated with short warm interglacial intervals. The transition from glacial to interglacial periods was marked by an increase in global temperatures on the order of about 12° C. However, warm intervals comprised less than 10% of the Pleistocene. Lands that are now the Prairies were covered by ice during the cold stages of the Pleistocene. At the same time, the territory that is now the Steppes was located south of the ice sheet, in the periglacial zone. During cold phases of the Pleistocene, the periglacial zone experienced a dry, cold climate that favoured tundra-steppe vegetation. The most extensive glaciation of northern Eurasia and North America, called the Dnepr/Don Glaciation and the Kansan Glaciation in the respective areas, began during the mid-Pleistocene, about 400,000 years ago. Until about 13,000 years ago, the massive ice shield extended south to 48° latitude in European Russia and to 37° latitude in North America. At this same time, far south of the periglacial zone, in Africa, homeland of the earliest hominids, the climate was warm and humid.

Throughout warmer phases of the Pleistocene, climate varied from modern-like conditions to much warmer. The warmest interglacial period (Mikulino in European Russia, or Sangamonian in North America) occurred about 120,000 to 130,000 years ago and was marked by an increase in global temperatures on the order of 12° C. During this period, the European Steppes were covered by broad-leaved forests. The first artifacts in the Steppes fall within this period.

The first inhabitants of the area that is now the Steppes were hunters and gatherers, who set their temporary camps along rivers and lakes, near the seasonal haunts of game animals. No human skeletal remains of this age have been discovered within the Steppes. However, vestiges of shelters and hearths have been found, in association with large stone tools, such as stone dart points, hammer stones, chipped stone knives for meat butchering, scrapers and perforators for hide working, along with stone nuclei, flakes and pre-forms, which are the by-products of stone working.

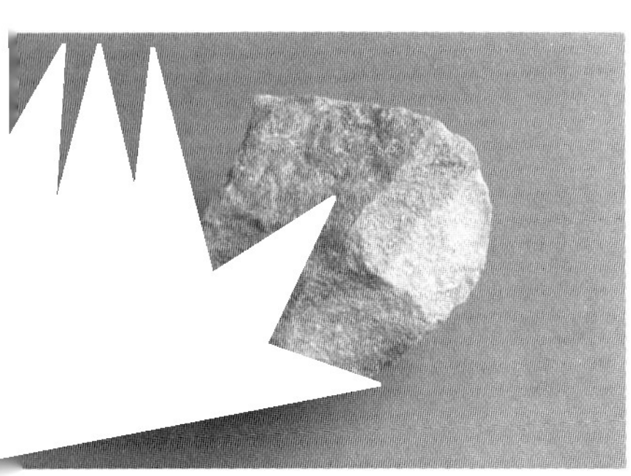

The Mikulino/Sangamonian Interglacial was followed by a new glacial stage called the Valdai in European Russia or the Wisconsinan in North America. Sporadic penetration into the Steppes by peoples of Mousterian culture continued during this period. Meanwhile, in North America, according to our current knowledge, the Prairies were not inhabited by humans until the last part of the Wisconsinan period.

# HUNTERS AND GATHERERS OF THE LAST ICE AGE (35,000 TO 11,500 YEARS AGO)

About 40,000 years ago, Mousterian cultures disappeared from the Steppes, and new Upper Palaeolithic cultures re-populated the area. Humans were thoroughly adapted to cold environments by this time, enabling their occupation of the northern parts of the Eurasian Steppes and, eventually, all of North and South America. The oldest Upper Palaeolithic sites in the Steppes and in Central Siberia are 35,000–40,000 years old, in Subarctic Siberia about 25,000 years old, and in Kamchatka around 14,000 years old. In North America, although predecessors are suspected, the oldest well-established archaeological culture dates to about 11,500 years ago.

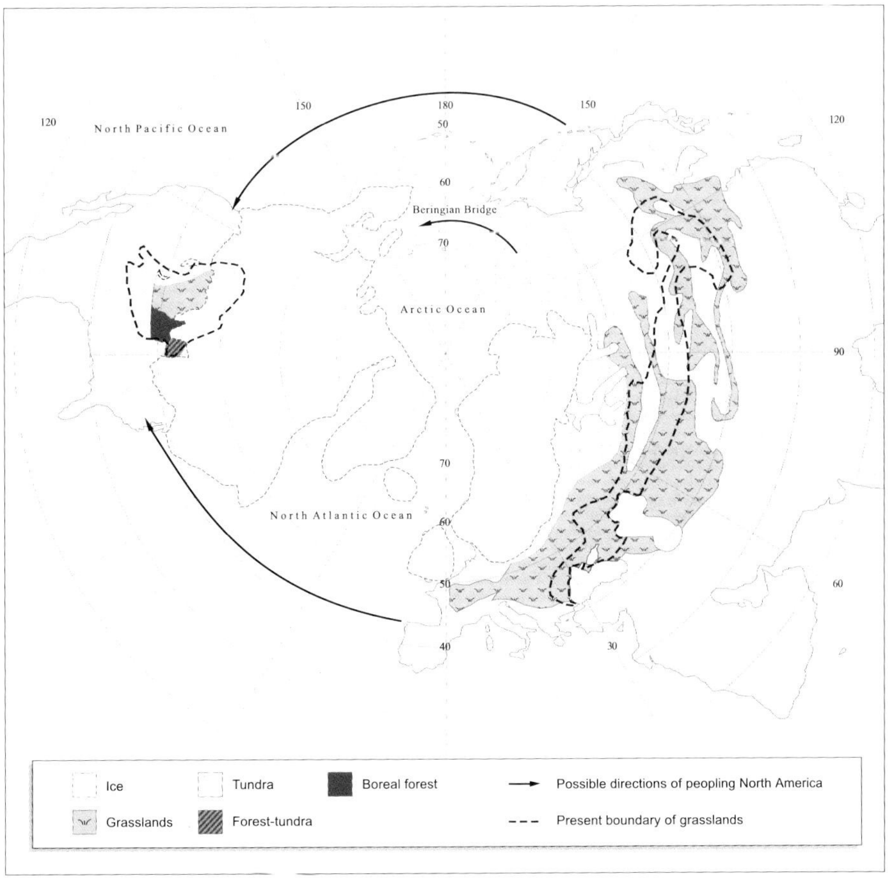


Extent of Northern Grasslands 20,000 years ago (Oleksiy Vasilenko, Canadian Museum of Civilization)

# The Steppes

By 35,000 years ago, the Steppes were located over 500 kilometres south of the ice sheet. The cold, arid climate supported vegetation that does not have modern analogues—a so-called periglacial steppe, which was dominated by grasses, sedges, sages and chenopods. Animal life included some gigantic, now extinct, forms referred to as "megafauna." Palaeolithic hunters pursued mammoth, wild horse, ancient bison, wild cattle and rhinoceros. The dominance of these species was associated with specific micro-environments. Therefore, hunting was somewhat regionally specialized: mammoth was the staple game in the central area of the periglacial Steppes, caribou in the west, bison and horse in the south.

The hunters of the Last Ice Age built dwellings using the bones and tusks of mammoths for a framework, and hides for a cover. These dwellings were heated by hearths and, since there was an insufficient supply of wood, broken bone was widely used as fuel. Mammoth hunters lived in long-term settlements, possibly base camps, in dwellings that contained many subsurface cache pits. Dwellings and cache pits were rebuilt many times, forming the typical "perforated" look of Palaeolithic mammoth-hunter sites. Long-term settlements of steppe bison hunters are not known. However, bison bone beds up to 10 metres thick, containing the remains of up to 100 bison, are evidence of successful bison hunting in the Steppes during this period. Tool kits included stone knife blades for butchering, stone end scrapers, stone perforators and bone needles for hide working and manufacture of clothing, chisels and hammer stones for tool making, and spearheads made of stone and bone for hunting. Shafts for spears were made mainly of ivory. Technological innovations of the period included bone and stone carving, drilling and polishing. Darts and throwing boards (a weapon called an atlatl in North America) appeared at least 15,000 years ago in Europe. Domestication of the dog was achieved both in South Asia and in the Steppes at about this same time.

Palaeolithic painting of mammoth, Capovaya Cave, Bashkiria (after O. N. Bader, *Capova Cave*, 1965)

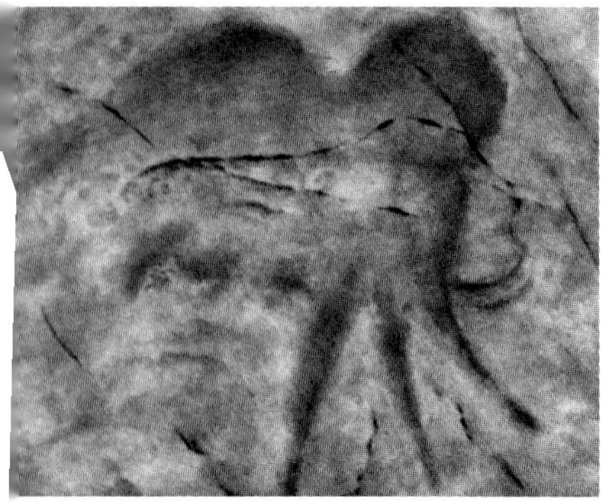

Visual art bloomed during the Upper Palaeolithic. People began to wear pendants and bracelets and to adorn their clothing with teeth, claws, and bone figurines of animals. Some groups used complex geometric ornaments such as meanders, labyrinths and spruce-like ornaments. The first images of humans and animals were created during this time. In sacred places such as caves, game animals were depicted for ceremonial purposes, in rituals that preceded hunting. Palaeolithic art was realistic and colourful. A wide range of colours was generated using pigments such as red ochre, yellow limonite, white chalk, black manganese oxides and charcoal. It is probable that similar pigments were used to decorate clothing and the human body. People created figurines of women with well-defined, and often exaggerated, gender traits. They also created animal figurines. Images could be three-dimensional, carved of bone and soft stone, or bas-reliefs on flat rocks. Music was part of Upper Palaeolithic ritualism. The oldest musical instruments are flutes made of mammoth tusks and percussion

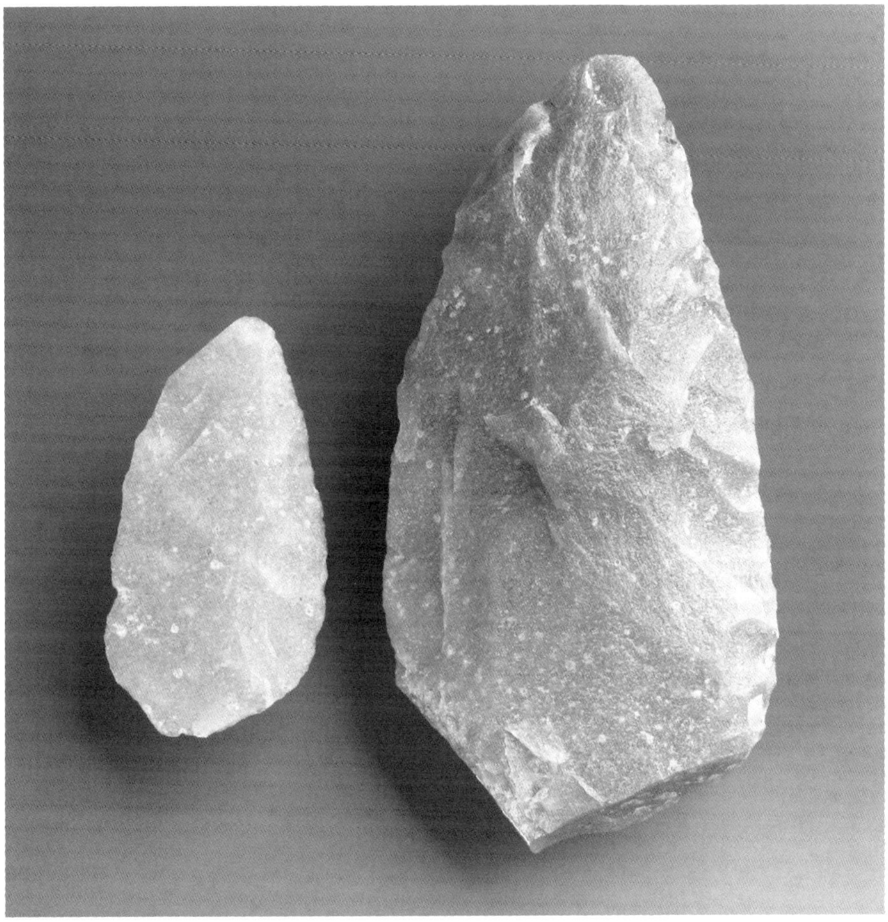

Quartzite dart head (right) and knife-projectile point (left), ca. 40,000 years old (Upper Palaeolithic)
(P. V. Alabin Museum of History and Regional Studies, Samara, KP-25405/1-2)

instruments made of mammoth bones. These were found in the Ukrainian Steppes and are about 20,000 years old. Upper Palaeolithic people buried their dead within their occupational sites, mostly in a supine pose, often along with their possessions.

## The Prairies

Much of northern North America, including the Prairies, was covered by ice and was not available for occupation until at least 13,000 years ago. Parts of Alaska and the Yukon remained ice-free and sustained a steppe-tundra type of ecosystem. The rest of Canada and the northern tier of the United States were covered with ice. Areas south of the continental glaciers were covered by grasslands and, at higher elevations, parklands—vegetation similar to that of the periglacial steppes of European Russia. The periglacial grasslands of North America also supported a megafauna like that of the periglacial Steppes, including mammoth, giant bison, giant sloth and mastodon. The Pleistocene animals of the Plains also included the camel and the horse.

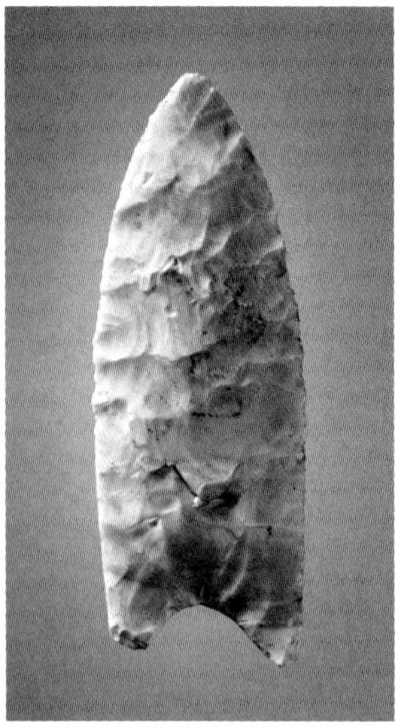

One reason that North America and Eurasia shared a similar fauna during the Pleistocene is because they were connected by a land bridge across the Bering Strait, between Alaska and Siberia, during parts of that era. The land bridge emerged from the shallow waters of the strait whenever the sea level was about 130 metres lower than it is today, the most recent emergence beginning about 20,000 years ago. Both ends of the bridge remained ice-free, due to air-mass behaviour and local rain-shadow effects associated with mountain ranges. Dry periglacial steppes with sages and willows dominated the area. Sea levels rose and fell several times due to changes in the size of the Earth's ice sheets and, as a result, the Bering land bridge appeared and disappeared several times during the Pleistocene, each time presenting opportunities for the intercontinental exchange of plant and animal life. Finally, about 11,000 years ago, the Beringian land bridge was again submerged, and remains so today.

The oldest evidence for human occupation of the Americas dates to between about 22,000 and 14,000 years ago. At sites such as the Bluefish Caves in the unglaciated part of the Yukon, Meadowcroft Rockshelter just south of the glacial ice in the United States, and Monte Verde in South America, artifacts have been found and dated to that time. The evidence is sparse and controversial. Little is yet known about these cultures, and there is no evidence for their occupation of the Prairies.

About 13,400 calendrical years ago (11,500 radiocarbon years), an archaeological culture known as Clovis radiated throughout North America south of the ice. As the Pleistocene began to wane and the ice receded, Clovis cultures also moved northward. In terms of age, the Clovis culture is contemporary with early Mesolithic cultures of the Steppes. At that time, the Eurasian megafauna

**Above** Chipped stone spear point, Clovis culture, ca. 11,000 years old (Canadian Museum of Civilization, VIII-G-82)
**Below** Woolly mammoth (*Mammuthus primigenius*) (Larisa Nikolaeva, P. V. Alabin Museum of History and Regional Studies, Samara)

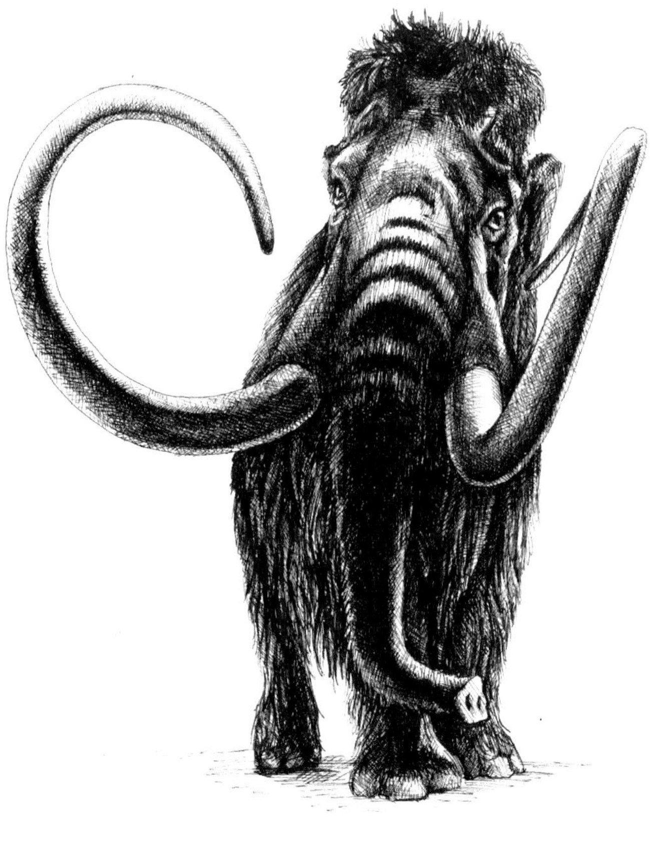

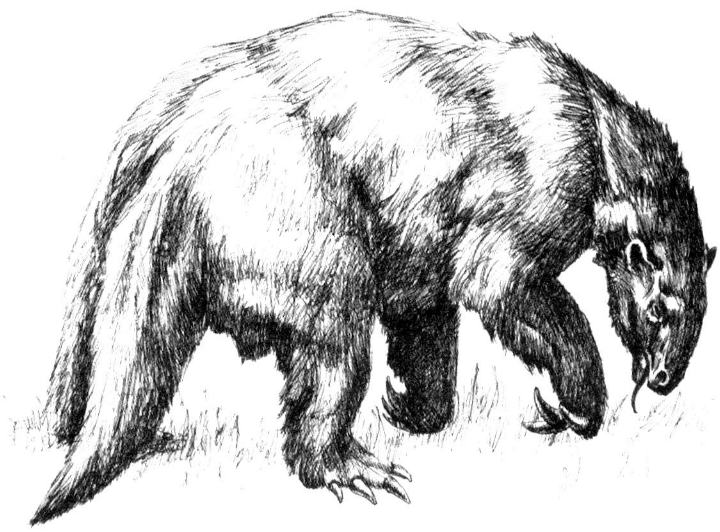

Jefferson's ground sloth (*Megalonyx jeffersonii*) (Larisa Nikolaeva, P. V. Alabin Museum of History and Regional Studies, Samara)

was already extinct, but in North America the megafauna lingered a couple of thousand years longer where it sustained Clovis populations until the end of the Pleistocene. Among the game animals were mammoth, ancient bison, mastodon and caribou. During the late Pleistocene wild horse and camel inhabited the Prairies and likely were hunted as well.

Clovis hunting was somewhat specialized by region, as mammoth and mastodon were more abundant in the central part of the continent, mammoth and giant bison in the southern part, and caribou in the eastern part. However, the set of Clovis tools was quite uniform throughout the continent. It included spears with large fluted projectile points, bifacial knives, unifacial scrapers, knife blades, flake tools, and bone and ivory projectile points and foreshafts. Other key Clovis diagnostics are bone rods and bone projectile points with bevelled bases. These artifacts, along with perforated "bone wrenches" used for straightening spear shafts, show close similarities to Upper Palaeolithic assemblages from the Steppes. It is possible that the atlatl was already used during Clovis times, but spear technology certainly prevailed. Stone chipping materials included quartzite, flint and obsidian of high quality, from sources that were often several hundred kilometres distant from the place where they were used. This suggests wide-ranging travel or trade and a thorough knowledge of stone resources covering large regions.

Archaeologists interpret certain nearly circular clusters of Clovis stone chipping debris, ranging from two to six metres in diameter and including a central hearth, as being traces of light dwellings. Other occupation features of the period include stone cairns used as food and tool caches. Some researchers interpret the caches under stone cairns as ceremonial features. Clovis people used domesticated dogs, the oldest example being at Jaguar Cave, Idaho. Clovis art is represented by engraved stone tablets with various ornaments, such as "checkerboard" and "wheatstone" patterns. Ochre was used as a pigment for ritual purposes and, possibly, for body and clothing decoration.

Currently, there are three main hypotheses concerning the original peopling of the New World; all presume northern Old World origins. The oldest and most deeply seated is that people came by land from Northeast Asia via the Bering land bridge. Once they had reached North America, people migrated southward, either down the West Coast or along a mid-continental ice-free corridor that opened between the Laurentian and Cordilleran ice masses about 12,000 to 13,000 years ago. Neither route has yielded hard evidence for the proposed migrations, in spite of years of research. A second hypothesis is that people crossed the Pacific Ocean in boats on an ocean current. There is little direct evidence supporting this hypothesis in North America. The third hypothesis is that people came in watercraft from southwestern Europe to the east coast of North America. According to this hypothesis, the passage made use of an Atlantic Ocean Gulf Stream that had been redirected from northwestern Europe by a barrier of ice. Although Clovis artifacts do show some interesting similarities to artifacts of the Solutrean culture of southwestern Europe, the age of Solutrean materials is at least 10,000 years older. Consequently, this hypothesis lacks a convincing temporal connection. Thus, we are left with uncertainty about the original peopling of North America.

## Time of Change: Hunters and Gatherers from 11,500 to 8,000 Years Ago

At the end of the last Ice Age, human populations of the Prairies and Steppes were at a similar level of cultural development: hunters and gatherers with similar tool sets, means of subsistence and lifestyles. But with the end of the Ice Age, their environments began to change. The boundary between the Pleistocene and the Holocene epochs, at roughly 11,500 calendar years ago (10,000 radiocarbon years BP), was marked by milder weather and increased precipitation. A belt of spruce-dominated boreal parklands covered both the Steppes and the Prairies for several centuries. That was followed by an abrupt increase in the temperatures of the northern hemisphere. Between 9,700 and 9,000 years ago, the temperature increased more than 10° C. Rapid warming entailed changes in flora and fauna. Forest vegetation started disappearing by 9,000 years ago and was replaced by grasslands vegetation. At the end of the last Ice Age, certain elements of the fauna of both areas went through significant extinctions, including horse and camel in the Prairies, and bison in the Steppes. Some researchers associate these extinctions with hunting pressure, others with changes in the environment. Deprived of all, or at least significant parts, of their megafauna, early Holocene people had to find other game to hunt, develop new hunting strategies, and explore other means of subsistence. As it turned out, the crisis required greater changes in the Steppes, as will be explained below.

Far south of the Steppes, in the Iranian Plateau and Tigris and Euphrates valleys, the first attempts at plant domestication took place about 12,000 to 10,000 years ago. During the same period, far south of the Prairies, in present-day Mexico, the first clearly recognizable cultivated plants appeared about 10,000

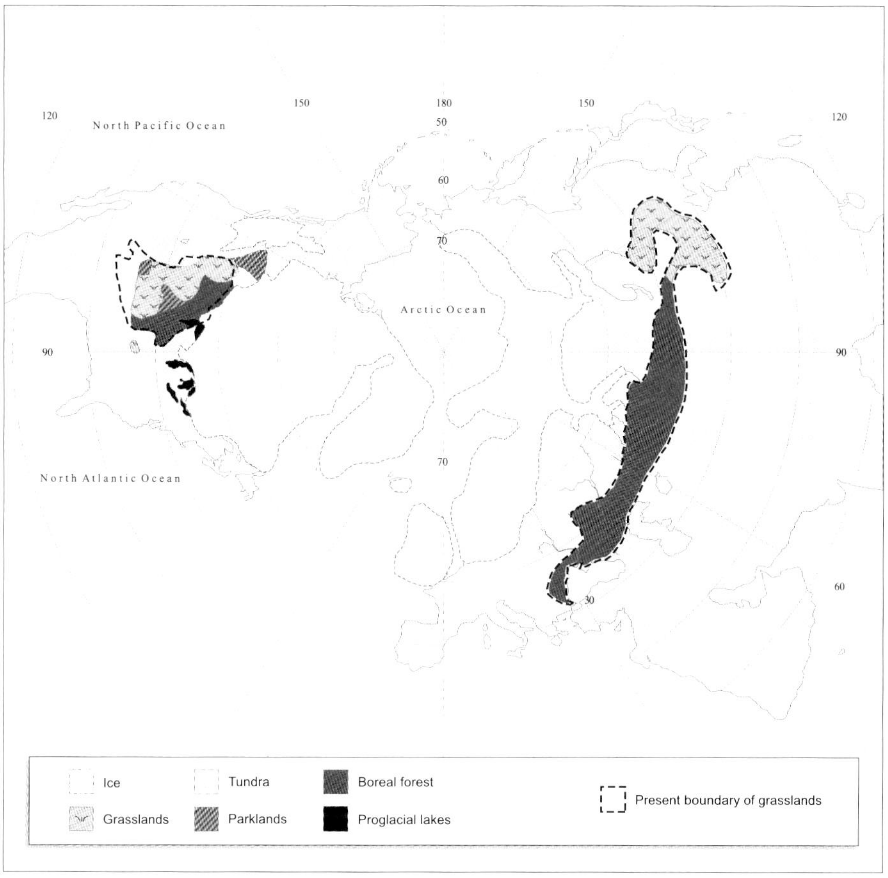


Extent of Northern Grasslands 11,000 years ago (Oleksiy Vasilenko, Canadian Museum of Civilization)

to 8,000 years ago. The Prairies, Siberia and the Russian Far East experienced their thermal maximum between 9,000 and 8,000 years ago. Toward the end of this period, the Prairies and the Steppes were sparsely populated. Only a few sites are recorded for this period. This may be explained by the rapidly changing climate, decline of water supplies and the lack of herd animals (in the Prairies, the decline of ancient bison).

## The Steppes

For a short time at the end of the Pleistocene (the Alleroed – about 9,700 to 9,000 years ago), the area now occupied by the Steppes was covered by spruce savannah, which was later replaced by grasslands vegetation. These environmental changes coincided with the extinction of all species of megafauna. Pleistocene grassland species that survived the extinctions were the horse, the camel and the smaller ungulates: saiga, dzhayran and onager. However, by the beginning of the Holocene epoch, while the Steppes were under open forest, all these herd ungulates inhabited grasslands to the south. The only animals to pursue in the Steppes during this period were moose, deer, elk, wild pig, rodents, birds and fish.

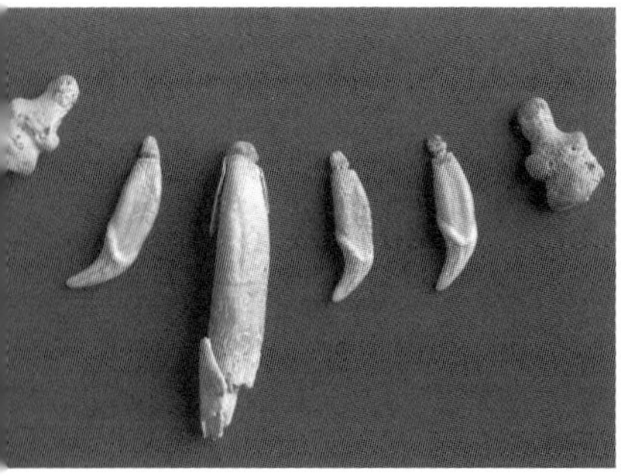

**Above** Necklace made of animal fangs, ca. 10,000 years old (Mesolithic) (P. V. Alabin Museum of History and Regional Studies, Samara, KP-26048/4)
**Below/Left** Flint arrowheads, ca. 10,000 years old (Mesolithic) (P. V. Alabin Museum of History and Regional Studies, Samara, KP-26048/1-3)
**Below/Right** Mesolithic drawings, about 12,000 years old, Cuesta de la Vie, Spain (after S. V. Oshibkina, 1999)

Deprived of megafauna and herd ungulates, the Mesolithic hunters of this period developed methods of individual hunting, started exploring alternative food sources, and invented a new tool kit. Fishing and plant gathering become important parts of subsistence in the Steppes, at least as important as hunting. Many sites are located close to water, reflecting the greater role of fishing. Nets, fishing hooks and dugout boats appeared in this period. As demonstrated by the analysis of human bone remains from Sidelkino (Samara region), plants prevailed in the diet of the local population at the beginning of the Holocene. Tools of this period included woodworking tools (chisels and axes), scrapers for hide working, hammer stones (for stone chipping), and knife blades. Stone tools became smaller: a new microlithic technology was developed, based on pressing out microblades from specially prepared nuclei and producing various geometric shapes (segments, triangles, squares, trapezoids) from the microblades. Bone, ivory or wood shafts with inserted microlithic blades were used as complex tools, for example, knives, sickles and spears. Bows and arrows were invented in Eurasia during the Upper Palaeolithic, but this invention reached the Steppes and became widely used only by the Mesolithic period. From this time on, arrowheads became a part of archaeological assemblages in the Steppes. First finds of travois and skis belong to this era. These reflect changes toward a much more mobile lifestyle in the Mesolithic, likely associated with a decrease in the size of a travelling group. There are some indications that people used light, portable, tipi-like dwellings during the Mesolithic, but in some areas semi-subterranean dwellings are recorded, and in others, light shelters appear to have been made of twigs and branches. The brief occupancy of campsites characteristic of Mesolithic sites is indicated by the thin occupation layers.

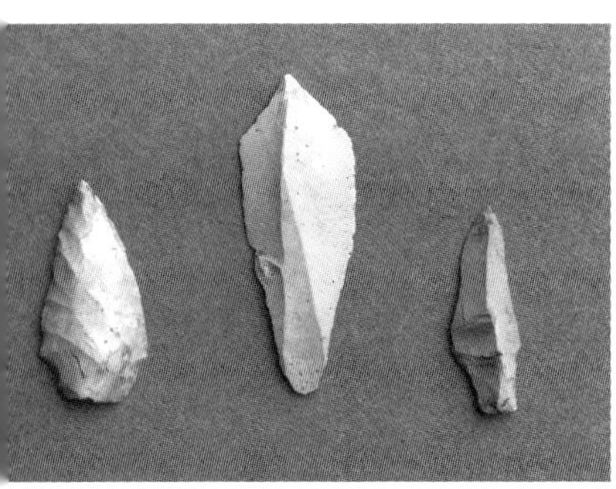

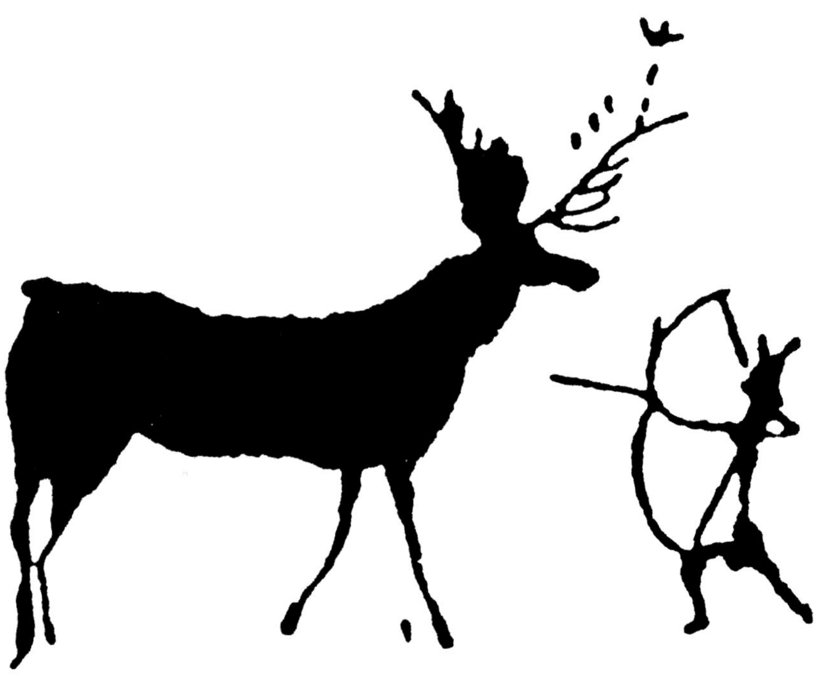

# The Prairies

From about 13,000 years ago on, the continental and mountain glaciers began to retreat from the Prairies, leaving a surface blanketed with stony silt, sand and clay deposits and large dammed glacial lakes immediately south of the ice sheet. By 11,000 years ago, all of the modern Prairies was free of ice, but a large area of what is now Manitoba and eastern Saskatchewan remained under the water of proglacial Lake Agassiz. During the last glaciation, rivers south of the ice sheet flowed either east-west or southward (e.g., the Missouri River), since any path to the north was blocked by ice. Only by about 8,400 years ago did the ice over Hudson Bay collapse, finally allowing the drainage of Lake Agassiz into the Atlantic Ocean. This event (known as the 8.2 ka event) had global consequences, causing a sea level rise of over a metre, flooded shorelines, a decrease in water salinity in the Atlantic Ocean, and a short-term cooling and drying of the climate in the northern hemisphere.

For a short period at the beginning of the Holocene, the area now occupied by the Prairies was covered with forest. Forest vegetation followed the retreating ice sheet northward at least in the eastern part of the modern Prairies: white spruce spread from some southern refugia northwards and formed a belt south of proglacial lakes from about 14,000 to 10,000 years ago. As the early postglacial forest moved north in a belt behind the glaciers, grasslands moved north to replace the shifting forest.

The Pleistocene-Holocene boundary was marked by the dramatic extinction of megafauna in the Prairies. Between 14,000 and 10,000 years ago, following the peopling the North America, 22 genera became extinct, among them camel, horse, mammoth, mastodon, ground sloth, sabretooth cat and tapir. The only species of megafauna that survived in the Prairies was the ancient form of bison. Bison is a Eurasian species that became extinct in the Steppes at about the same time that it became a focus of human attention in the Prairies. The most recent find in the Steppes dates to about 10,000 years ago.

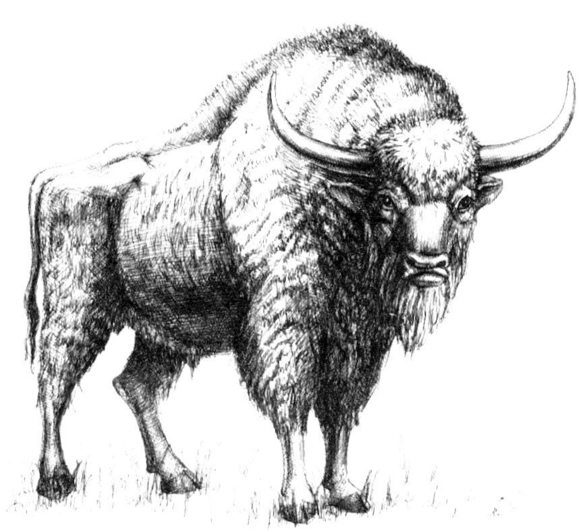

Ancient bison (*Bison antiquus*) (Larisa Nikolaeva, P. V. Alabin Museum of History and Regional Studies, Samara)

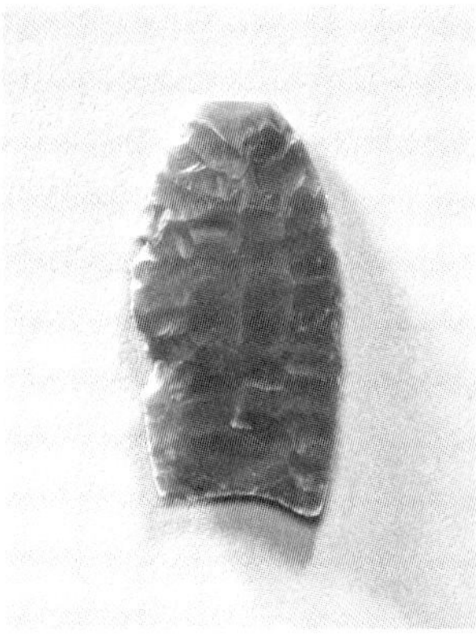

By about 12,600 years ago (10,500 radiocarbon years), Clovis was replaced by regional cultures. From that time on, local game animals and regional sources of raw materials came to play a much greater role. In the Prairies, bison became the subsistence staple of Palaeo-Indian hunters. The bison economy did not necessitate any major changes in hunting tools: spear technology still prevailed. The tool kit of this period included lanceolate and stemmed projectile points, various scrapers, gravers, burin-like tools, drills, biface (butchering) knives and rough-stone tools: hammer stones, choppers and anvils. In comparison to the Clovis culture, later Palaeo-Indian assemblages contain more local materials, such as cherts and quartzites, and no ivory, but little else had changed. In contrast to the Steppes, the Prairies exhibited no use of microblade technology.

## TRANSITION TO NOMADISM 8,000 TO 5,000 YEARS AGO

The period between 8,000 and 5,000 years ago was marked by a prolonged and severe drought in both grassland regions.

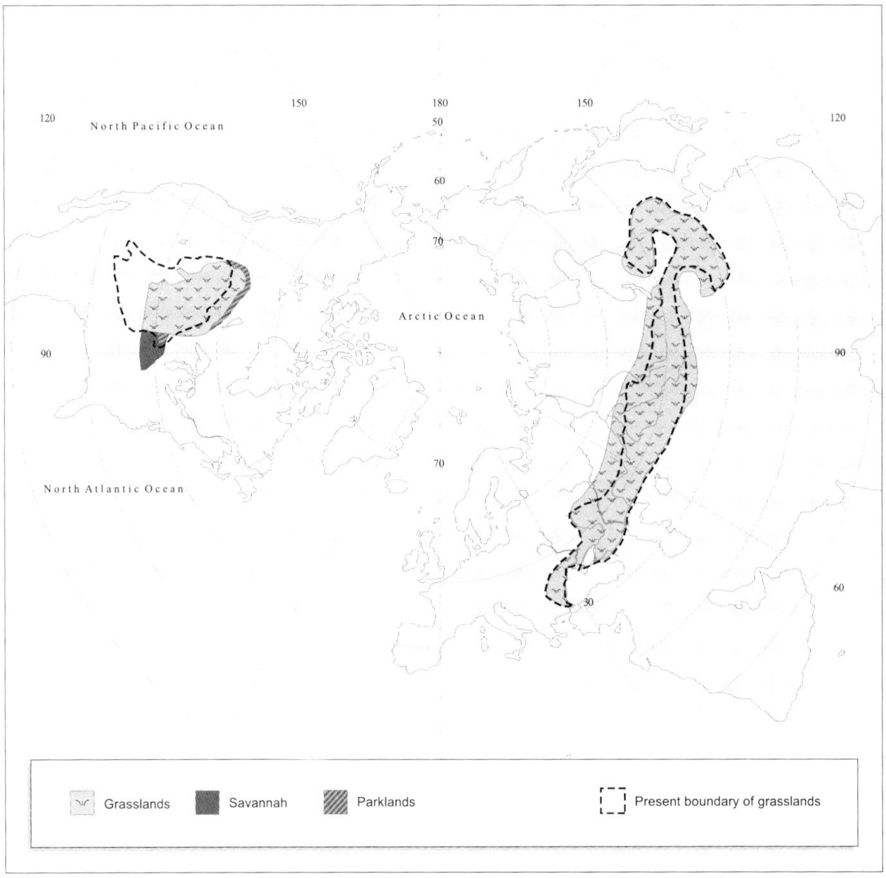


**Above** Folsom culture chipped stone spear point, ca. 10,600 years old (Canadian Museum of Civilization, X-C-161)
**Right** Extent of Northern Grasslands 8,000 years ago (Oleksiy Vasilenko, Canadian Museum of Civilization)

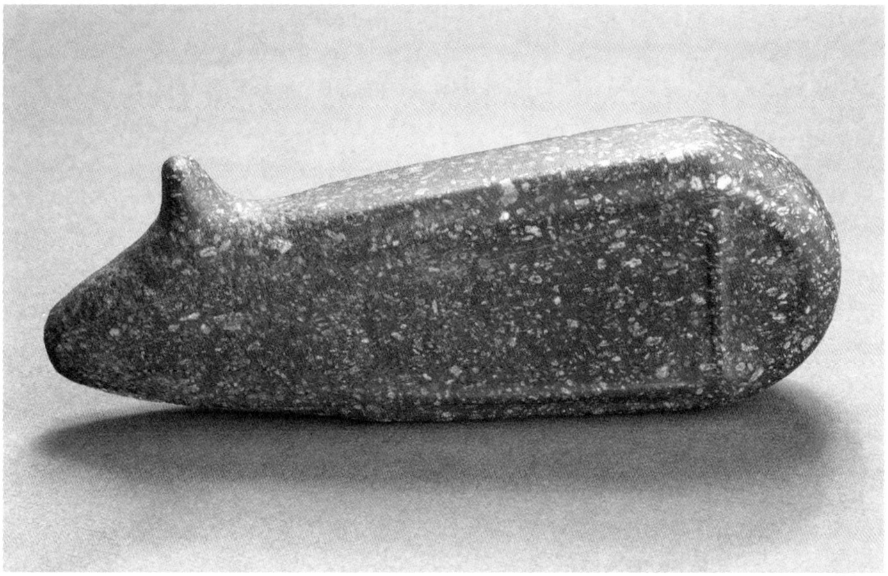

Horse-shaped sceptre made of diorite, ca. 5,000 years old (Eneolithic) (P. V. Alabin Museum of History and Regional Studies, Samara, KP-18485/1)

# The Steppes

Between 8,000 and 6,000 years ago, grasslands expanded 200 to 250 kilometres north and 200 kilometres west of the modern perimeters of the Steppes. During this time, Neolithic newcomers entered the Steppes from areas to the south where domestication of ungulates had already been achieved (see Table). The first domesticated animals brought to the Steppes were sheep and goats. Later, domestic cattle also arrived for use as draft animals and beasts of burden in long-distance migrations. The idea of stockbreeding was rapidly assimilated in Europe where sedentary stockbreeding husbandry was established between 7,000 and 6,000 years ago, but in the Steppes, hunting remained the preferred form of subsistence at the beginning of this period. Bones of domestic oxen have been found in some Early Neolithic sites within the Steppes, but they represent only one generation of animals. The bones of domestic animals were replaced by the bones of game animals in subsequent occupation layers. Later, a firm shift toward pastoralism recurred between 5,400 and 5,200 years ago, recorded archaeologically as a steady high proportion of domestic to wild animal bones.

Neolithic sites in the Steppes were seasonal, and usually near rivers or lakes. Dwellings were mostly semi-subterranean and square in plan, with supporting poles at the centre, hearths off-centre and storage pits around the perimeter. Pottery appeared in the Steppes during this period. The new technology rapidly became widespread, as it allowed for better food preservation and transportation of prepared food. The pottery was mostly flat-bottomed, made of clay with admixtures that varied from region to region, and richly decorated with geometric patterns incised or impressed on exterior surfaces. Along with clay pottery, ceremonial stone objects, such as sceptres and bracelets, appeared in the Steppes at this time. Presumably, these objects reflect connections between the populations of the Steppes and those of the Caucasus and Mesopotamia.

The tool kit of this period includes polished adzes and drill bars (woodworking tools), polished and drilled axes, and end scrapers (hide working tools). Spindle whorls first appear in the Steppes during this period—evidence of weaving. Pestles and mortars also appear for the first time in the Steppes, likely indicating an attempt to include wild plants in the diet. Raw materials used for stone chipping were regional cherts and quartzites. Bone tools and tools for bone-working became diverse and numerous. By about 6,000 years ago, the first copper objects began to appear in the Steppes, and are assumed to have been imported from the Balkan-Karpatian metallurgical province. The first copper objects were mainly jewellery—necklaces, rings, pendants and bracelets. Shortly after the arrival of copper objects, copper-making technology was also imported into the Steppes.

Clay pot, ca. 5,000 years old (Neolithic); the small paired holes indicate ancient repairs. (P. V. Alabin Museum of History and Regional Studies, Samara, KP-25964/130)

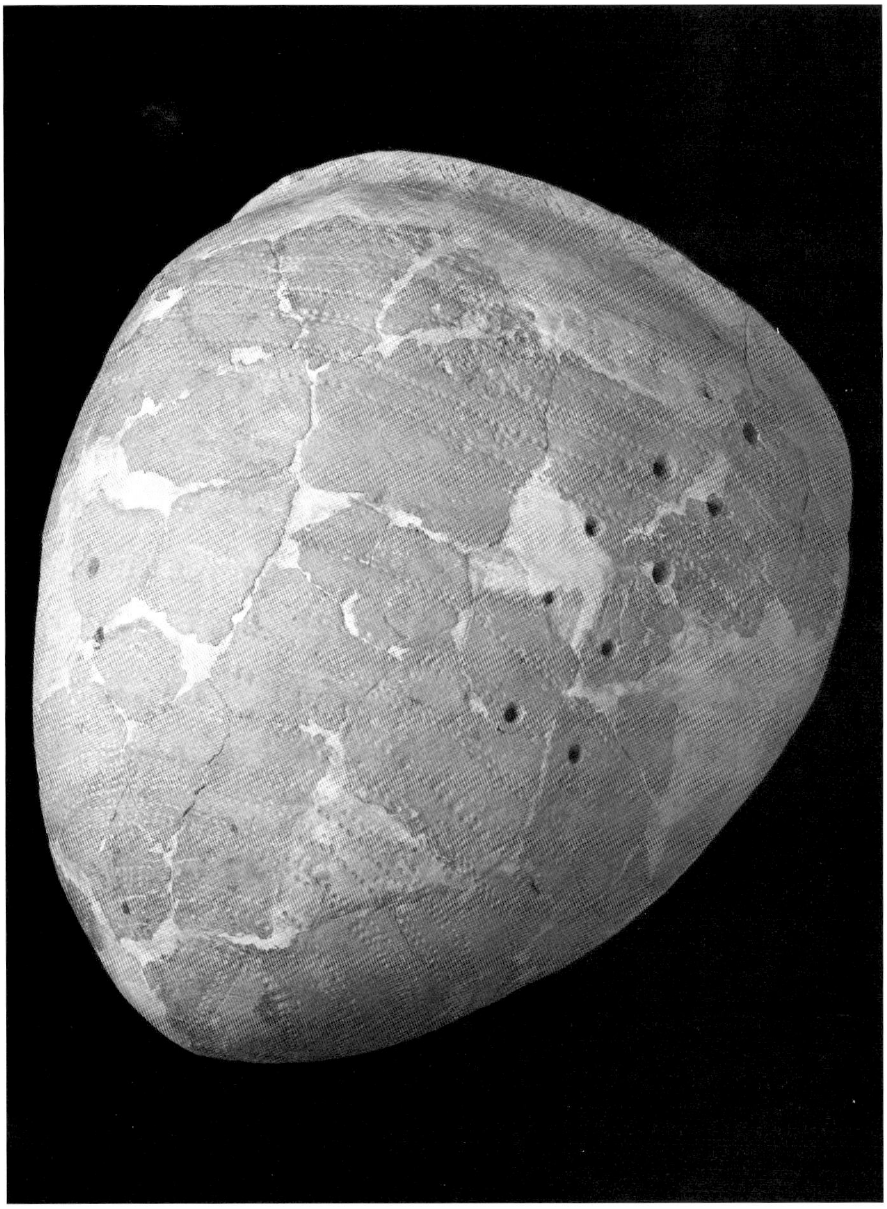

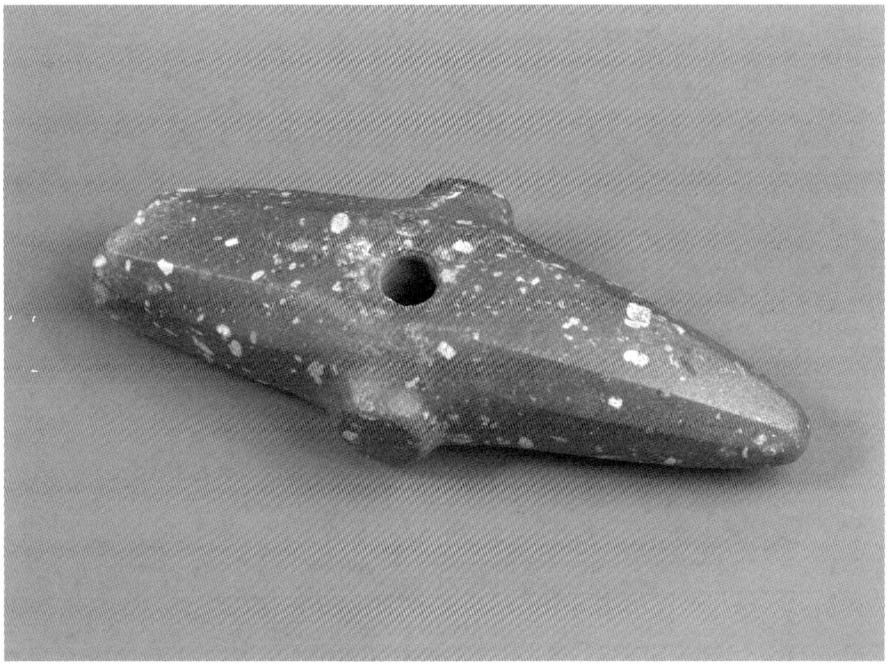

**Left** Polished stone axe, 4,000 years old (Bronze Age) (P. V. Alabin Museum of History and Regional Studies, Samara, KP-22974/1)
**Below** Eneolithic drawing, about 5,000 years old, Okunev Culture, Chernovaya burial site near Krasnoyarsk, Russia (after Vadetzkaya *et al, Sites of Okunevskaya Culture*, 1980, p. 121)

Sometime between 7,000 and 5,000 years ago, the horse was domesticated in the Steppes. Its wild ancestor was either the tarpan or the Przhevalsky horse, both native to the Steppes. The horse became a central feature of steppe cultures, as it allowed for great improvements in the mobility of populations. From this time on, the cult of the horse is recorded archaeologically in many ways, one example being caches, within occupational sites, bearing horse teeth arranged around copper bars. Only after domestication of the horse did a mobile form of stock-breeding become possible.

Art during this transition period is represented by images of various animals (elk, bear, horse, etc.) carved three-dimensionally in wood, bone and stone (stone figurines and finials of stone axes, batons, etc.) and as bas-reliefs on rock surfaces. During this period steppe peoples began to establish large burial grounds with hundreds of individual burials.

| **Animals** | **Place of Domestication** | **Time of Domestication** |
|---|---|---|
| *Sheep* | *Iranian Plateau* | *10,000 to 9,000 years ago* |
| *Goat* | *Mid-East and Caucasus* | *9,000 to 8,000 years ago* |
| *Cattle* | *Anatolia and/or southeastern Europe* | *9,000 to 8,000 years ago* |
| *Horse* | *East-European Steppes* | *7,000 to 5,000 years ago* |
| *Camel* | *Arabian Peninsula and Baktria (Mid-East)* | *4,000 years ago* |
| *Donkey* | *Turkmenistan/Afghanistan* | *4,000 years ago* |

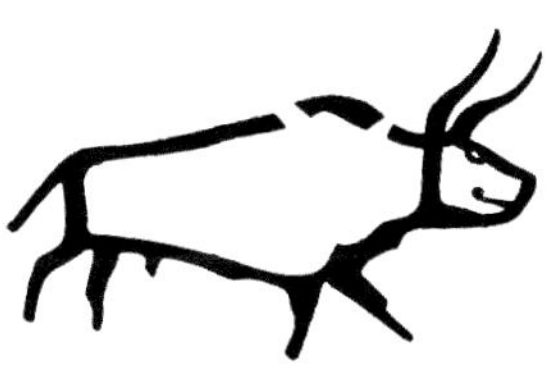

# The Prairies

The early- to mid-Holocene in the Prairies was marked by a prolonged drought (from 9,000 to 6,000 years ago) that extended the grasslands 200 to 250 kilometres north and about 200 kilometres east of their present boundary. During this period, surface and groundwater sources were severely decreased. The salinity of water in seasonal water bodies increased and many water bodies disappeared or became ephemeral. Climate-induced changes in vegetation peaked about 6,000 ago. Arboreal vegetation disappeared from lowlands and riverbanks, and xerophytic, short grass vegetation replaced tall grass prairies. There are some indications that overall vegetation density was reduced while aeolian activity leading to sand dune destabilization and movement increased at this time. It has also been suggested that both human and bison populations were reduced during this harsh period. However, throughout the period, bison remained the subsistence staple in the Prairies although the appearance of the animals was changing, with larger forms giving way to progressively smaller ones.

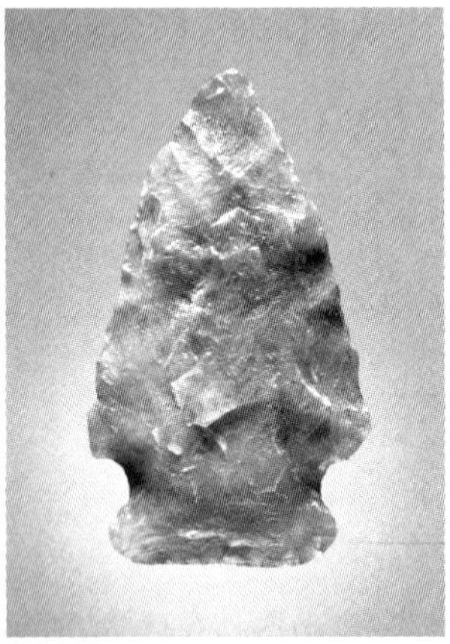

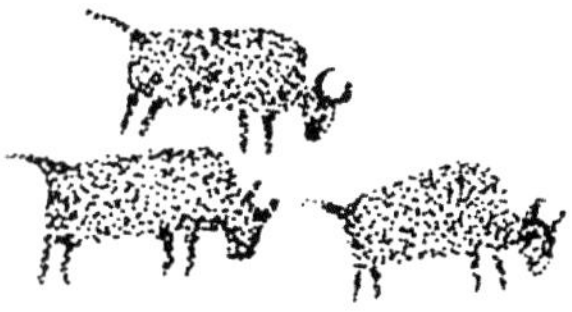

**Above** Mummy Cave complex chipped stone dart point, ca. 7,000–6,000 years old (Canadian Museum of Civilization, X-B-2355b) **Below** Pictograph at the western edge of the Northern Prairies, showing three bison (after Keyser and Klassen, *Plains Indian Rock Art*, 2001, fig. 7.2)

By about 8,000 years ago, lanceolate and stemmed projectile points were replaced by smaller side-notched points. It is presumed that the points were attached to atlatl darts and that the atlatl became the major hunting device during this period. An atlatl consists of a dart with a projectile point, and a throwing stick with a hook against which the rear end of the dart shaft rests. While spears could be thrown up to 15 metres by hand, an atlatl, or spear-thrower, allowed a hunter to hurl a dart up to 30 metres with enough power to injure or kill an animal. A small (60- to 80-gram) weight, a so-called atlatl weight or banner stone, was attached to the midsection of the throwing stick. The weight added accuracy to the dart launch and may also have had value as a hunting charm. The chronology of finds suggests that the atlatl spread northwards from the southeastern United States, where it has been recovered from sites up to 11,000 years of age. Other stone tools included hafted bifaces, biface knives, uniface knives, side scrapers, gravers, drills, spokeshaves, flakers, anvils, hammerstones, grinding stones, cobble spall tools and choppers. Bone tools, such as fleshers, awls, stone flakers, needles, as well as bone beads became a little more common. Chipped stone tools of this period were made mainly of local materials. They were not as finely crafted as in the previous period, and often recycled and retouched. During this period, fire-cracked rocks became abundant in campsites and bison processing sites, marking the beginning of the use of heated rocks for boiling liquids and probably the beginning of pemmican production. The dog remained the only domesticated animal in the Prairies during this time.

Archaeological sites of all kinds are relatively rare for this period in the Prairies and are generally located close to reliable water sources. Records of dwellings are sparse as well; examples are vestiges of subterranean houses, approximately 3 x 3 metres, and stone-weighted lean-to shelters. Toward the end of the period, around 5,000 years ago, vestiges of dwellings are more numerous. These were mainly tipis, whose outlines are preserved as circular rings of stone. About 6,000 years ago, there was an increase in the number of sites in the foothills of Colorado and the Wyoming Front Range at the southwest corner of the Prairies. In this region, pithouses and earth baking ovens appeared and disappeared several times between 6,000 and 3,500 years ago. The earth ovens were used for baking plant tubers. In the same setting, the presence of grinding and milling stones, together with storage pits, likely reflects attempts to incorporate seeds, tubers and other plant resources into the diet. Hand-dug wells become more common in these areas during the two-millennial drought. In combination, these finds may indicate an expanded breadth of diet related to reduced settlement mobility.

By the end of this period, the population of the Prairies came into contact with copper artifacts from the Lake Superior area and started exploring the use of this metal for ceremonial purposes.

# becoming nomads

In both areas, the prerequisites for the nomadic, herd-based lifestyle were in place by about 5,000 years ago. Climate was ameliorating in both areas. Grasslands were becoming more hospitable to people and to animals. At this time, herds of domestic ungulates were brought into the Steppes from the Near East, along with the first wheeled transport and a new diet of milk and milk products. In the Prairies, bison had become smaller and more numerous. Preserved meat and grease had been invented to supply food when fresh bison meat was not available. By 5,000 years ago, the now extinct forms of bison (*Bison antiquus* and *Bison occidentalis*) had been replaced by a smaller form of bison (*Bison bison*) that became more numerous and possibly wider ranging through the Middle and Late Holocene. By about 5,000 to 6,000 years ago, mass bison killing sites, known as jumps, traps and pounds, come into frequent use in the Prairies. Some jumps were reused successfully and repeatedly for the next several millennia. High mobility within certain territories is evidenced by the dominant use of the portable tipi-type dwelling and the short-term use (but frequent reuse) of campsites. Above all, human populations began to rise as bison hunting became a more consistently rewarding lifestyle.

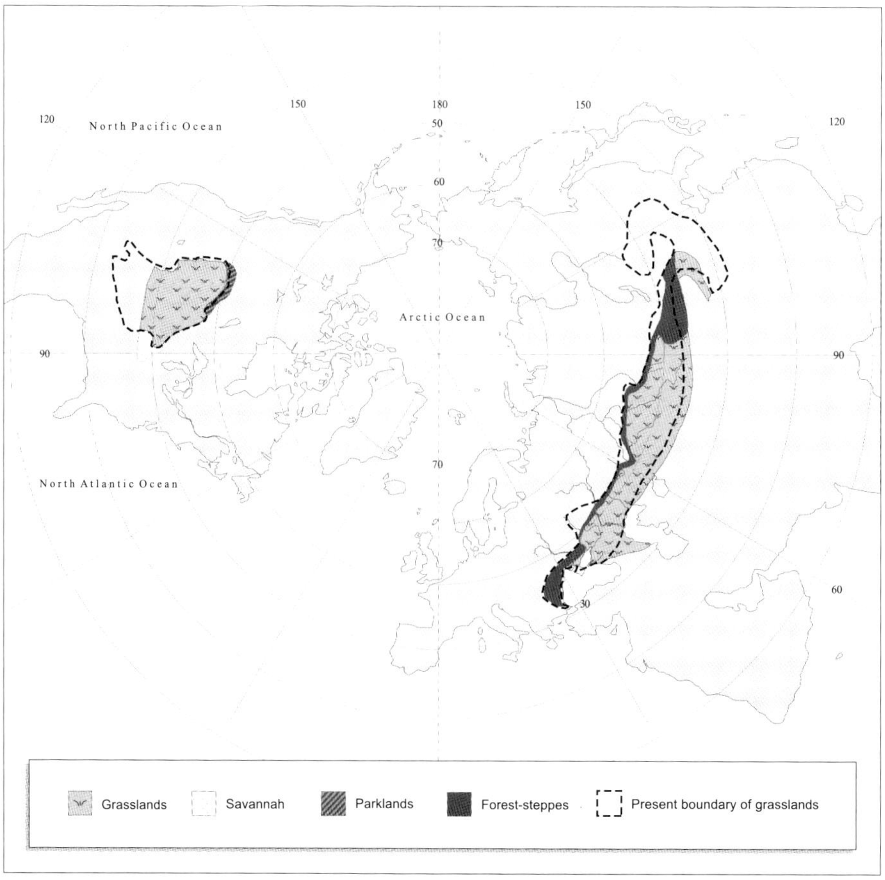


Extent of Northern Grasslands 5,000 years ago (Oleksiy Vasilenko, Canadian Museum of Civilization)

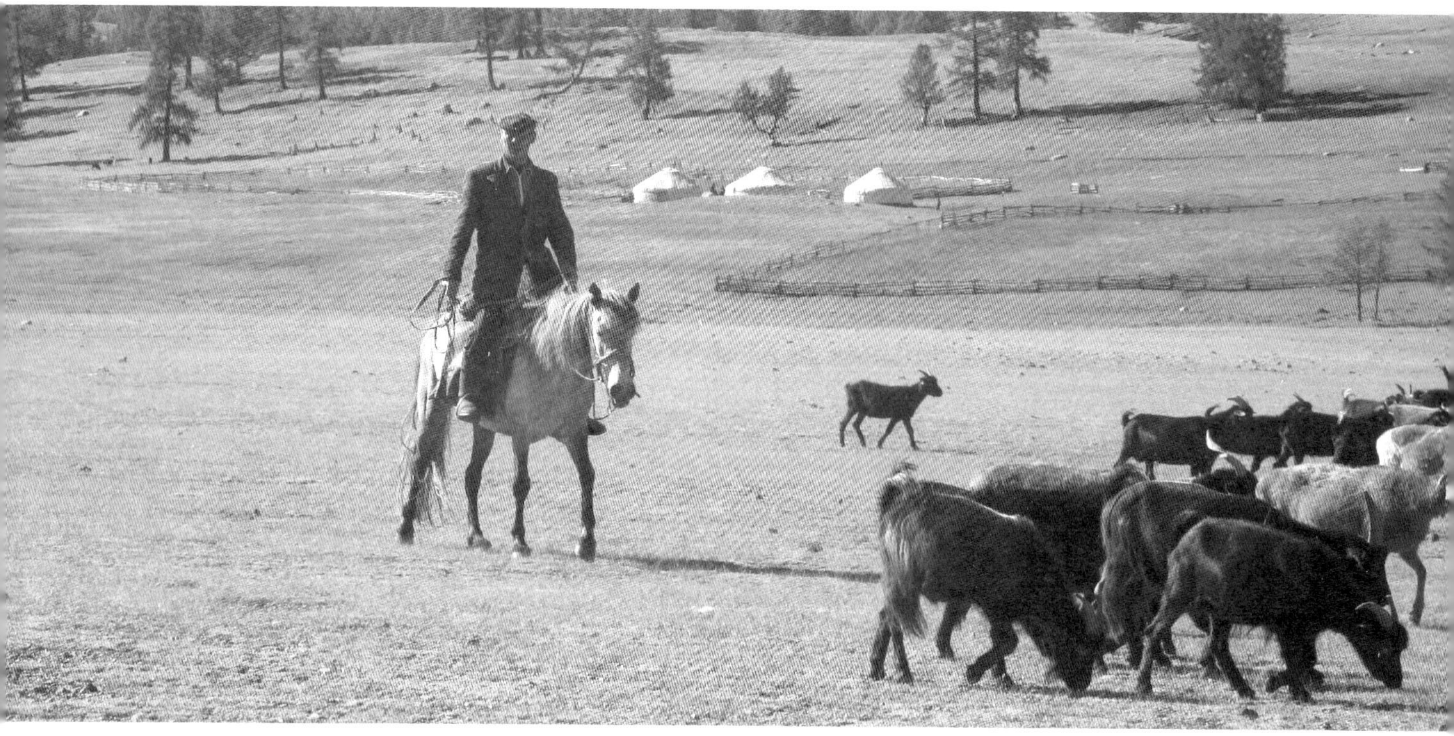

**Above** Mixed herd, Mongolia (courtesy of Matt Reichel)
**Below** Small herd of bison in a water hole (K. Desrochers, Canadian Museum of Civilization S71-2203)

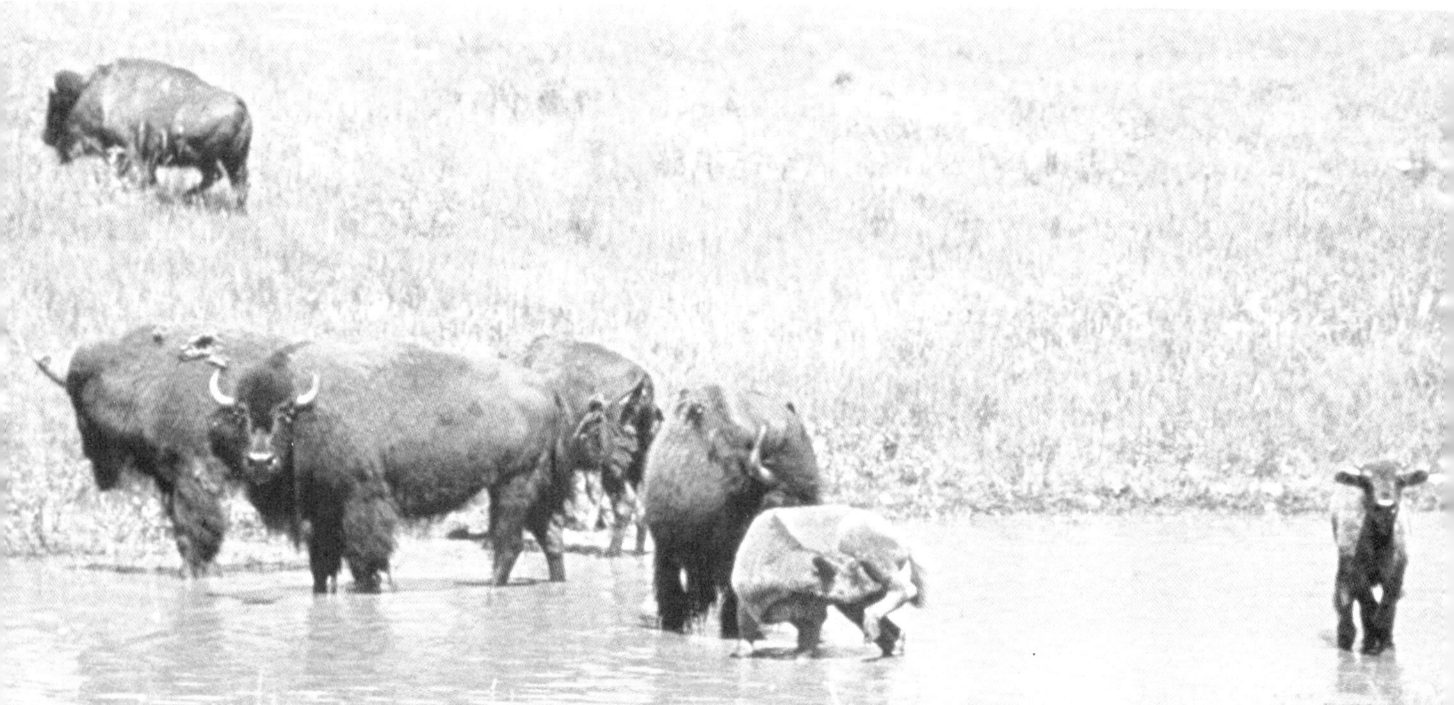

# subsistence

By 5,000 years ago, human populations in the Russian Steppes and Northern Plains had become highly dependent on mobile herds of grass-eating ungulates (hoofed animals). In the case of the Steppes, all the key ungulates were domesticates: horses, sheep, goats and cattle; in the Northern Plains they were wild, primarily bison. In both areas, people shifted their residence seasonally as they followed herds of ungulates into areas where grass quality and quantity were optimal.

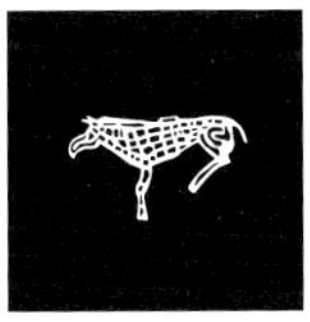 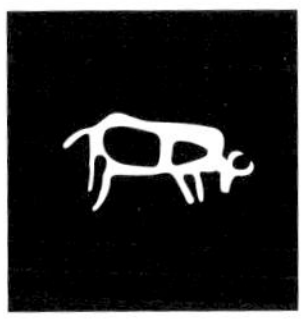

Dwellings were movable, taken with the people as they followed the herds. The most important resources for ungulates, grass and water, were available in different parts of the grasslands in different seasons. Seasonal movements of herds to optimize the use of these resources were either self-driven (in the Northern Plains) or directed by humans (in the Russian Steppes). To migrate with all their goods and chattels, people needed the help of draft animals. Only their domestication made the nomadic lifestyle possible.

In dry grassland landscapes, human migration and occupation is constrained by available water sources. Because the landscape of the Northern Plains is geologically quite young (postglacial), drainage is poorly developed. The land is covered with a network of glacial lakes and potholes that can serve as local water sources for most of the summer. This allowed for slow, non-linear migrations with dogs and people as the sole beasts of burden. The much older landscape of the Russian Steppes is dissected by deep ravines and river valleys that rapidly drain melt water into a relatively small number of permanent water sources. This distribution of water required fast linear, movements of herds and people from one water body to another. It also necessitated improved means of transportation, which steppe people were able to put in place using cattle and horses as draft animals for vehicles, and eventually, horses as riding animals.

In both areas, the growth of human populations was limited by the availability and quality of pastures for their herds. This, in turn, varied according to ten-year, hundred-year, and thousand-year climatic cycles. As a result, human populations grew during wet periods and shrank during prolonged droughts.

The nomadic lifestyle fostered certain group traits. The family group was the most stable and self-sufficient unit in nomadic society. Nomads co-operated willingly and effectively within bands and tribes, but the nomadic lifestyle did not sustain long-lived centralized social structures. Even when such formations appeared in nomadic history, they lasted only a few generations and, then, even the greatest of them dissolved again into loose tribal aggregations.

## steppe nomads

By the end of the Last Ice Age, the surviving herd ungulates of the Eurasian Steppes were horse, saiga and, in southern regions, camel, dzhayran and onager. By about 5,000 years ago, herds of wild horse and saiga had been nearly eliminated by over-hunting. The lifestyle of steppe populations in this time was rather sedentary, with sites located near major water sources, such as river valleys.

The first herds of domesticated ungulates—sheep, goats and cattle—appeared in the Russian Steppes about 5,000 years ago, likely brought by migrants from the Near East. Along with domesticated ungulates came wheeled transport. Two-axle carts with large, heavy wheels made of solid wooden disks were pulled by pairs of oxen. Burials of that time included wheels, whole carts, clay models of carts, and harnessed oxen. Thereafter, regular migrations became possible, and pastoralism began to develop as a form of economy.

However, the use of oxen as principal draught animals put certain limitations on the mobility of the grasslands population. Large cattle are not able to migrate long distances—they move very slowly, need fine forage and large daily amounts of water and are very susceptible to cold winters. In the Near East, use of cattle as the principal draft animal was supported by agricultural production of plant crops in societies with a combined pastoral-agricultural economy. In the western part of the Steppes, attempts were made during the Bronze Age (4,500 to 4,000 years ago) to obtain agricultural products either through agriculture or trade. Sacks of emmer and spelt grain have been found in Catacomb culture burials.

In the Steppes, a cattle-oriented economy could be effective only in river valleys, where fodder was richer than in the open steppes and water was available throughout the year. Permanent settlements of wooden longhouses located close to water were characteristic of the pastoralists of this period. During winter, when snow cover was deep and often crusted with ice, cattle had to be fed with stocked hay, which required hay collection and preservation during the summer. Bronze sickles found in burials of this era confirm the importance of winter provision.

A new stage of pastoralism was achieved with the domestication of the horse, which apparently happened within the Steppes region. The first evidence of horse domestication—changes in the form of teeth, their occlusion or bites, and finds of cheek pieces (psalia)—is dated to about 5,000 years ago. However, the horse was not widely used as either a draft or a riding animal until after the invention of harness specific to them and lightened wheels with spokes. Before these inventions, the horse was a less desirable means of transportation than large cattle. It was inferior in productivity and carrying capacity; small cattle reached sexual maturity faster: one year as opposed to three years in horses. Yet, horses needed less food and water. They could survive on tall, dry, poor-quality forage. Moreover, their grazing stimulated the growth of more nutritious grasses for bovids (cattle, sheep and goats). Most important, however, the horse could paw for food beneath deep snow. Horses can get fodder in pastures covered by 30 to 40, and sometimes even 50 centimetres of snow, whereas small stock can get fodder

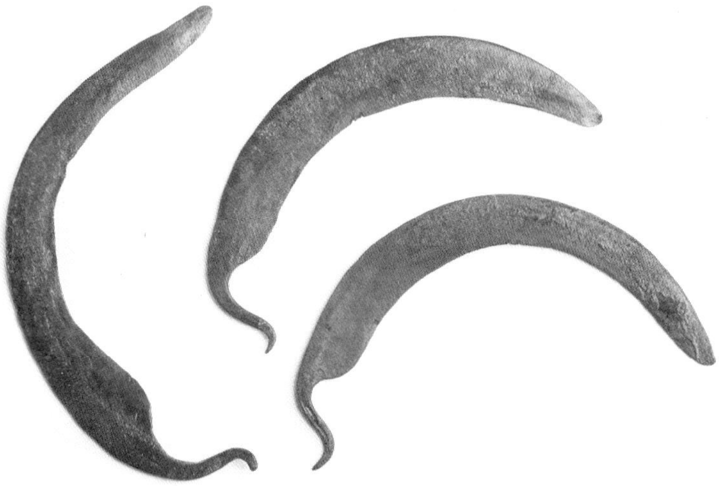

Bronze sickles, ca. 4,000 years old (Bronze Age) (P. V. Alabin Museum of History and Regional Studies, Samara, KP-6/625, 626)

only if the snow cover is less than 15 to 17 centimetres. And, by breaking the snow crust in winter, horses created feeding grounds for sheep and goats. Finally, horses can move faster and for more hours during a day than cattle. Thus, the domestication of the horse and the invention of the harness and vehicles adapted to horses gave pastoralists the means to exploit the open Steppes on dry watersheds. This led to the replacement of the semi-nomadic pastoralist communities of the Bronze Age by the fully nomadic communities of the Early Iron Age. Intriguingly, no occupation sites have been found in the Russian Steppes dating between 2,500 years ago and the formation of nomadic empires about 1,000 years ago.

Seasonal changes of pastures were necessary to provide herds with water and fodder, and to protect them against cold in the winter. Water was the main priority in summer, whereas grass was the main priority during other seasons. The amount of time spent in camps, as well as the number, distance and direction of migrations, depended on these resources. Other factors that could govern migrations were the search for supplementary resources, such as plants and metal, and avoidance of blood-sucking insects. According to historical descriptions, steppe migrations were north-south oriented and regular, the routes remaining generally unchanged over 2,000 years. The regularity of migrations was determined by seasonal changes in vegetation cover. To maintain herds, nomads needed to have fodder along the entire migration route at the stage when the fodder was most nutritious. During spring, nomads began to move their herds toward the northern Steppes where pastures were richer. Winter pastures were located in the southern Steppes where snow cover was shallower. Wintering grounds were near estuaries and lakes, for example in the Manych valley, or at the Caspian Sea coast. The total distance of annual migrations could reach up 2,000 kilometres.

The north-south direction of migrations was governed by the meridional flow of the main rivers. Rivers were major impediments to migration, because most domesticated ungulates did not swim well. On large rivers, crossing places were not numerous. There were, according to historical descriptions, only three river crossings on the mid- and lower Volga River. Nomads used pontoons made of inflated hides, woven reed mats, or hide-covered baskets to move herds across major rivers. Large-scale latitudinal migrations did occasionally happen, shifting people east or west. The preferred destination of such movements was the area west of the Don River, where the climate is more humid and pastures are richer than in the rest of the Steppes.

According to historical observations, steppe nomads spent four to five months on winter pastures, two months on summer pastures, and five to six months travelling between them. On summer and winter pastures, herds were moved one to three times per month, depending on the quality of pastures and herd composition. During migrations between summer and winter pastures, herds were moved once every several days, or even every day, except while fawning.

A characteristic feature of steppe nomadism was the mixed composition of herds, which included sheep, goats, horses and cattle. Proportions among species varied from one region to another, but generally, small stock prevailed. Sheep were the most universal animal, supplying meat and milk, the food staple of the steppe nomads, wool for weaving and trade, skins for clothing and felt for yurt coverings. The animals themselves were valuable trade items. Goats were less

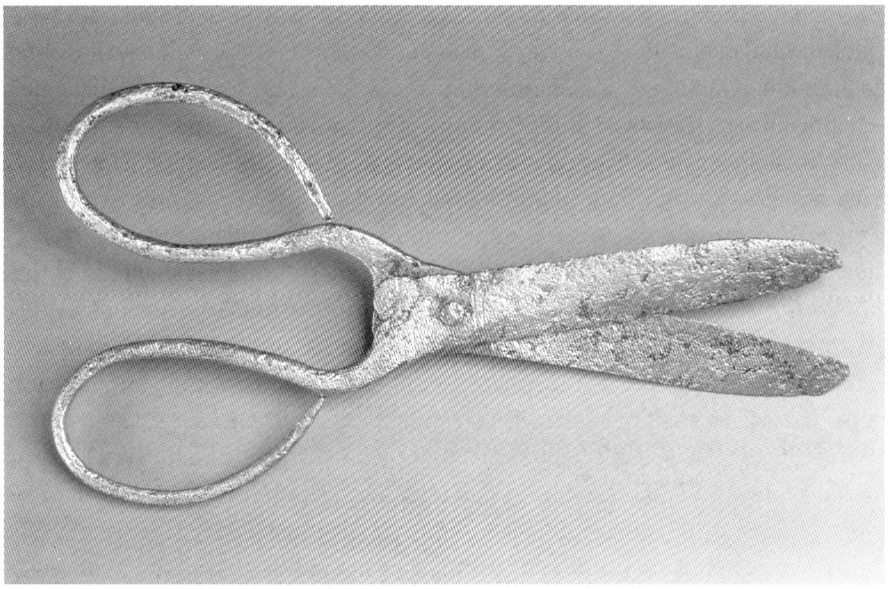

**Above** Iron scissors, late 13th–14th century (Middle Ages, Golden Horde) (P. V. Alabin Museum of History and Regional Studies, Samara, KP-26049/5)
**Below** Bronze horsewhip knob, late 13th–14th century (Middle Ages, Golden Horde) (P. V. Alabin Museum of History and Regional Studies, Samara, KP-23/370)

valuable than sheep, being more difficult to raise and having hair that was not as useful as wool. However, goats were more resilient than sheep and provided insurance against losing an entire herd in a bad year. Goats and sheep are able to graze on the same pastures, using a wide variety of plants and little water (small stock can survive by drinking once in two days). In addition, goats are capable of guiding sheep, making herds easier to control. Cattle need finer fodder and more water than small stock and horses, and are therefore poorly suited to long-distance migrations. According to ethnological descriptions, the proportion of cattle never exceeded 4% of nomadic herds. The proportion of horses in nomadic herds increased through time, reaching a maximum of 20% during the era of the Golden Horde, roughly from 850 to 650 years ago.

The everyday work of nomads was herding. The herder directed the feeding of the herd, moving it so that the area was grazed evenly, while preventing the animals from scattering. This seems like monotonous work, but every decision on herd movement was crucial to the fate of the herds and their owners, and the head of a nomadic group had to make such decisions quickly and independently. Most other types of nomadic work, such as breeding, milking, shearing and slaughtering, were seasonal.

Spring was fawning time, critical for the growth of the herd and, therefore, for the well-being of herd owners. Lambs, foals, kids and calves are born in early spring when the Steppes are still cold and windy and wet newborns are at risk of freezing. Herders had to watch all animals about due to give birth, even sleeping near them at night in order to protect the newborns. Providing salt supplements to herd animals during pregnancy and lactation was another important activity.

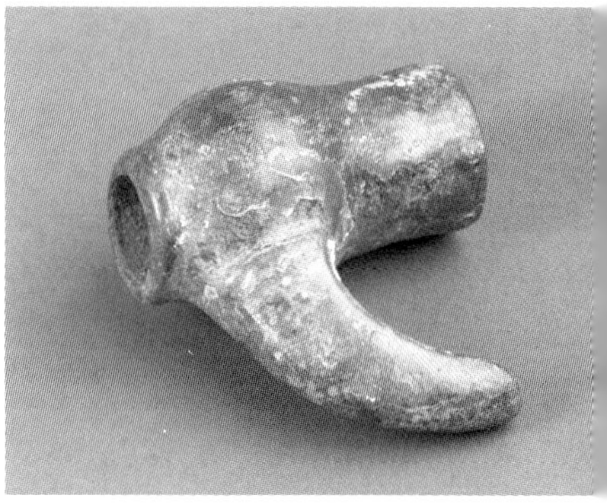

Steppe nomads were heavily dependent on milk and milk products. Their herds supplied milk for only part of the year: horses for six months, sheep for three and goats for four and a half months—all in summer. During these months, animals were milked regularly and part of the milk was preserved in the form of butter and cheese/curd. In summer, sheep and goats were milked one to three times a day, and horses as often as five times a day. At this time of the year, the

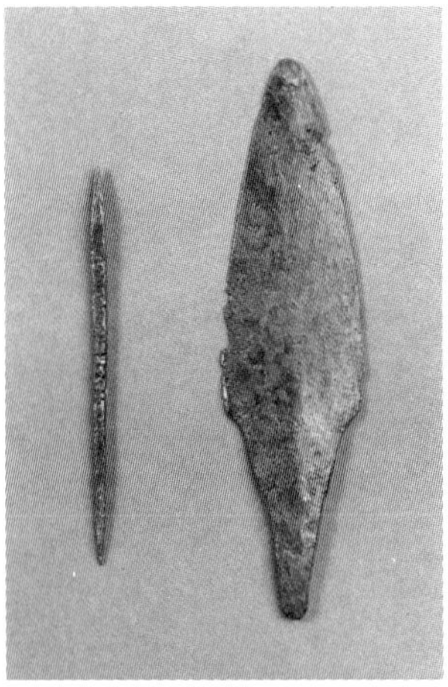

Bronze knife (right) and awl (left), ca. 4,500 years old (P. V. Alabin Museum of History and Regional Studies, Samara, KP-18544/2)

yield per animal and the number of animals milked daily were maximal. Such dairy work could require over six hours per day, and according to ethnological evidence, was done exclusively by women.

Sheep and, to a lesser extent, goats provided wool as well. In different areas, sheep were shorn once in spring, or twice in spring and late summer. The spring shearing removed the winter coat, which was of poorer quality. The second shearing was of better quality, and where possible, women did most of the felt making after the second shearing. Shearing was a productive time for steppe nomads, similar to farmers' harvests, and its completion was celebrated by feasting.

Meat of all domestic animals except camels was used for food. Animals were usually slaughtered at the end of fall and during winter. By late fall animals had gained their maximal annual weight and their fur was at its best. The annual slaughter was actually a culling process, which aimed to achieve or maintain a certain composition of the herd. For example, in a natural population of horses, a family group is composed of a stallion, his mares (commonly five or six per stallion) and their young. The nomads increased the proportion of mares, reaching up to 15 per stallion. All male horses not required for breeding were castrated in order to achieve better obedience. Riding horses were mostly geldings; mares and stallions were saved for breeding and production of milk and meat. Horses were slaughtered either at one to four years of age, when there was a surplus of young animals not needed for breeding and working, or after 15 years of age when fecundity and strength had declined.

Once the decision to begin slaughtering was made, the work could be completed over the span of a few days. Meat harvested in late fall could be eaten fresh, or frozen for later use. The factor limiting meat preservation was storage space, as an average group of five nomadic families would have to deal with 20 to 50 carcasses each winter. One solution was to store meat in dug-out pits within dwellings; another was to build special shelters for meat storage. The former method has been recorded both archaeologically and ethnologically, the latter only ethnologically.

A certain minimum number of animals was required to maintain the herd and to provide food and transportation. According to eighteenth-century ethnological sources, the average Kazakh family of five needed about 20 horses, 50 sheep, and 6 head of large cattle to survive. To ensure identification, each nomadic group marked their animals. This could be done by cutting one ear in a distinctive way, marking the animals with paint, or branding them. Larger herds provided a more stable food supply. They were also easier to control because animals tend to behave more gregariously in large numbers. Just one herdsman on horseback helped by dogs could look after 400 to 500 sheep and goats, while two herdsmen were needed to control 300 to 400 horses. However, during the summer, the livestock was divided into several sub-herds, such as lactating sheep and goats, nursing infants, non-lactating females and young males. To direct such sub-herds, each group of nomads needed several herders.

Beside epidemics, the major external factor limiting the increase of herds was the availability of pastures. Each nomadic family needed at least 200 to 400 hectares of pasture. The number of nomads, the number of livestock, and the abundance of grass were interrelated. The size of nomadic populations was limited by the carrying capacity of pastures in the least productive years. Carrying capacity was lowest during droughts, which hit the Steppes once every six to ten years. Under the effect of drought, the biomass of wild plants might drop fivefold, causing a somewhat smaller decrease in the herd size. Large-scale losses could be caused by other natural disasters, such as heavy snowfalls. Historical sources indicate that between 2,000 years ago and the nineteenth century, losses of up to 50% of animals in a herd happened approximately once a decade. Food shortage in the ensuing years resulted in mortality in the nomadic populations, starting with the children and the old. Populations sometimes decreased by 50 to 70% during the times of famine. The greatest steppe population occurred during the Golden Horde period (750 to 650 years ago), when there were about one million people.

Once the grass resources had been used to their maximum extent, the human population reached its maximum and no further population growth could be achieved. The only possibility for expansion was to turn forests and agricultural

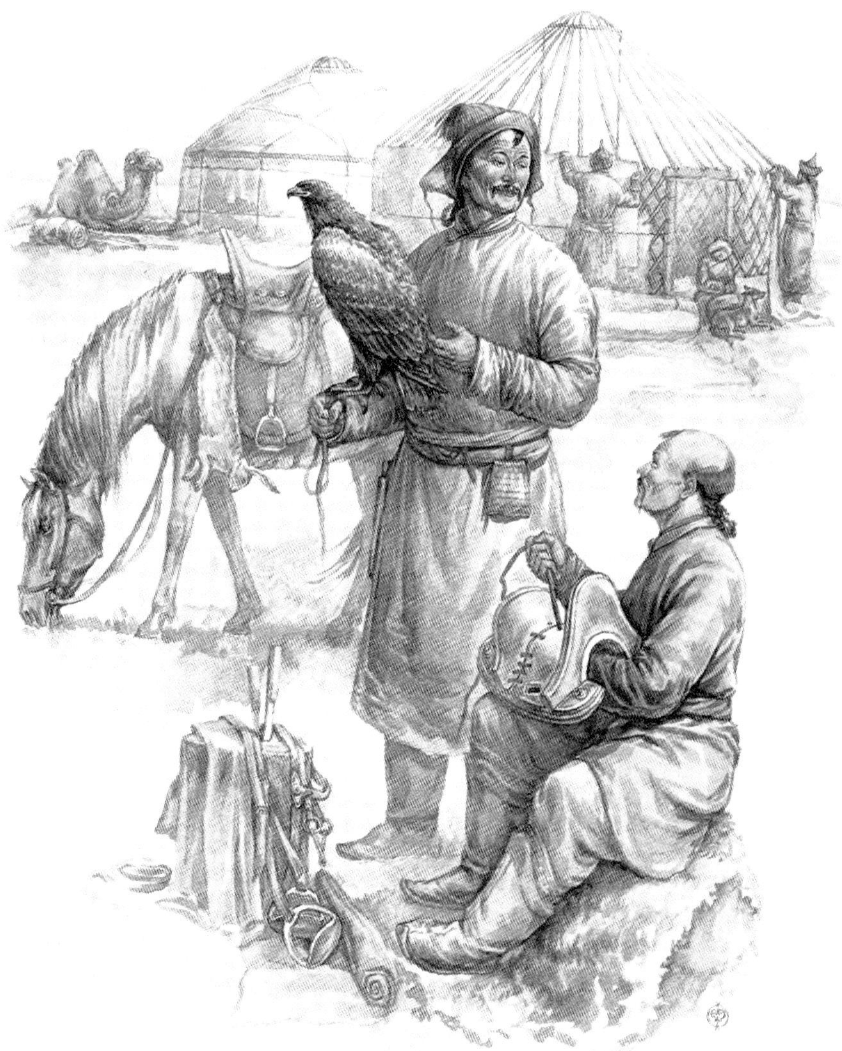

Mongols, 13th century A.D. (courtesy of Oleg Fedorov)

areas into pastures, at the cost of one's neighbours. Traces of repeated burnings of surface vegetation are typical for soils buried under various embankments made by nomadic pastoralists, such as the burial mounds of the Bronze Age. Burning was widely used to maintain and improve the existing pastures and to expand pastures into forested areas.

Although pastoralism was the subsistence base for steppe nomads, they also hunted wild game. Seasonal hunts in spring and summer were the main source of meat during the periods of breeding, parturition and lactation of domestic animals. Wild animals were also hunted in emergencies, for instance during war marches. The main methods of hunting were the chase (bay hunting) and round-up (battue). Ad hoc groups used the former; groups of militarized nomads practiced the latter. Large amounts of meat could be obtained in one hunt using these methods, and at the same time, people developed warrior skills and polished their social status as warriors. Hunting could be done not only in a group, but also by individuals, in which case it was performed with the help of dogs or falcons. Nomadic populations also practiced fishing, judging by archaeological finds of fishhooks and of human bones whose isotopic composition reflects the frequent consumption of fish.

Grass resources were used most efficiently by small groups of nomads, because large aggregations of people and stock necessitated almost continuous travel, which was too exhausting for lactating animals. Therefore, for most of the year, nomads migrated in small groups. A number of groups bound by real or fictitious kinship formed a tribe. Tribal areas were usually bordered by rivers. However, the nomadic lifestyle did not preclude a centralized social organization, such as a state. In such formations, which appeared repeatedly in the Russian Steppes from the Early Iron Age on, administrative techniques borrowed from sedentary agricultural societies were imposed on the nomadic lifestyle. Yet, the longevity of nomadic states was very short. Even the greatest of them was eventually replaced by fluid tribal aggregations.

## PRAIRIE NOMADS

The only large Northern Plains ungulate to survive the last Ice Age was the bison. From 10,000 years ago until the late 1800s, bison remained the subsistence staple of Northern Plains societies. Bison is a Eurasian species that evolved in the Steppes and entered North America about 300,000 years ago. Early forms of bison were generally larger than modern bison, and had longer, straighter horns. Between 10,000 and 5,000 years ago, the bison's appearance underwent significant changes, and by about 5,000 years ago, it had evolved into its present form (*Bison bison*). In just a few thousand years, body size decreased by 10%, and skull and horn dimensions decreased even more, with horns becoming shorter, more curved and more forward-pointing. The latter trait is believed to be associated with defence against increased wolf predation. At the same time, human predation probably played a role in increasing the bison's habit of flight (rather than standing and fighting) as a defence mechanism. The long period of drought during the first part of the Holocene decreased the value of Great Plains pastures and forced bison to expend more energy searching for food. By the end of the drought, the bison were smaller, more numerous, more gregarious and more mobile.

The bison is a grazer with a preference for short and middle-height grasses, such as Blue Grama Grass and Spear Grass. Unlike many ungulates, the bison does not browse shrubs, twigs or leaves of trees. Another trait that sets the bison apart is that it does not need salt licks. Although bison are not able to paw like horses, they can make craters in soft snow by sweeping it with their heads. The ability of bison to feed throughout the winter in the Northern Plains is facilitated by shallow snow cover, and strong winds that expose low-lying vegetation. Bison suffer most in winter after a freeze-thaw-freeze cycle or after freezing rain when the snow is covered by a hard crust and fodder is not available. By the 1700s when the first Euroamericans began to live in the Northern Plains, bison were the most numerous, dominant and thriving game animals in the world, numbering as many as 30 million animals for the whole Great Plains, with 15 to 18 million in the Northern Plains.

Depending on the microenvironment, each bison required from one-half to three hectares of grassland to supply sufficient forage for a month. Living in herds, bison consumed grass quickly, which kept them constantly on the move in search of fodder and water. Although described by early travellers as chaotically roaming animals, bison herds maintained certain seasonal directions to their movements, with the annual distance of travel being about 500 to 1,000 kilometres. In spring, herds began moving from their wintering grounds in the parklands on the fringes of the Northern Plains toward open grasslands and, later in the summer, further south, to mixed prairies. Two to three months were spent on summer pastures in the open prairies, where mating occurred. In richer pastures, herds were large and their migrations were minimal. In areas with sparse vegetation, herds were smaller and migrations were greater.

Water was another important resource that governed summer migrations. Because the Northern Plains landscape is young, drainage systems are weakly developed, leaving a network of lakes and potholes that can serve as local water sources for most of the summer during years of average precipitation. During periodic droughts, however, most seasonal sloughs disappear early in summer. In such years, large numbers of bison gathered near the few permanent water sources available and overgrazed the surrounding area. In the fall, when water supply was at its minimum (and salinity was increasing) herds began moving to winter ranges in parklands, forested river valleys, uplands and sand dune regions, where blizzards and snow crusting were less severe. The movement to wintering grounds generally began in late October or early November. However, migrations were not totally predictable and depended on the weather pattern. When winters were mild or produced little snow, bison herds remained in the open prairies.

Bison tended to retrace their paths, treading trails that also became convenient passages through the Prairies for nomads. Rivers posed no barrier to bison migration. Herds were often seen crossing major rivers such as the Missouri and Saskatchewan. Such crossings were marked by well-established trails leading to each side.

The composition of bison herds changed with the annual cycle. The mating season continued from late July to early September and occurred in open prairies. During this period, while the biomass of grasses was greatest and most nutritious, bison aggregated into large herds that stretched for kilometres. Historic travellers who passed through the Northern Plains during the mating season reported that bison covered the whole country for several days of travel. During the mid-1800s, two separate populations of bison (eastern and western) were described, occupying the Grand Coteau-Red River range and the Saskatchewan range, each with different rutting grounds.

After the rut, the big herds dispersed and formed small groups in search of food and shelter. Large bulls formed male herds in which they recovered from injuries and slowly regained weight. Females roamed in separate herds with calves, yearlings and young bulls. Male and female herds selected somewhat different pastures. The bison is a fast runner, but only on hard ground. On soft ground, it is vulnerable and can be overtaken by wolves. Bulls preferred areas with richer fodder, which often had softer soil and therefore were less secure in case of predator attack. On such grounds, bulls grazed in small groups, staying far apart. Cows selected poorer, but harder and therefore safer, grounds for pastures. They tended to forage in large herds, staying close together. Bull groups ranged from 5 to 15 animals in a group; cow groups averaged around 20 animals, but occasionally reached up to 100.

Although bison are well adapted to winter weather, survival during that season could be difficult, especially for calves, due to lack of forage and severe predation. During winter, herds were large, although not nearly as large as for the mating season, and migrations were minimal whenever fodder could be easily obtained.

Calves were born in late May or early June, just before the appearance of the first new grass. At this time, bison moved out into the open prairies. The composition of groups was quite variable. Animals separated or aggregated according to the quality of pastures, which was affected by such local factors as fires, droughts or overgrazing.

Prairie nomads adapted their movements to the migrations and biological cycles of bison herds. A certain degree of regularity in bison migrations allowed the nomads to predict roughly where the animals would be grazing in each season. The pace, distance and direction of human movements was generally controlled by those of the bison. Nomads were unable to control bison movements other than by burning grass. The use of dogs as shepherds was not possible, as bison had strong defensive mechanisms for use against both wolves and dogs.

The well-being of prairie nomads depended on the quality of pasturage for bison. They often fired the prairies deliberately to improve the grass. When set in spring, fires helped to reduce shrubs and accelerated new growth of fine fodder (grasses) that attracted the bison. However, fires could also destroy pastures if they were set, or occurred accidentally, at the wrong time of year. In fall, fires could spread swiftly for many hundreds of kilometres, leaving bison without fodder for the coming winter. Even worse, entire bison herds that were overtaken by wild fires could be destroyed by the flames.

Prairie nomads moved, gathered and dispersed through the year as the bison herds aggregated and dispersed. In summer, just before the bison mating season, large tribal gatherings brought hundreds, and sometimes thousands, of people together for ceremonial, social and recreational purposes, and for trade. In autumn, nomads divided into bands and radiated out to track migrating bison, later recongregating into large enough groups to commence the late fall communal hunts. Large quantities of meat and fat were processed and preserved during communal hunts against periods when winter hunting might fail. These hunts were sometimes continued well into winter and drew large aggregations of people as long as the bison remained in the area. Nomads preferred to winter in sheltered areas such as river valleys with plenty of wood for fuel. However, when bison failed to come to such areas, or deserted after a short visit, the nomads would have to hunt in wider and wider circles and eventually move to a more successful hunting area.

Except during winter when dogs could pull sleds on the run, the rate of travel was generally a walking pace. Try as they might, people could not keep up with a fast-moving bison herd, so they spent considerable time just locating herds that might be exploited until they were frightened away or moved off to find better pasturage.

Finding the bison, or better yet, having them come into the locality in which one was living, did not always happen when people needed fresh supplies of food. Consequently, nomads performed various ceremonies meant to attract the animals to them and to ensure success in hunting. Early observers called one such ceremony "the Bull Dance." A dozen or more young men, holding their weapons and wearing the skin of a bison head or a mask with bison horns, danced to the beat of drums, rattles, songs and chants. When they were exhausted, the dancers fell like killed bison and were dragged out of the dance area by the heels. The dance was performed day and night until the bison finally came to the hunting grounds. Small pieces of fossil ammonites, called iniskims or buffalo stones because they resembled bison, were also used to attract bison. Iniskims were painted red, set in a nest of bison hair and wrapped in the skin of a bison fetus. This medicine bundle was placed on a tripod outside the owner's tipi, and tribute was paid to it by smudging sweetgrass twice a day. As they

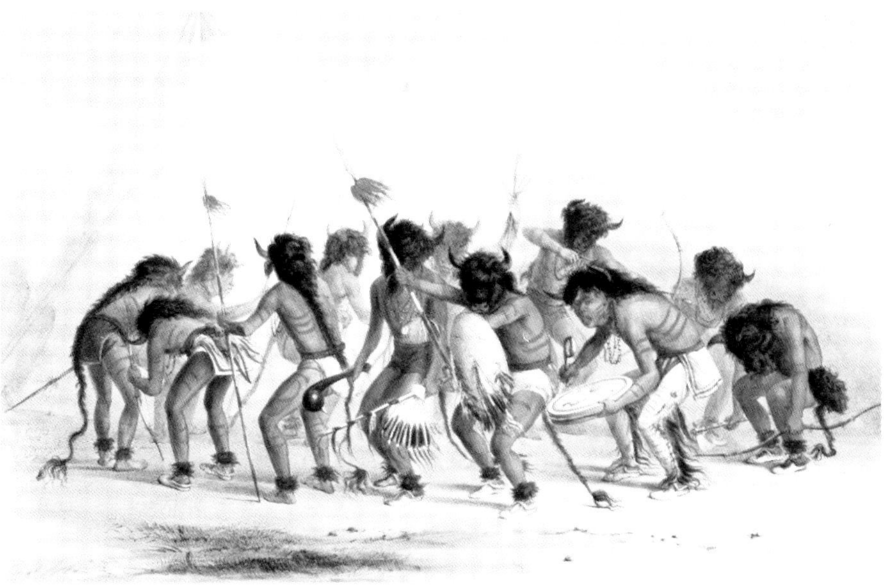

Bison dance (George Catlin, 1830s, Library and Archives Canada C-100019)

travelled, nomads occasionally encountered huge, solitary erratic boulders in spectacular landscape situations. Often used by bison as "rubbing stones" and sometimes even resembling bison, these boulders were regarded by the nomads as sacred and were propitiated with offerings. In places where such natural monuments did not exist, nomads sometimes built a stone cairn surmounted with a bison skull as a landmark honouring the bison. It may also be noted that the majority of large ceremonial structures created by prairie nomads, such as stone medicine wheels, rock and cairn alignments, and animal effigies, are associated with rutting season pastures.

Bison herds have social defence mechanisms, for example, special poses and dense packing of the group, which they use to protect themselves from attack by single or small groups of predators such as bears, wolves and large cats. However, when attacked by a pack of wolves or a group of hunters, bison react by fleeing. The modern bison can be goaded into running more easily than any other cattle species, and that trait was exploited by nomadic populations of the Prairies in their hunting practice.

According to historical descriptions, often confirmed by archaeological studies, nomads used a variety of techniques to hunt bison.

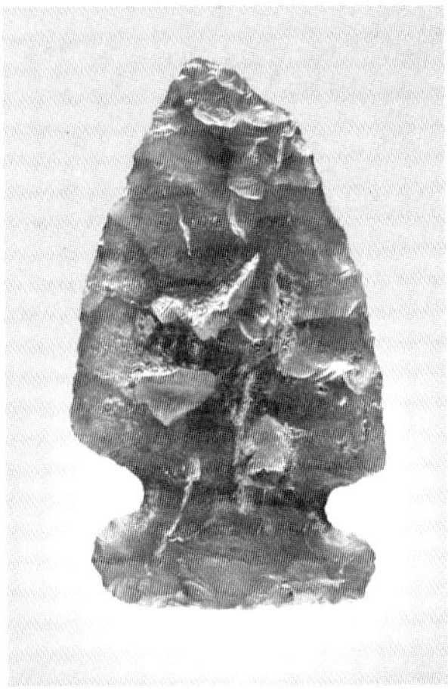

Late side-notched chipped stone arrow point, ca. 1,400–1,100 years old (Canadian Museum of Civilization, X-A-2837)

**Surround hunt.** According to historical descriptions, pedestrian hunters surrounded a small herd of bison and began to close the circle, yelling. When frightened, bison tend to veer to the right. The surrounded animals would begin to circle clockwise, sequentially spooked by the hunters who tried to keep them running in a circle. Once the circle of running bison was sufficiently tight and within bowshot, the hunters picked their targets and shot the bison with arrows. Such hunts were usually held on still days, when the animals were less likely to scent the approaching humans. Bison have an acute sense of smell, but poor vision.

**Wolf tactic.** Since the beginning of the Holocene, the major predator of bison was pack-hunting wolves. Bison were accustomed to wolf packs following their herds (up to 70 in a pack, as described in the 1800s). For the most part, wolves subsisted on the sick, the injured and the young. Bison were well able to defend themselves against single wolves. Indeed, they could kill or drive them off with relative ease. Therefore, bison were quite tolerant of small numbers of wolves, even in fairly close proximity. Hiding under a wolf skin, a hunter could crawl toward a bison herd on hands and knees, approaching to within shooting range of the bow or atlatl. In winter, a hunter covered with a wolf skin could penetrate a herd on a sled pulled by a couple of dogs, and shoot several bison at a time.

**Bison pound.** The herd could also be driven into a corral, where the animals were quickly slaughtered. Hunters made a circular corral, fenced with wooden posts interwoven with branches, with a ramp-like gate and a funnel-shaped corridor-entrance. A large cut tree or pole was set in the centre of the corral. On it, a spiritual leader of the hunting group placed objects that were believed to attract bison; among them often were painted bison skulls. Two rows of people spread in a long line extending out from the entrance to the pound, hiding under robes or leafy branches. Once the bison herd appeared, the hidden people jumped up, waved their robes and yelled, trying to spook the herd toward the pound. When the animals entered the pound, they circled around the tree until all the animals were in or the pound was full. Then the hunters

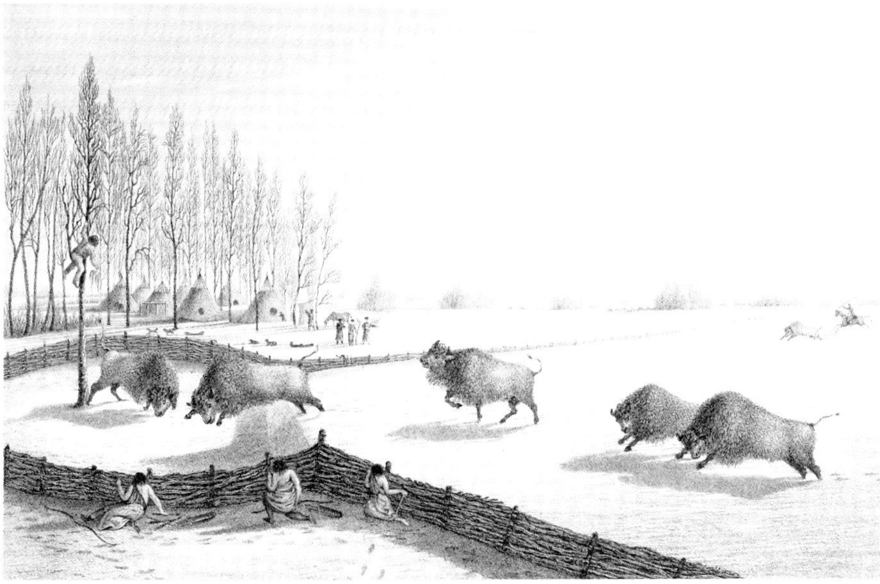

A bison pound (George Back, 1820, Library and Archives Canada C-033615)

closed the gates and the killing began. Another method of driving the herd in a desired direction was by setting small fires downwind to frighten the bison toward the pound. However, fire was not always manageable in grasslands conditions, as the wind could change direction unpredictably, driving the herd away from the pound.

**Bison jump (*piskun* in Blackfoot).** In western parts of the Plains, nomads drove bison to steep cliffs over which they cascaded to serious injury or death. Successful jump sites were not easily detected by the bison as they approached. The landform that assured this had a surface that rose slightly just before the herd reached the cliff. To channel the bison toward the cliff, hunters constructed long rows of stone cairns leading to the jump. Cairns were sometimes topped with branches, behind which the hunters could hide. As the bison moved between two lines of cairns, hunters rose to frighten them along in the right direction and to prevent any deviation from the necessary path. The ideal situation occurred when the bison ran so hard as they approached the cliff that they would not see it until the very last moment and then would be pushed over it by those behind them. At the bottom of the cliff, hunters killed any animals that survived the jump. Jumps were used mostly in fall and winter. In bison jumps that were used repeatedly, the bone beds were burned before reuse in order to eliminate the stench of previous kills.

**Hunting on snowshoes** was possible after a heavy snowfall. When bison became mired in snow they were easily dispatched.

Many hunts failed when wary bison escaped out of the ambushes that hunters had laid for them. Nomads came to believe that when they were successful in hunting, it was because the animals gave themselves up to be killed. This belief underlay bison ceremonialism, as people tried to propitiate bison spirits. They also believed that if some animals escaped from a communal hunt, they would tell other animals about the human's intentions and bison would become very hard to obtain as a result. Consequently, when hunters did manage to get a herd into a mass kill situation, such as a pound, they killed all the animals so that word of what had happened would not escape to other bison.

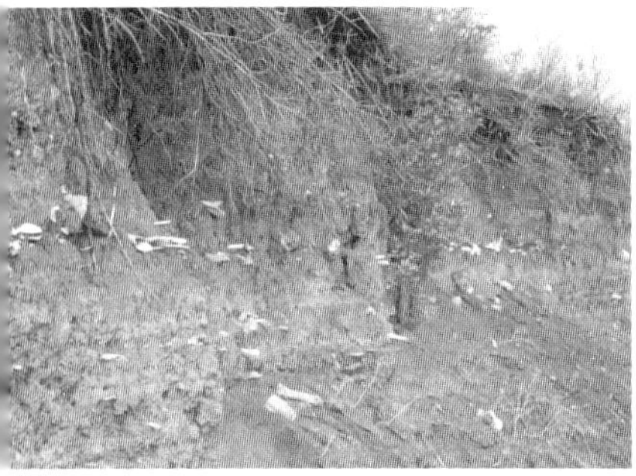

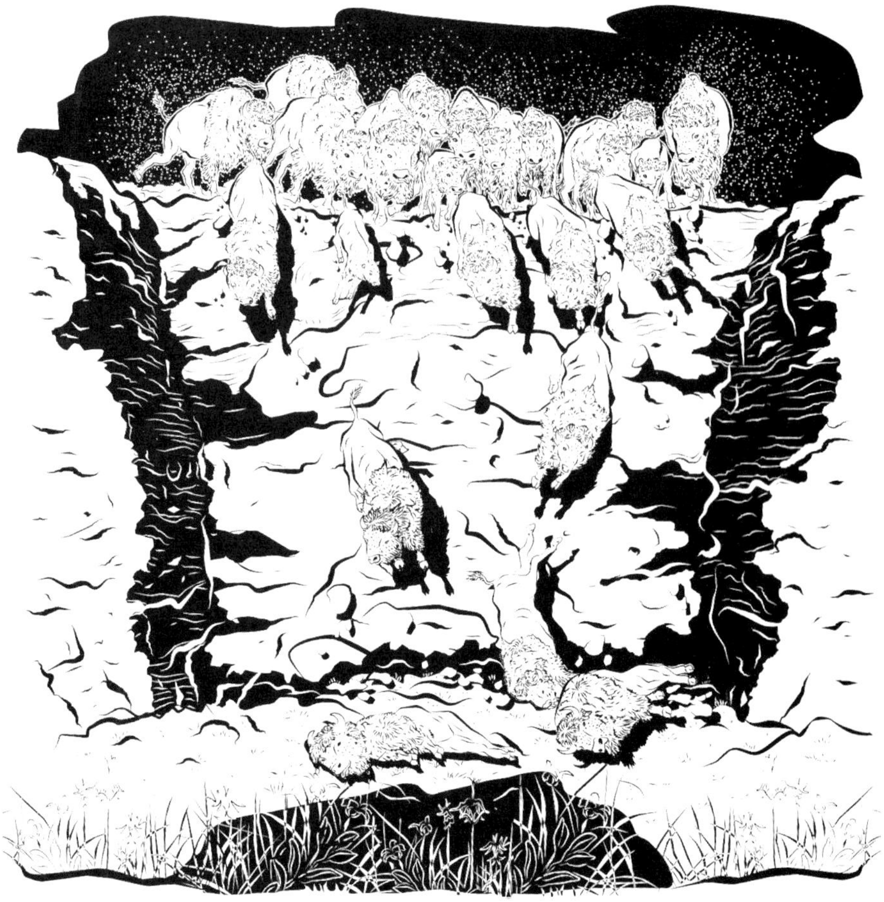

**Above** Bison bones indicate the location of a buried site used by prairie nomads (Royal Alberta Museum, 15A108) **Right** Bison jump at Head-Smashed-In site, Alberta (Susan Laurie-Bourque, Canadian Museum of Civilization, after J. Nickol in *The First Albertans*, 1987, p. 86) **Below** Loaf-shaped atlatl weight (Canadian Museum of Civilization, X-B-290)

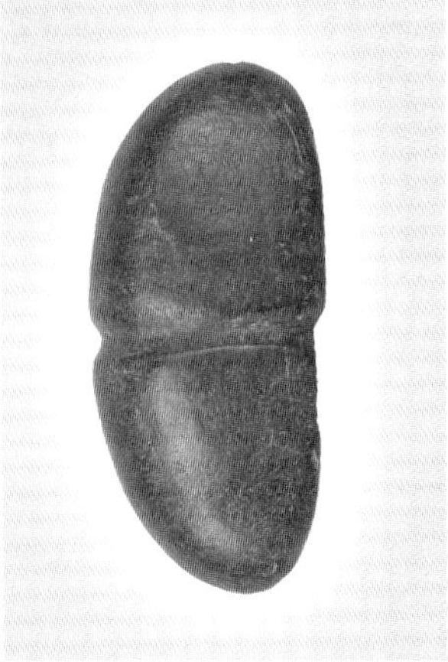

The earliest archaeological evidence of communal bison hunting, using natural traps, is dated to about 12,000 years ago. The first large, complex bison jumps appeared in the Prairies about 5,500 years ago and in some cases, such as the famous Head-Smashed-In bison jump in Alberta, were used successfully for thousands of years. In such places, bone beds at the base of the jump may be up to six metres in depth and dozens of metres in length. However, communal hunting seems not to have been a primary strategy in most of the Northern Plains throughout the early millennia of the Nomadic era, but only to have become so about 3,000 years ago with Pelican Lake, Besant and later archaeological cultures. The number of bison jumps and pounds increased dramatically between 3,000 and 1,800 years ago, which coincided with changes in weaponry. At the beginning of this period, the atlatl was the main hunting weapon, whereas toward the end of the period, the bow and arrow become dominant in the Northern Plains.

A full-grown male bison weighed from 700 to 1,200 kilograms: it provided prairie nomads with plenty of meat after a successful hunt. Butchering techniques reflected hunters' preference for fat animals. Female bison tend to be depleted of fat in spring, males in the late summer after the rut, and most animals, but especially the young, during late winter. As a result, many kills contained animals that were lean and therefore of lesser nutritional value. Some bison were only partially butchered, to obtain fatty body parts, such as the tongue and front portions of the hump. When transportation was a consideration, as

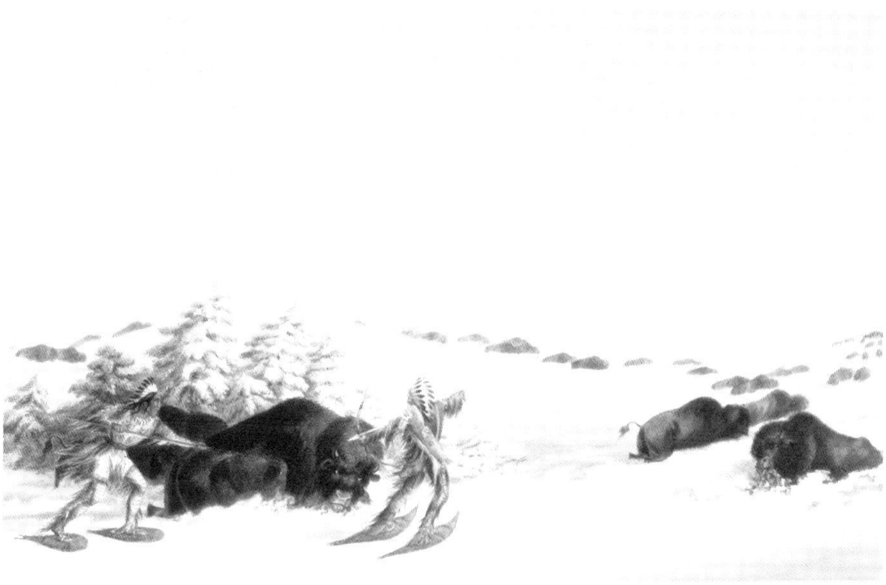

when kills were a considerable distance from camp, hunters discarded heavy bones with little meat or marrow fat, such as the skull and pelvis.

Following a hunt, depending on the circumstances, meat was cached, or cooked and eaten, or preserved for later use. According to archaeological evidence, prairie nomads developed a technology for preserving meat and fat about 5,000 years ago. Meat was sliced thin, sun-dried and then pounded into a granular flour. Fat was rendered into grease by boiling fat deposits or greasy bones in large hide vats with hot stones. Dried meat and rendered grease could be stored separately in bags, or they could be mixed together in large rawhide containers to make a product later know as "pemmican." This extremely nutritious, long-lasting, and very lightweight type of preserved food formed a surplus that allowed people to continue to feed themselves when hunting failed. It was easy to transport and facilitated travel when speed and secrecy were of the essence, as during times of war. It also became a commodity for exchange.

Bison provided prairie nomads with much more than meat. All parts of the bison, from horns to hooves, could be utilized: hides for clothing, bags, ropes and tipi covers; sinews for thread; the paunch for cooking; bones for tools such as scrapers and awls; horns for spoons; and hoofs for glue making. The dried dung was used as fuel in the open prairies where no wood was available and, in

**Above** A winter bison hunt on snowshoes (George Catlin, 1830s, Library and Archives Canada C-006288)
**Below** Use of the atlatl dart-throwing device (Larisa Nikolaeva, P. V. Alabin Museum of History and Regional Studies, Samara)

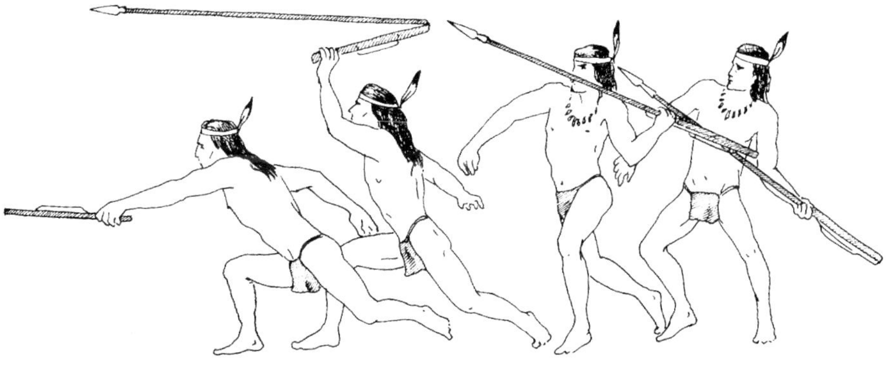

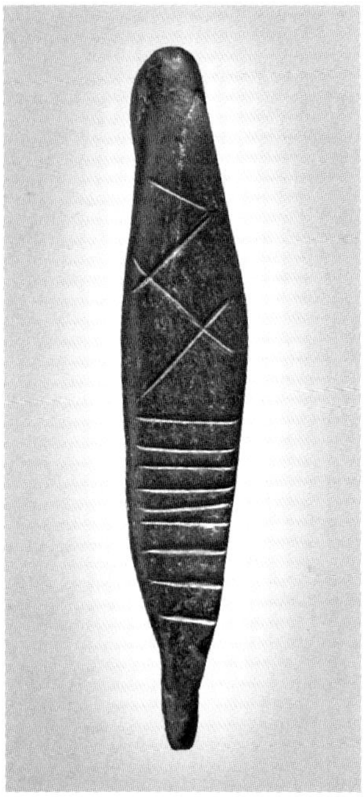

**Above** Incised atlatl weight (Canadian Museum of Civilization, X-A-435)
**Below** Oxbow culture chipped stone dart point, ca. 4,500 years old (Canadian Museum of Civilization, X-B-178a)

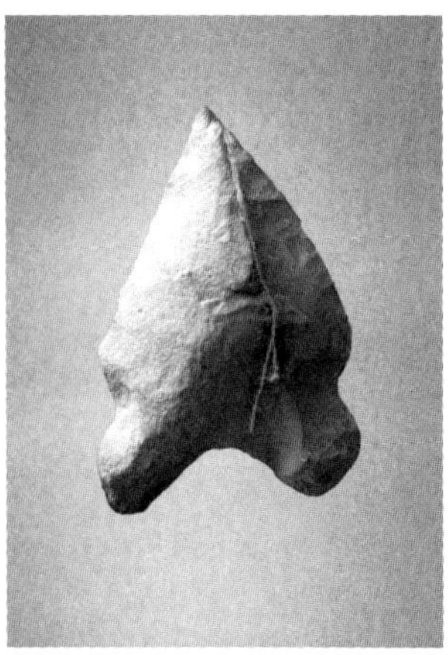

pulverized form, as an absorbent in baby's cradleboards. It has been estimated that each nomad required at least six or seven bison per year to obtain sufficient food, lodging, and clothing.

Other ungulates such as elk, mule deer and pronghorn antelope, were hunted by prairie nomads as well. Elk and mule deer were not as numerous and not nearly as sought after as bison. Antelope, although quite numerous in southern parts of the region, was utilized only occasionally, as indicated by the proportion of its bones in archaeological sites. Many other animals were hunted and trapped for special manufacturing, decorative or protective materials as well as for food, such as weasels, martins, beavers and muskrats for furs; hawks and eagles for feathers; eagles and bears for claws and teeth.

Gathering and scavenging were important seasonal activities that supplemented hunting. In the fall when ice was still thin, or in the spring when ice began to thaw, bison drowned in large numbers while crossing rivers. Nomads often scavenged the carcasses when they reappeared from beneath the ice. Gathering berries, fruits, tubers, and wood for poles were important warm-season activities. Gathering stones for tool-making and water-boiling was another important activity. Because stones suitable for these purposes were widely available in surface deposits, on valley slopes and in river and creek beds, much of this gathering was done on an ad hoc basis in the course of hunting, travelling or even camping. In general, there was no need for mining, except for a few very high quality chipping materials, such as are found in the Knife River Flint Quarries in North Dakota. Travel routes were shaped and camping places chosen simply to make the most efficient use of natural resources.

The nomads' intimate knowledge of the grasslands and their dwellers allowed them to make almost any young animal a pet, but attempts to take the next step and domesticate these animals, particularly bison, were not recorded. During the middle of the nineteenth century, the bison population was almost exterminated (approximately 30 million animals were killed in less than 100 years); but several dozen wild calves were rescued, and the small, protected herd they produced saved the bison from extinction. In recent years, some farmers and ranchers have begun raising and breeding bison for commercial purposes. This experience has shown that bison have many similarities with domestic cattle, but due to several biological peculiarities, they have never become a popular domesticate. In particular, milking the bison cow is impossible.

Social organization consisted of local bands (20 to 50 people in 3 to 7 tents), regional bands (350 to 800 people in 50 to 115 tents) and tribes (many regional bands). The composition, size and number of local bands shifted often as people adapted to bison movements and population dynamics. People could leave their band and join another one freely. Regional bands were more stable and tended to be associated with certain geographic regions for longer periods. They did not own or mark their territories. Other regional bands might hunt in their neighbour's territory with relative impunity. However, other tribes, unless they were in alliance, had to have permission for such hunting or they would suffer aggressive retaliation. Regional bands gathered together when bison herds coalesced for mating, then dispersed as the herds divided into smaller, more scattered groups. Beginning about 1,500 years ago, more centralized forms of social organization, chiefdoms, were formed near the southeast corner of the Northern Plains among village cultures of the Hopewellian and Mississippian traditions where corn, beans, squash and sunflower agriculture was supplemented with bison hunting. These chiefdoms occupied permanent earthlodge villages during the growing season, and lived in tipis when they were hunting bison.

The maximum population that could be achieved in the Prairies within the bison economy was limited by the number of bison and the amount of grass resources. These parameters changed through time from one extreme to another. Under average conditions, the Northern Plains probably sustained a nomadic population of about 35,000 to 40,000 people.

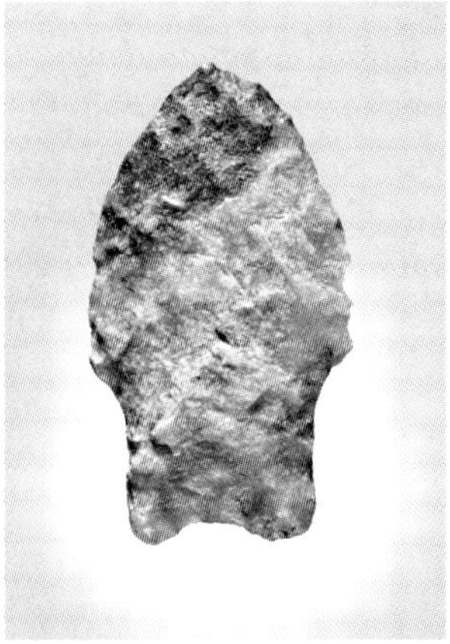

McKean series chipped stone dart point, ca. 4,200 years old (Canadian Museum of Civilization, X-A-1562b)

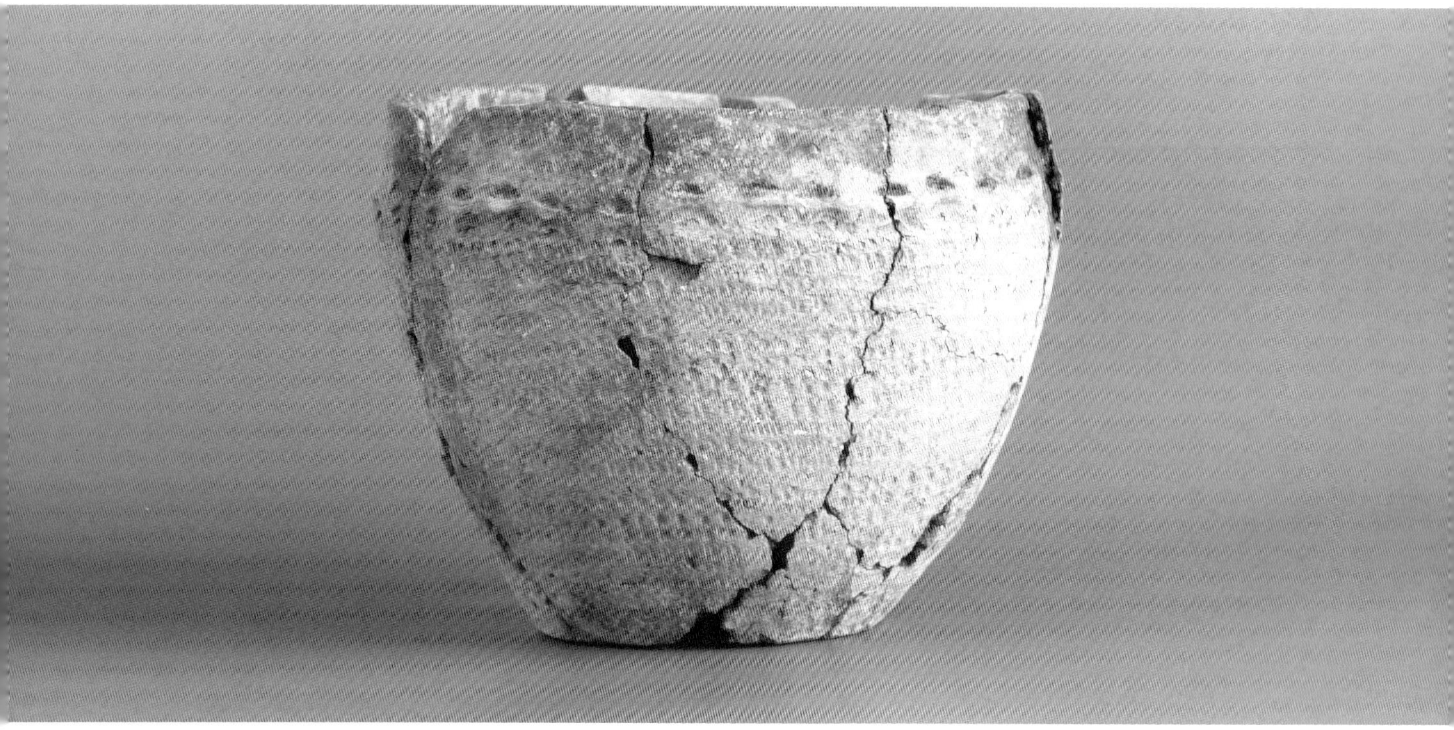

**Above** Clay pot, ca. 5,000 years old (Bronze Age) (P. V. Alabin Museum of History and Regional Studies, Samara, KP-25961/6)
**Below** Bison horn spoon, ca. 100 years old (Department of Archaeology, University of Saskatchewan specimen A L3973.2: Canadian Museum of Civilization photo)

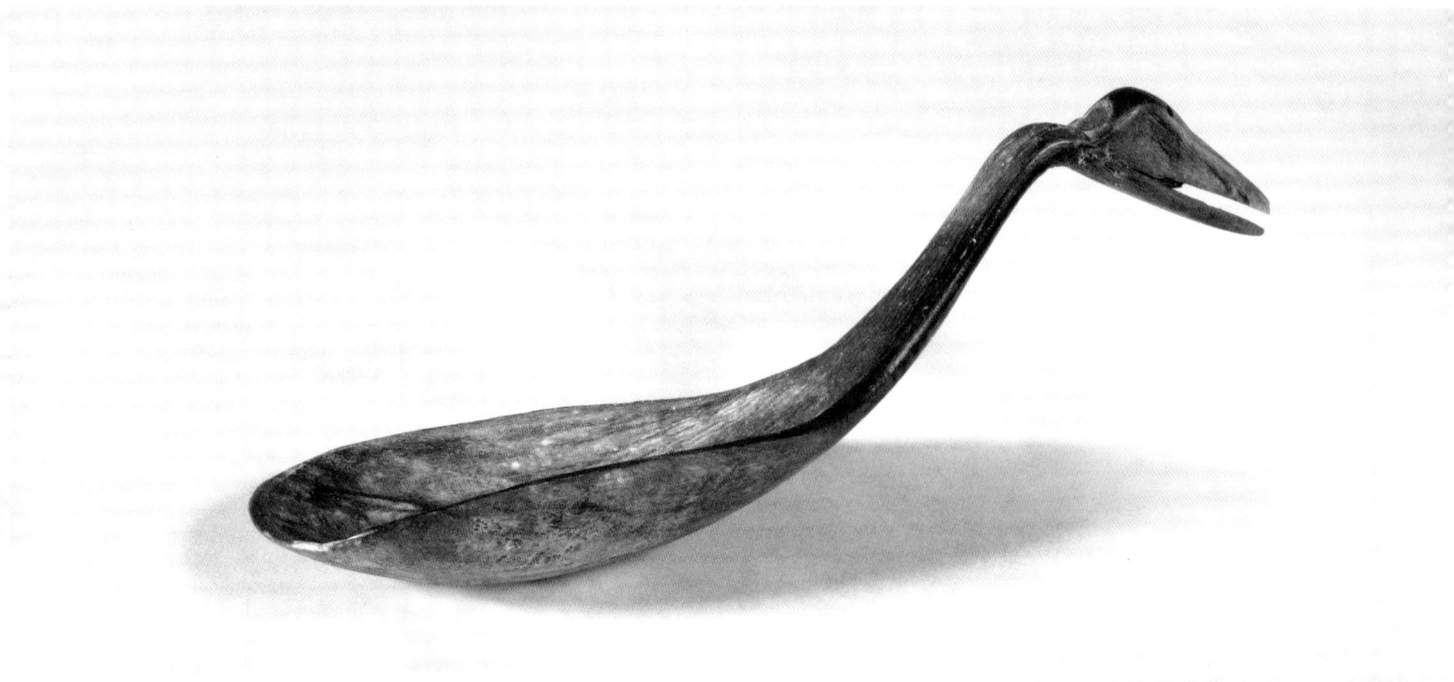

# FOOD

People need reliable sources of protein, fats and carbohydrates to sustain themselves. In the Steppes and Prairies, nomads relied on herd animals for proteins and fats, and on wild plants, berries and tubers for carbohydrates. Yet, there were significant differences in the foods of the two regions. The diet of steppe nomads was centred on milk and meat, whereas that of prairie nomads was focused on meat.

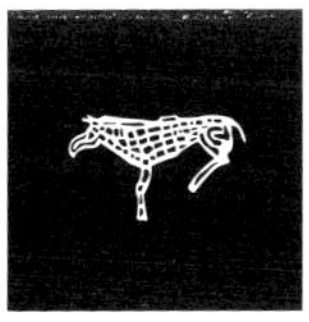

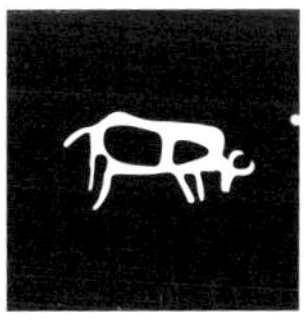

Food preservation reflected these biases, being concentrated on milk in one region and on meat in the other. In the Steppes, salt was a key element in food preservation, whereas in the Prairies, food was preserved mainly by drying. Many of the nomads' techniques for preparing, preserving and storing milk and meat remain in use today.

Since the major foods were high in protein and low in carbohydrates, the teeth of nomadic peoples in both regions were generally healthy, bearing fewer caries than the teeth of people in agricultural societies, but showing considerable signs of wear due to the infusion of omnipresent silt and sand into their food. In both areas, leather and wood were the preferred materials for storing and transporting food. Pottery was also made and used by nomads in both regions, although in relatively small quantities as compared with their more sedentary agricultural neighbours.

## Steppe Nomads

Most of our knowledge about the food and eating habits of steppe nomads comes from ethnological data. However, the analysis of bones from archaeological sites shows which animals were utilized; and the analysis of food residues on pottery gives a general idea of the kind of food the vessel contained (for example, a beverage vs. meat vs. kasha). In addition, radioisotope analysis of human bone collagen reveals the proportions of animal and plant-derived foods in the peoples' diet. In the Steppes, milk products predominated in the summer and meat in the winter.

Raw milk and various milk products were staples of the steppe diet since at least 2,500 years ago. According to ethnological data, milk contributed 80 to 90% of the nomads' summer diet. Sheep and goat's milk was not only consumed, but also transformed into long-lasting and easy-to-preserve summer products such as butter, kefir, yogurt, cheese and curd. Sheep produce 300 to 600 grams of milk per day and goats about 1,200 to 2,400 grams. As goats produce four times more milk than sheep, their milk was more important for cheese making. Dried dairy products made of sublimated sour milk, such as cheese and curd balls, contained a high proportion of salt. Salt was a key ingredient for the preservation of these products. Curds and young cheeses were made and eaten during the milking season. Once salted, they could be preserved in oil for several months. For longer preservation, cheese was sun-dried rock-hard and stored in wooden containers or cured in sheep stomachs for use in winter and spring. With the use of salt, such cheeses could last for years.

Clay pot, ca. 2,500 years old (Early Iron Age) (P. V. Alabin Museum of History and Regional Studies, Samara, KP-18548/21)

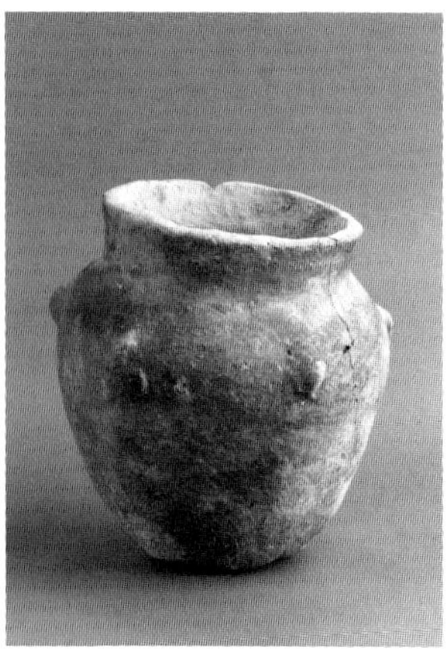

Most of the Steppes region is rich in salt sources, such as salt lakes. In areas where salt was not available, it was obtained through trade, a practice which may go back to Palaeolithic times.

Mare's milk is very lean (1 to 2% fat) and therefore cannot be used to make most dairy products. It was used mostly to make a fermented beverage known as kumys (or ayran). Kumys is very nourishing and, with about 2% alcohol,

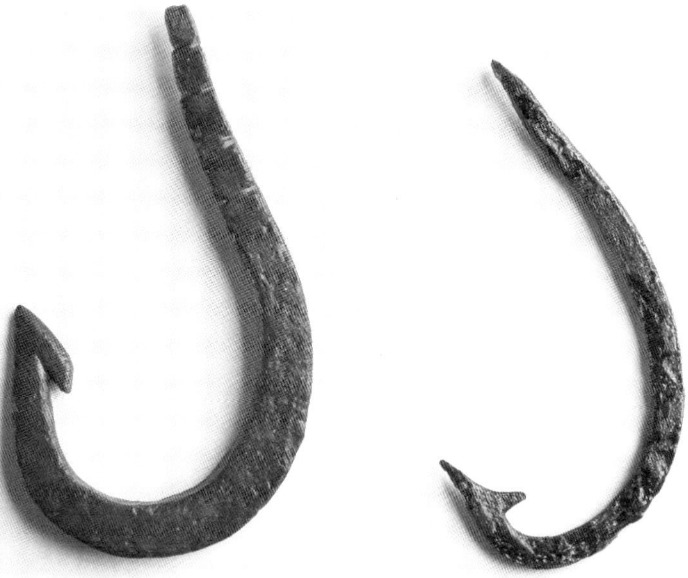

Fishing hooks made of bronze, ca. 4,000 years old (left) and of iron ca. 7th century A.D. (right) (P. V. Alabin Museum of History and Regional Studies, Samara, KP-18483/4, KP-26135/20). In summer, fish was an important source of protein for steppe nomads.

slightly intoxicating. It contains four to five times as much vitamin C as cow's milk, as well as vitamins A, D, E, B1, B2 and B12. In Russia, it was used as a remedy against tuberculosis (and malnourishment in general) until recent times. Fermentation was achieved by churning and could be done in a day. The kumys was prepared in leather vessels with a capacity of up to 200 litres. The neck of a vessel was attached to the frame of the dwelling (yurt) with its bottom resting on a special wooden bench. The milk was poured into the vessel, then churned and beaten until it became pungent and began bubbling. Early European travellers to the Steppes mentioned the constant rhythmic sound of milk churning coming from the yurts. About 2,500 years ago, Herodotus wrote that blind slaves churned mare's milk to make kumys; later, this was women's work.

A wide range of utensils was used to receive, pour and skim milk, and to store milk products. Most of these utensils were made of leather and wood. Steppe nomads preferred light, unbreakable utensils to those made of ceramics and metal. Moreover, using metal buckets to collect milk was believed to scare the animal, resulting in a smaller milk production. To create a leather vessel, a hide was cleaned, softened in sour milk, kneaded, and then smoked for several days for waterproofing. Then, the leather was cut into appropriate pieces, sewn together using animal sinews, and filled with salt or damp ash to give it the desired shape. Finally, it was thoroughly washed with salt and grease. A great variety of shapes was used, from vessels resembling horse heads to flasks. Animal organs, such as intestines, stomach, and even the scrotum, were used to create bags of various sizes and shapes for storing food and small personal belongings, such as a woman's sewing kit. Wood was used for buckets, ladles, scoops, dishes, bowls and spoons. Leather and wood are not well preserved in grassland archaeological sites, but recent archaeological finds have confirmed that a great variety of leather and wood vessels was used in the Steppes in prehistoric times.

Meat and meat products were made and consumed in winter, especially on festive occasions. Domestic ungulates were slaughtered mostly in late fall and winter. All but camels were used for food. Mutton was the preferred meat and sheep tail fat was especially prized. Goat meat was not eaten as much as mutton, because its fat solidifies at ambient temperatures.

Horse meat and fat were also regarded as important foods. Horse meat is richer in protein and essential fatty acids than that of ruminants. Steppe nomads regarded horse fat as the best fat yielded by any of their domesticates and used it as weaning food for their babies. All parts of the horse (hair, skin, sweat, bone, excrement, etc) were used in medicine. The meat was usually eaten fresh. Unlike beef, horse meat cannot be dried effectively. Other meats could be dried, but there was little need to do that. Since the slaughter took place during the cold season, meat could be kept frozen as long as the nomads stayed on their wintering grounds. A small proportion of meat was preserved as jerky or made into smoked sausages for use in summer. For smoking, meat and meat products were hung high in the yurt, close to the smoke hole. During marches, jerky could be prepared by placing a piece of fresh meat under a horse's saddle: the meat was salted by absorbing salt from the horse's sweat. Fresh meat was roasted on skewers, baked, or cooked in leather bags (during war excursions) or, more commonly, in ceramic and metal vessels. Greek historians described nomadic war parties putting fire-heated stones in leather bags to boil meat. Stone boiling was practiced in stone-rich areas in the southeastern Steppes. In the Caspian lowlands, people still prepare food by rolling meat and hot stones in large milk tins. In the Steppes, after the invention of clay pottery, food was cooked mostly in pots, but stored and transported in vessels made of wood and leather.

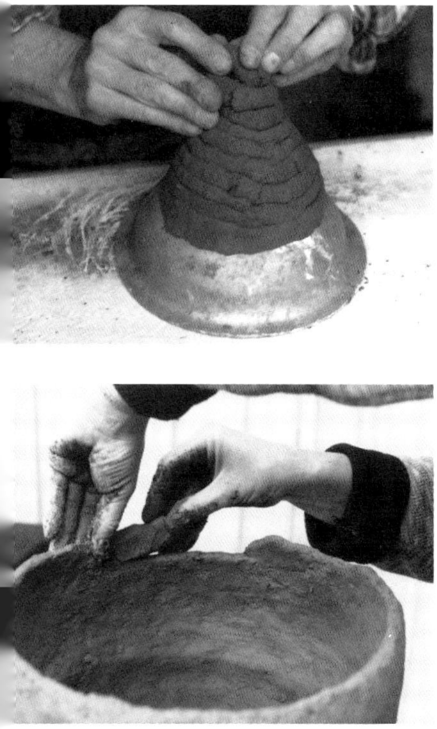

Experimental production of hand-made pottery (Samara Project of Experimental Archaeology, photos by Irina Vasiljeva and Natalia Salugina)

During the entire nomadic period, pottery was hand-made. The first pottery, introduced to the Steppes by newcomers from agricultural regions, was flat-bottomed. By the Early Bronze Age, round-bottomed pottery was also in use. The round-bottomed pottery was more effective for cooking over an open hearth, whereas flat-bottomed pots were more convenient for storage and transportation. Toward the end of the Bronze Age, pottery became more abundant and varied, but also simpler in form and decoration. Simple geometric ornamentation prevailed. Clay was tempered with manure, shells, grit (gruss), or grog (ground pottery or chamotte). During the Iron Age, nomads started to replace their ceramic pots with metal vessels. Metal pots were mainly flat-bottomed. Beginning in Medieval times, pots were set on a special support (a hoop on feet) instead of hanging over a hearth. Beside cooking pots, a few metal objects related to cooking were used by the steppe nomads, including perforated ladles, hooks for kettles, and "forks" (hooks for lifting meat from a kettle). Metal pitchers, goblets and bowls were used mostly for ceremonial purposes.

The berry plants and shrubs of the Steppes are not diverse, the common species being blackthorn, wild cherry and strawberry. Wild crops within the Steppes also included the tubers of several species. Not much is known about the nomads' use of these indigenous plant crops. However, Bronze Age nomads did inter grindstones, mortars and rolling-pins as grave goods in their burial mounds; and these tools were likely used for grinding or mashing plant products such as berries and cereal grains (either wild or domesticated). The mountainous

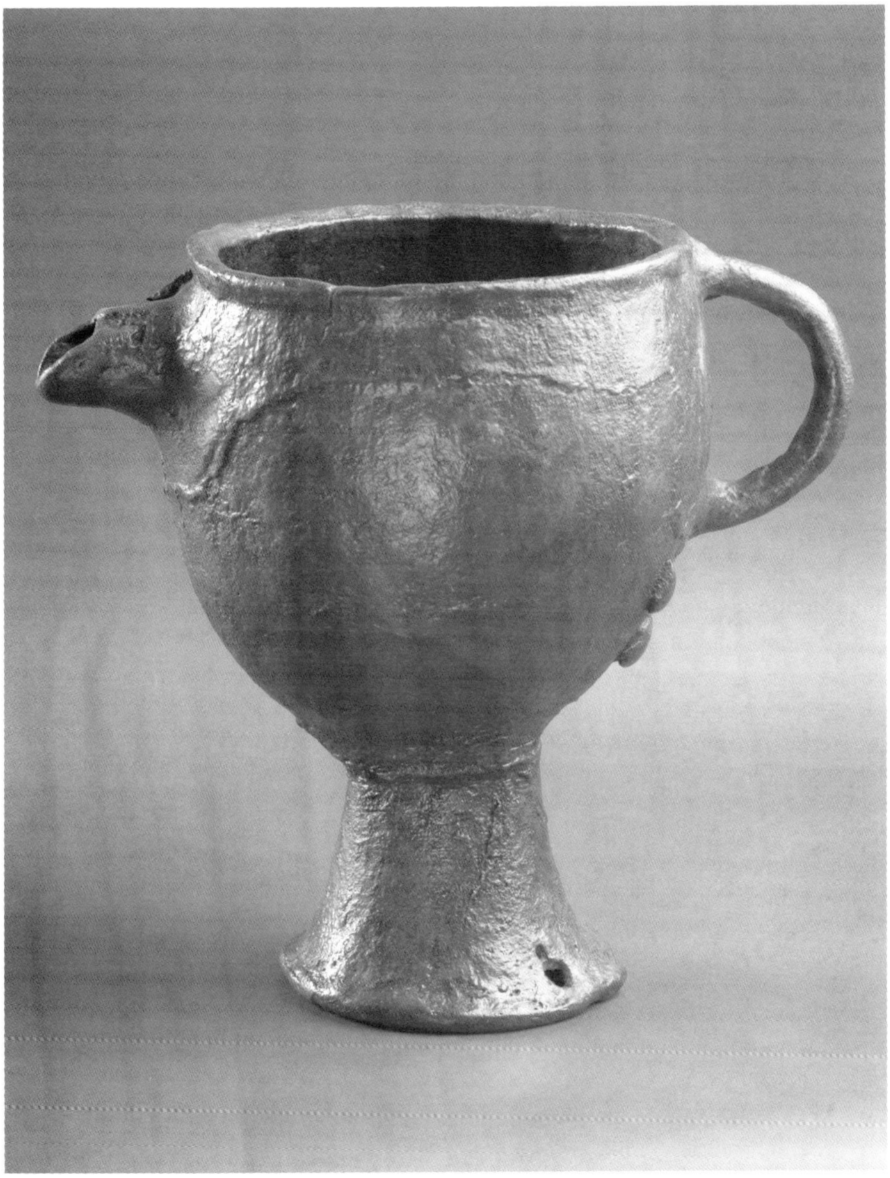

Bronze cauldron, 2,500–2,400 years old (Early Iron Age) (P. V. Alabin Museum of History and Regional Studies, Samara, KP-173/1)

region bordering the area of modern Kazakhstan contains forests of wild fruit and nut trees, including apple, apricot, plum and walnut. Dried fruits from this region, such as *kuraga* (dried apricot), may have been obtained by steppe nomads through trade. In the foothills of this region, the diversity of wild crops is much greater than in the Steppes, supporting over 100 wild relatives of cereals, vegetables, and nut and fruit trees; 70 wild relatives of forage crops; and 20 wild relatives of industrial crops. By the Bronze Age, cereals had definitely become an object of trade in western parts of the Steppes. In some fortified metallurgical sites, newcomers from agricultural regions, probably from the Caucasus, even began cultivating cereal crops for a short period.

Plant products were cooked over an open hearth or on portable braziers. During historical times, earth ovens (tandyrs) were used as well, but mostly in southern areas, and mostly for making bread. Dung was used as the fuel in outdoor hearths; in indoor hearths firewood was preferred. Cooking was done outdoors whenever possible. The ancient fire-making method was wood-on-wood friction either by hand-twirling a stick or by using a bow-drill. Nomads used this technology until about 1,400 years ago when they obtained the first fire-steels, the use of which rapidly replaced the old methods. Fire-steels, flint, and tinder were carried in a small bag attached to the belt.

## PRAIRIE NOMADS

In the Prairies, major foods consisted of cut meat; soups and stews of meat and wild plants; tubers eaten uncooked, boiled or roasted, or dried and crushed to a powder for soup; berries eaten fresh or dried, or combined with other foods; and maple syrup and sugar eaten as a delicacy, mainly by children. Despite the diversity of foods, the dietary system of prairie nomads was very much centred on meat.

Bison was a main source of meat, but many other animals were eaten as well, including antelope, elk, deer, moose, wolves, beavers, foxes, dogs, skunks and mice. Dogs were particularly important as an ultimate food reserve during famine. Most birds, excepting eagles, were eaten as well. Migratory waterfowl, such as geese and ducks, and their eggs were important during spring or fall. Most nomadic tribes avoided fish and snakes as sources of food.

Some parts, such as the liver, were often eaten raw; other parts, such as the kidneys, eyes, brains, testicles, and gristle of the snout, were occasionally eaten raw. Other parts were cooked. Meat cooking was achieved by roasting on a spit, boiling or baking. A common meal consisted of a thick soup containing meat, berries, fat and prairie turnips. To boil ingredients, a hole was dug in the ground and lined with a raw hide, or a paunch was suspended from a circle of sticks stuck in the ground. Meat, water, fat, turnips and berries were added. Then hot stones were dropped into the vessel to cook the meal. For baking, a hole was dug in the ground, lined with a fresh hide, hair-side down, and meat was placed on the flesh side. Then the hide was folded over, and heated stones from a nearby hearth were placed on top of it. The hot stones were covered with soil and left for several hours until the meat was cooked.

Old Women's phase ceramic pot, ca. 1,200–300 years old (Manitoba Museum specimen DjMg-2-161: Canadian Museum of Civilization photo)

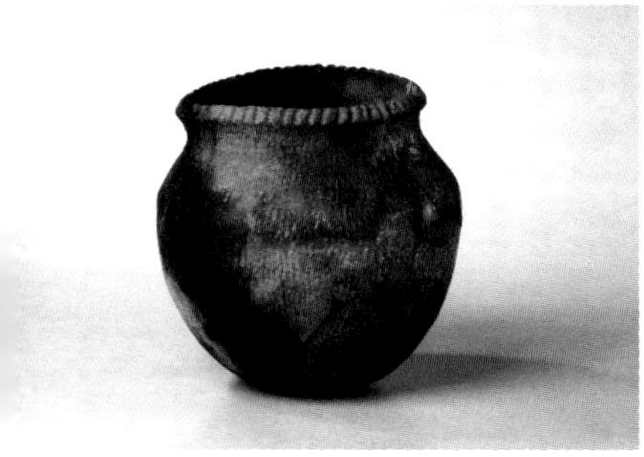

After the introduction of pottery, ceramic vessels were also used for boiling foods. Ceramics were adopted by prairie nomads about 1,500 years ago from Woodland cultures to the south and east. Nomadic pottery was hand-made and round-bottomed. When decoration was present, it consisted of simple geometric designs, which were pressed, incised or stamped onto the exterior rim, and sometimes also the shoulders, lip or interior rim. The shape of vessels evolved from rounded bottomed with no neck (conoidal–about 1,500 years ago) to round-bottomed with a neck (globular–about 1,300 years ago). Flat-bottomed pots, made either of clay or steatite, appear in the southwestern part of the region about 800 years ago. These vessels seem to have an intermountain origin and spread only a short distance onto the Plains. Clay pottery was most abundant in eastern parts of the region and declined toward the west. Vessel size varied

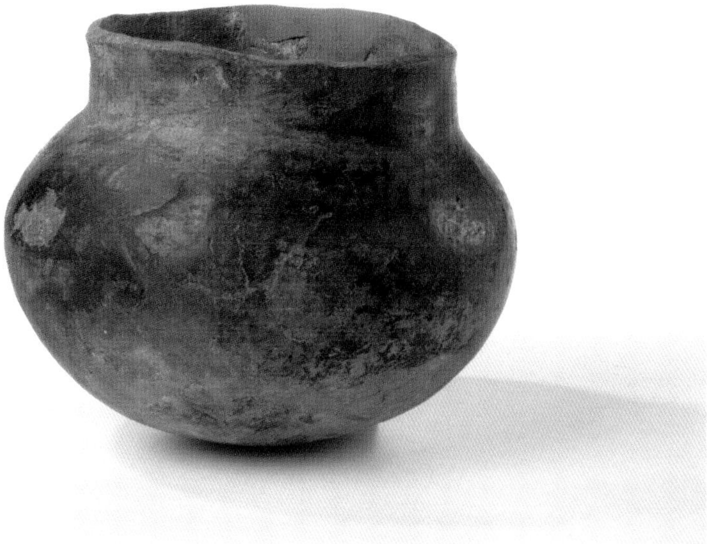

from half a litre to many litres in capacity. Historic nomads used horn spoons and wooden bowls as eating utensils; no record survives of their prehistoric counterparts.

According to ethnographic data, salt was not used for food preservation. Instead, the nomads' main method of food preservation was by drying. Systematic drying reduced weight, but not nutritional value, and it extended the life of foodstuffs for months or even years. Durable, lightweight food reserves stabilized the otherwise unpredictable food supply of bison hunters. The process involved cutting the meat in very thin slices and hanging them on drying racks made of two tripods joined by a number of horizontal poles. The meat was cut so thin (less than 0.7 millimetres) that flies could not blow it. In fair weather, this was done outdoors in open sunshine. During inclement weather, the drying rack was erected on four poles or simply suspended from the tipi frame, in both cases over the hearth and about midway to the smoke hole. Several days were needed to cure the meat sufficiently for storage. In the hot sun, meat strips became hard and dry in a couple of days and could be packed away in small bales or in rawhide sacks. Subsequently, the dried meat was flailed into a granular sort of meat flour, called "beat meat," and stored in leather bags for later use.

Reserves of dried lean meat had to be supplemented with reserves of fatty food to sustain a balanced diet. The main sources were animal body fat, bone marrow and bone grease. Masses of fat from the animal's shoulder, rump or hump were placed near a fire where they dripped into a hide container as they melted. The grease in bones was obtained by crushing the bones into pieces and rendering grease out of them in stoneboiling vats. The grease that rose to the surface was skimmed into buffalo-paunch bags. This technology is recorded archaeologically by a combination of fire-cracked rocks, bone boiling pits, hammerstones, stone anvils, crushed marrowbones, and masses of pulverized bison bones in prairie sites ranging from 5,000 to 130 years of age, terminating with the disappearance of the bison.

**Above** Old Women's phase ceramic vessel, ca. 1,200–300 years old (Canadian Museum of Civilization, EhPg-1-1)
**Below** Hammerstone and broken bison bones (Canadian Museum of Civilization, X-A-78)

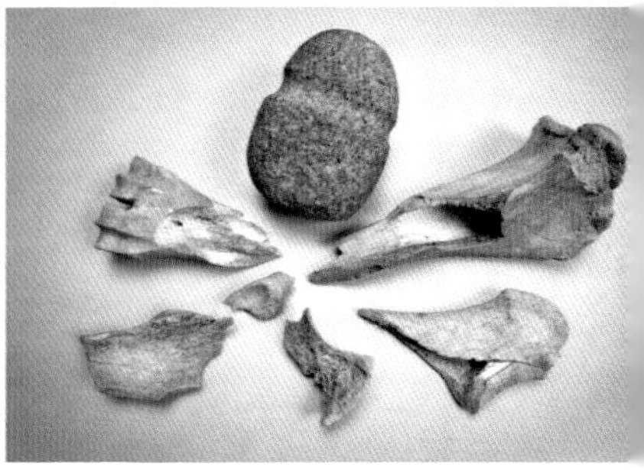

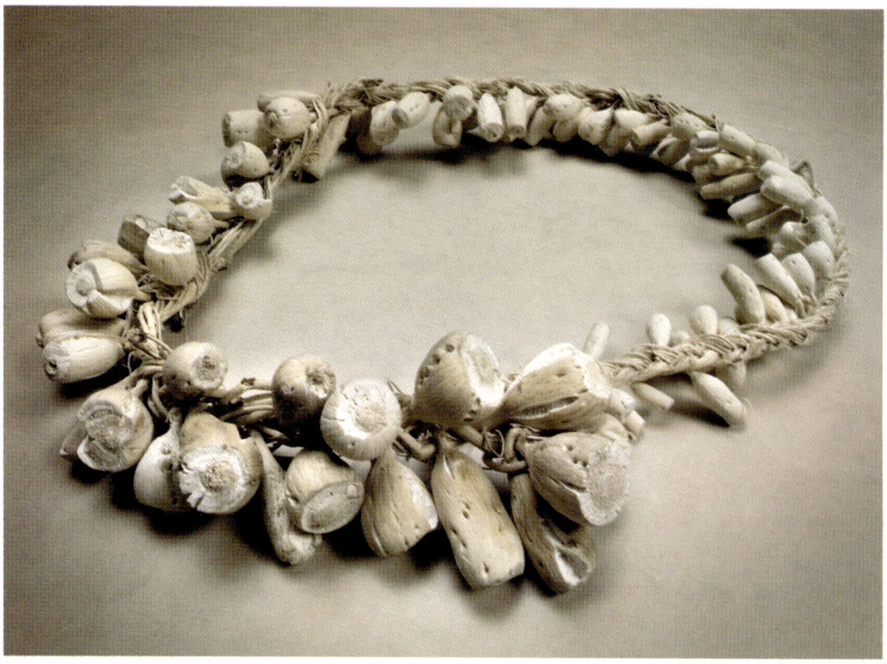

Dried prairie turnips (Canadian Museum of Civilization, V-E-420)

Beat meat and rendered fat might be stored separately. However, they were often immediately combined into a highly nutritious preserve called pemmican. Pemmican was prepared in a trough made of bull's hide, in which beat meat and rendered fat/grease were mixed together with a wooden spade. The finer kinds of pemmican also contained large quantities of dried berries, such as chokecherries or service berries. After it was thoroughly mixed, the pemmican was shovelled into large hide bags, which were rammed tight with a big stick to remove all the air. The meat and fat of two prime cows would produce about 50 kilograms of pemmican; that from one large bull about 40 kilograms. With a little care, pemmican would last months or even years.

When there was a considerable surplus of meat and meat products, bison nomads built a tipi-like storehouse comprised of closely laid poles covered with brush and weighted with stones, or they built a platform cache out of poles. Occasionally they made a grass-lined, stick-floored cache pit in a hillside, which they closed with a covering of grass and earth, or they enclosed the meat in stone cairns. For short periods in winter, foods were also preserved simply by freezing.

Plants were an important source of food and medicine. Some plant parts were eaten raw, some were cooked; many were dried and preserved for future use. The Prairies are very rich in berries, such as service berries, chokecherries, currants, bull berries, sand-cherries, gooseberries, red plums and strawberries. Some of these, such as wild strawberries, were eaten ripe. Others, such as service berries and chokecherries, were collected in large quantities for immediate consumption or to be dried and pounded into a sort of mash, which was pressed into small flat cakes for storage. In winter, such cakes were soaked in water and made into a sort of compote, or used as ingredients in soups, stews and other recipes.

Wild prairie turnip was another important and abundant food source. The tubers were dug out using a digging stick sharpened to a flat point. The collected tubers were either cooked and eaten fresh, or sun-dried. Fresh prairie turnip was either boiled or roasted on embers before eating. If the tubers were to be dried, they were put out in the sun for a couple of days, then braided by the root tails and put away, or crushed to a powder with a stone maul before being stored in skin bags. Prairie turnip powder was used in soups during winter; with dried service berries, it also made a very palatable sort of pudding. Some tubers, such as camas or bitter-root, which grow on the higher lands of the Western Plains, needed special processing before they could be consumed. Camas bulbs were roasted in large pits over heated rocks, which were covered with grass. More grass and twigs were laid over the bulbs, and then a covering of earth. On this a fire was built to complete the roasting. In areas along the eastern edges of the Plains and in the lake regions of Minnesota and Manitoba, wild rice (*Zizania aquatica*) was collected by local tribes.

Maple sap was used to make sugar. Most maple species in Canada contain a high proportion of sugar in their sap, including Manitoba maple, which is a common species in the parklands zone north and east of the Prairies. From ethnological data, the technology is known to have started with horn cups or birchbark baskets collecting the sap, which was then poured into a large hide vessel for boiling. After much heating and stirring, the resulting syrup was poured into birchbark boxes whose sides and bottom were greased with frozen fat. The sugar, eaten as a delicacy or sprinkled over meat as a condiment, was consumed mostly by children. Aside from the broths of soups and stews, the main beverage was water.

All kinds of food preparation involved the use of open hearths. The preferred fuel was wood, but when that was not readily available, people used dried bison dung instead. Cooking was done outside whenever weather permitted. Fire was made with a fire-drill, a hard stick spun—between the palms or by means of a bowstring—against another piece of hard wood with a small hollow that held the point of the drill. The friction generated heat, which eventually ignited the tinder.

The pattern of food availability in prairie nomadic communities has been described as one of feast or famine. However, recent analysis of body measurements of Plains Indians showed that in the late 1800s, they were the tallest people in the world, with an average male height of 173 centimetres (nineteenth-century European males were several centimetres shorter). This has been interpreted as a sign of sufficiently good nourishment, given the disease and environmental pressures they were under.

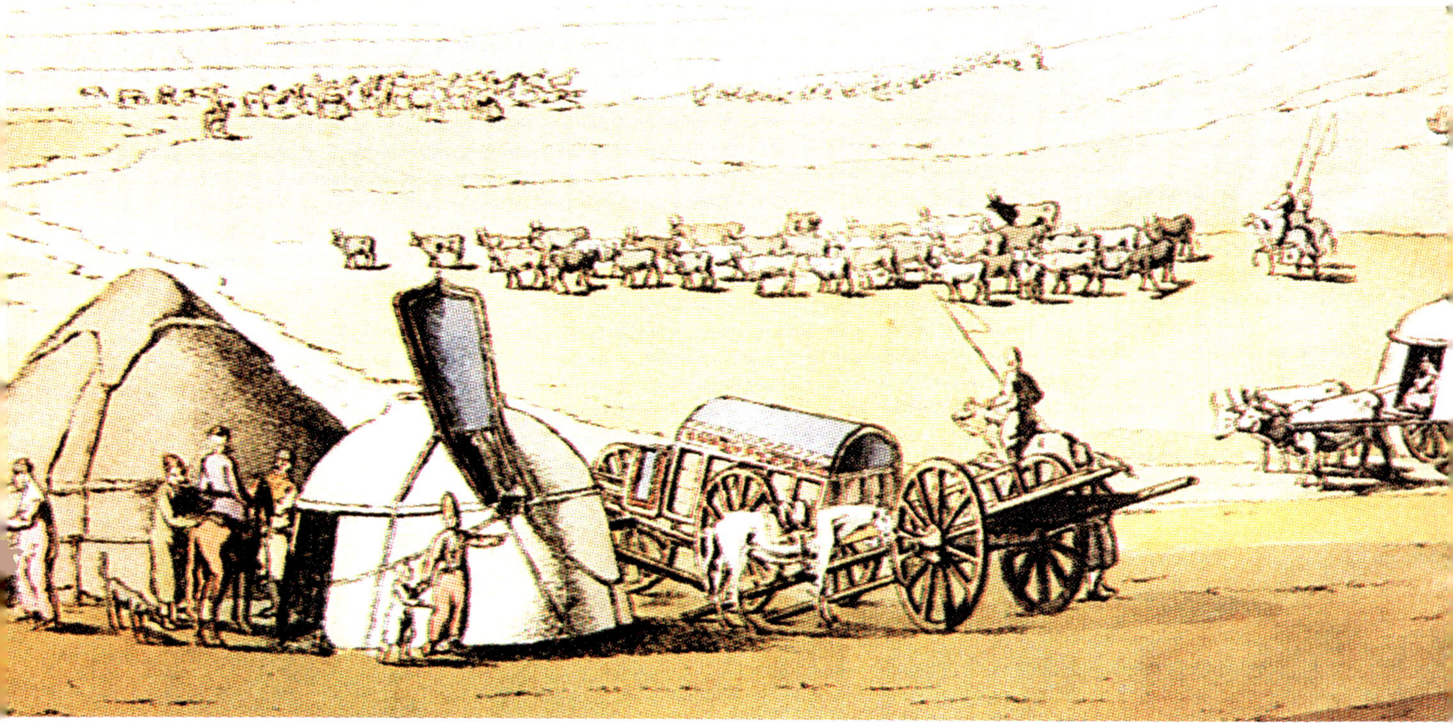

**Above** Miniature of an eighteenth-century nomads' camp
**Below** Saulteaux family on the move in winter, 1820s, near Lake Winnipeg (Peter Rindisbacher, 1820s, Library and Archives Canada C-040820)

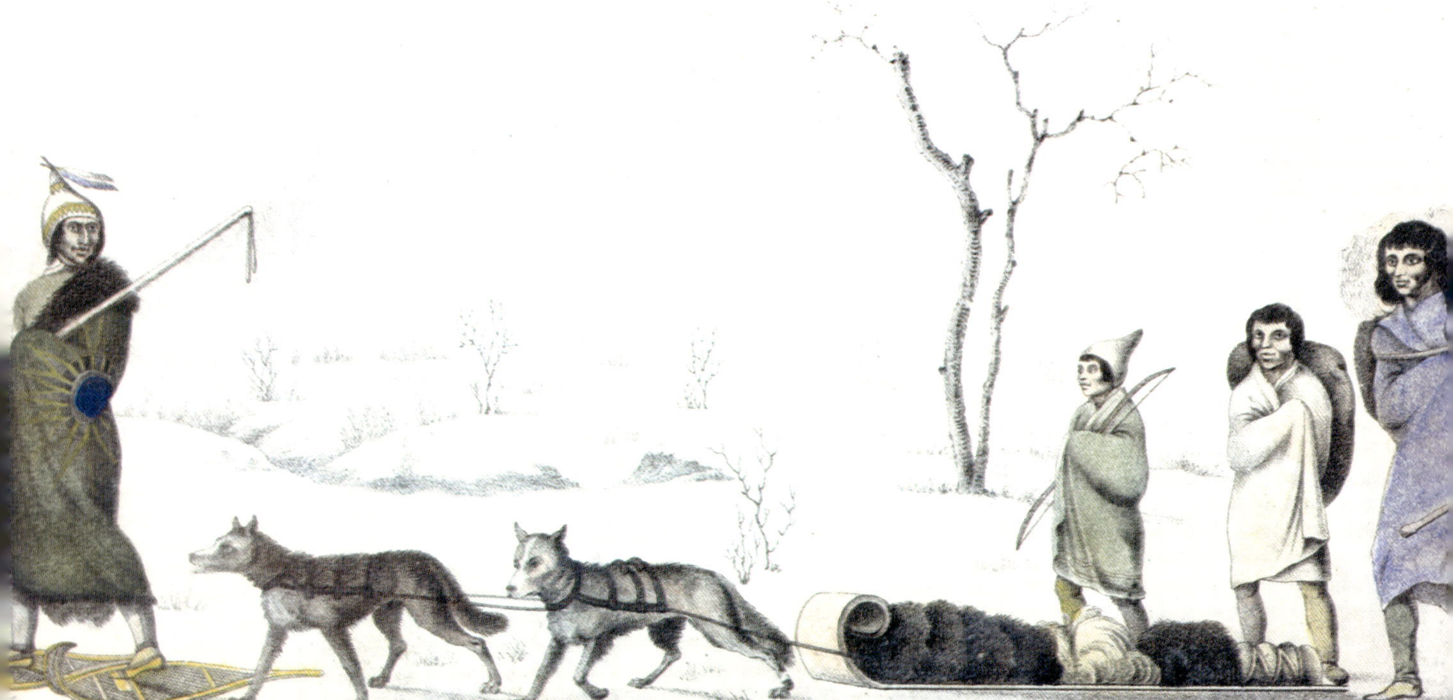

# TRANSPORTATION

Nomads in both regions made regular long-distance journeys to keep close to the animals on which they depended. Except for occasional obstacles, such as ravines and rivers, and irritants, such as biting insects and foot-piercing cactus spines, passage through the grasslands was relatively unimpeded. The chief problem was carrying baggage. Many choices had to be made to minimize the number and weight of belongings.

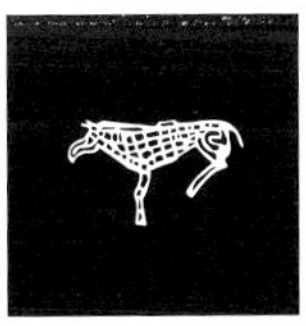

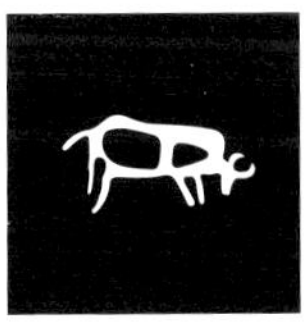

However, even after making those choices, nomads still had to transport a suite of essentials from one camping place to another—portable dwellings, food, clothing, a few tools and weapons. In the Great Plains, they relied partly on their own carrying power and partly on the assistance of dogs, which served both as beasts of burden and as draft animals. In the Russian Steppes, nomads used cattle and horses as draft animals; later they also made horses into riding animals. In both regions, people occasionally made short passages across or along waterways, but by far the greatest amount of travel was by land.

## Steppe Nomads

The first millennia of the early Holocene were marked by increasing mobility of the Eurasian population. Several important inventions reflected this: the appearance of the first dugout boats, skis, snowshoes and travois. By the beginning of the Holocene, the dog had already been domesticated in Eurasia and was being used as a beast of burden. No archaeological record for such use of dogs is available for the Steppes area, but in northern Russia the first finds of travois, presumably pulled by dogs, date to about 8,500 years ago. Far south of the Steppes, in the Middle East, cattle were domesticated about the same time. About 6,000 to 7,000 years ago, migrants from the Middle East began penetrating the Steppes, introducing cattle as a new beast of burden and draft animal,

**Right** Wheel in a nomad burial, ca. 4,700 years old, Shumaevo Burial Mound, Orenburg Region, Russia (courtesy of N. Morgunova)
**Below** Oxen pulling two-wheeled carts, modern Mongolia (courtesy e-Mongol.com)

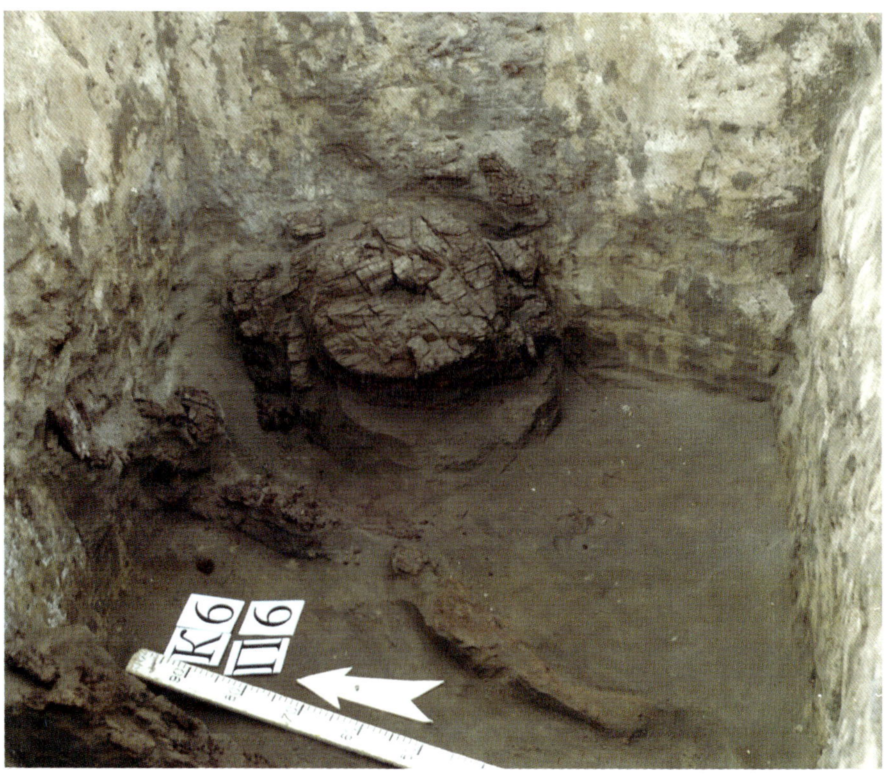

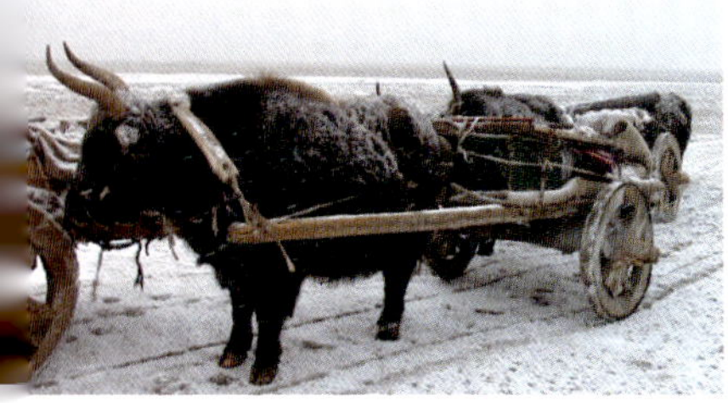

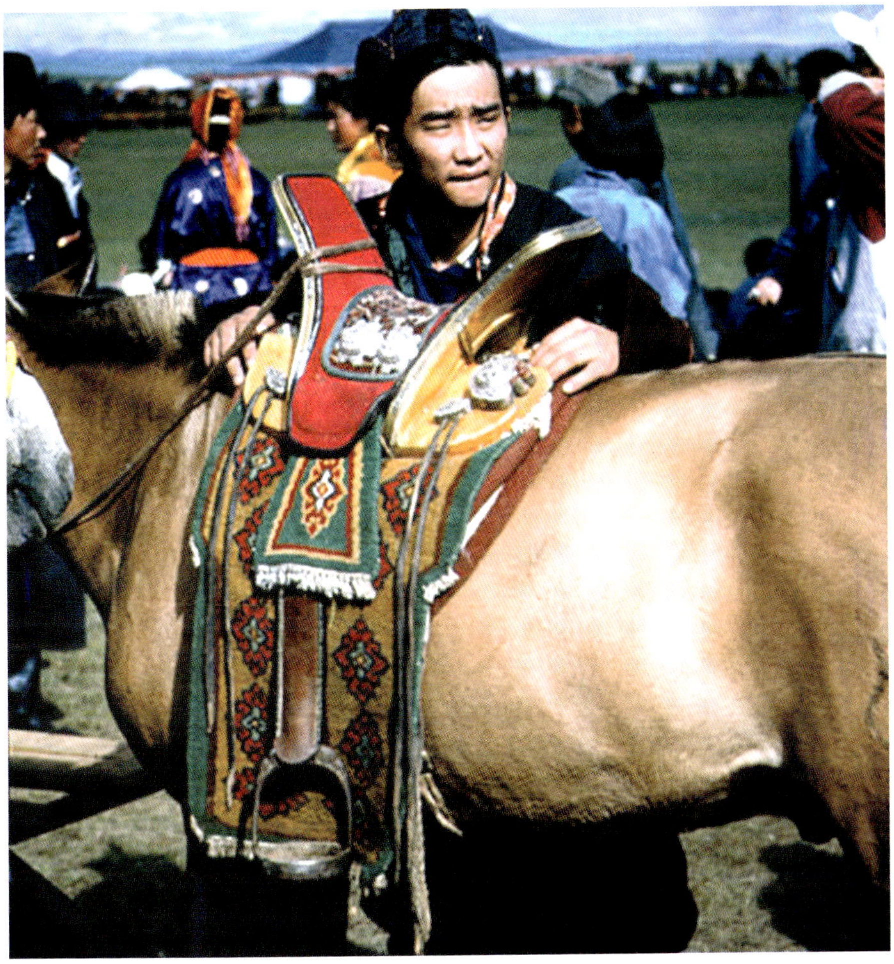

**Left** Mongolian saddle with overlays on pommels, leather straps for attaching cargos, and metal medallions—status and protection items (courtesy of Jan Wigsten, www.nomadicjourneys.com)
**Below** Iron stirrups, 13th–14th century A.D. (P. V. Alabin Museum of History and Regional Studies, Samara, KP-18793/1,2)

as well as a source of meat. Long migrations became possible with the invention of wheeled transport. The first wagons had four heavy wheels made of solid disks of wood up to one metre in diameter. These were pulled by a pair of oxen and were likely adopted from the Danube region, where sedentary stockbreeding was established earlier than in more eastern parts of the Steppes.

Sometime between 7,000 and 5,000 years ago, the horse was domesticated in the Steppes. Its wild ancestor was either the tarpan or the Przhevalsky horse, both native to the Steppes. This event marked a new era. Horses had less pulling force than oxen and required more care, but they travelled about 50% faster and could move for more hours in a day. A load of up to 50 kilograms could be transported on horseback. During the last 2,500 years, two breeds of horses were maintained—a stumpy, heavier one for pulling carts and wagons, and a lighter, taller one for riding. The use of the horse as a draft animal required lighter vehicles. Lighter, faster wagons with spoked wheels were invented about 5,000 years ago. A four-wheeled, felt-covered wagon became not only a means to transport all goods and chattels, but also a mobile home for steppe nomads while they were migrating. The covered wagon proved to be very practical, as the same model was used by steppe nomads for over 3,000 years. The maximum load of a horse-pulled wagon reached 500 kilograms. Typical possessions of a nomad family included rugs, pillows and blankets, extra sets of clothing, kitchenware and utensils, a tripod for

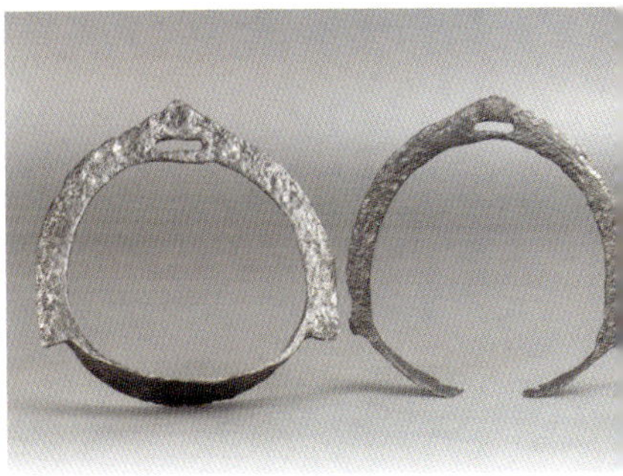

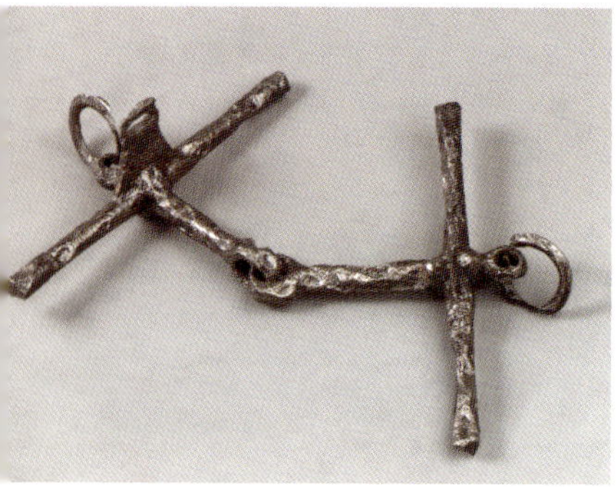

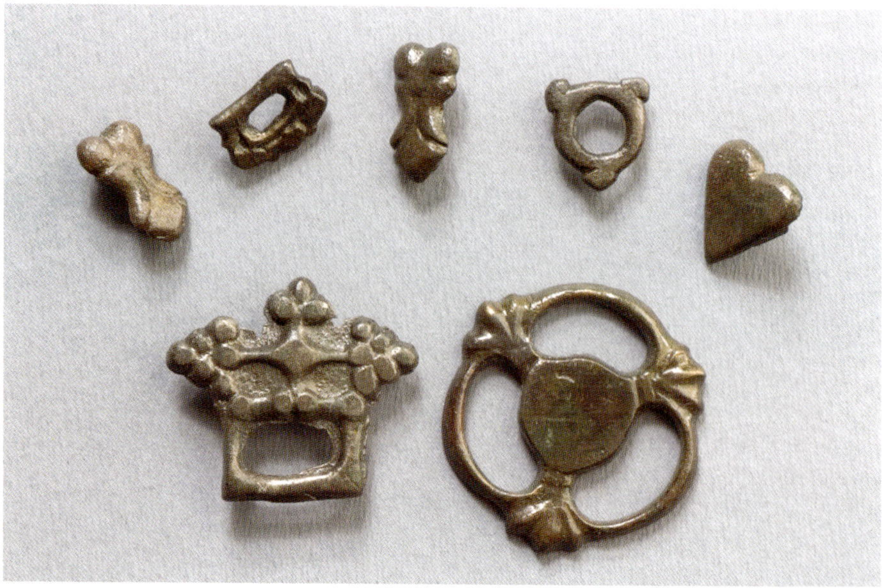

**Above** Iron bit, 7th–8th century (Early Middle Ages) (P. V. Alabin Museum of History and Regional Studies, Samara, KP-25963/2)
**Right** Bit ring and inlays from a bridle, 9th century A.D. (Middle Ages) (P. V. Alabin Museum of History and Regional Studies, Samara, KP-18461/6-12,13)
**Below** Bone overlays (saddle trim), 7th–8th century A.D. (Early Middle Ages) (P. V. Alabin Museum of History and Regional Studies, Samara, KP-26136/32-36)

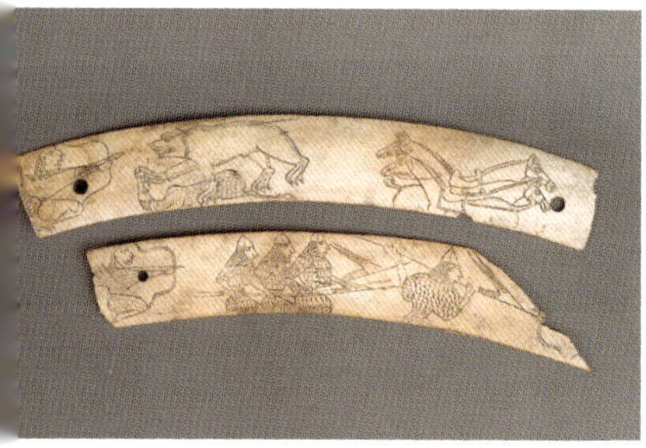

a kettle, a low table, extra harness for horses, weaponry and tools. Breakable objects were stored in wooden, leather or felt cases. Wooden chests were used for clothes, fabrics and dishware, and also as places on which to sleep. Most of the rest of the belongings were packed in bags made of leather or felt. Most possessions were transported in wagons, but men carried their personal belongings and some food in saddlebags. The heaviest, most voluminous objects to be moved were components of the yurt, a portable dwelling used in base camps. According to historic records, three to four horses, or one to two oxen, were required to move a yurt from one camp to another. With the domestication of the horse and the invention of wheeled transport, nomads were able to occupy new areas that were remote from the major rivers, such as the vast steppes between the Volga and Ural rivers.

For steppe nomads, the horse became more than a draft animal: nomads developed a horse cult. Whole horse skeletons, or sometimes just skulls and parts of the legs, were placed in human burials. In royal burials of the Scythian epoch, up to 10 horses were put in a human burial, with the body of a groom next to them. Horses were richly decorated by "reshmas"—forehead and breast jewellery and plumes. Horse harnesses were adorned with gold, silver and bronze trim. In steppe folklore, a horse was called a warrior's brother—it could talk to its master in a human voice, or leave its master if it felt hurt.

The dog survived the domestication of the horse, but its former multifaceted role became more restricted and specialized. Where once the dog had been a beast of burden, draft animal, source of meat, and hunting helper, from the Bronze Age on it had only two purposes: large dogs were used for keeping herd animals together and smaller dogs for hunting. As a result, their prestige declined. Images of dogs in hunting scenes, which were common in rock art from the Mesolithic to the beginning of Bronze Age, became rare later.

According to historical data, during the past 2,500 years, the annual migrations of steppe nomads reached round-trip distances of up to 2,000 kilometres. Migration routes were decided upon in winter camps, and were strictly adhered to. Later in nomadic history, between 1,200 and 600 years ago, regional governors decided on the migration routes for particular groups. The loops were generally oriented longitudinally (north to south) with the northernmost limit in the parklands at 53° north latitude, and the southernmost limit on the Caspian Sea shore at 47° north latitude, a one-way distance of 800 kilometres.

River crossing, especially of major rivers such as the Volga, was avoided as much as possible. Migration routes generally ran parallel to river valleys. Most rivers served as boundaries between tribal territories or (later) states. Since most domesticated ungulates do not swim well, rivers were major migration barriers for domestic herds. When crossings were deemed necessary, they were accomplished at fords, or by means of rafts and inflated hide bags used as floats.

Distance and speed of movement were governed by the capacity of the herd and did not exceed 30 kilometres per day. Commonly, while on the move, nomads set up camp every third day to give their animals a chance to graze and rest. Nomads made long-term camps on winter and summer grounds; their other camps were short-term stops en route to winter and summer pastures. Only one day was needed to set a camp and one more to pack for renewed travel.

Travelling groups generally included 20 to 30 people (three to five families). On summer grounds, up to 200 people gathered together; on winter grounds, up to 2,000 people. Women and children travelled in covered wagons, while men spent most of their time on horseback. With the nomads went their animals. An average family possessed four horses, five to eight cattle, and 20 to 40 sheep, goats and pigs. The herd was guided and kept together by shepherd dogs, and herdsmen on horseback. Newborn animals that could not keep up with the herd were put into wool bags and carried either on people's backs or on horseback until they were capable of travelling independently.

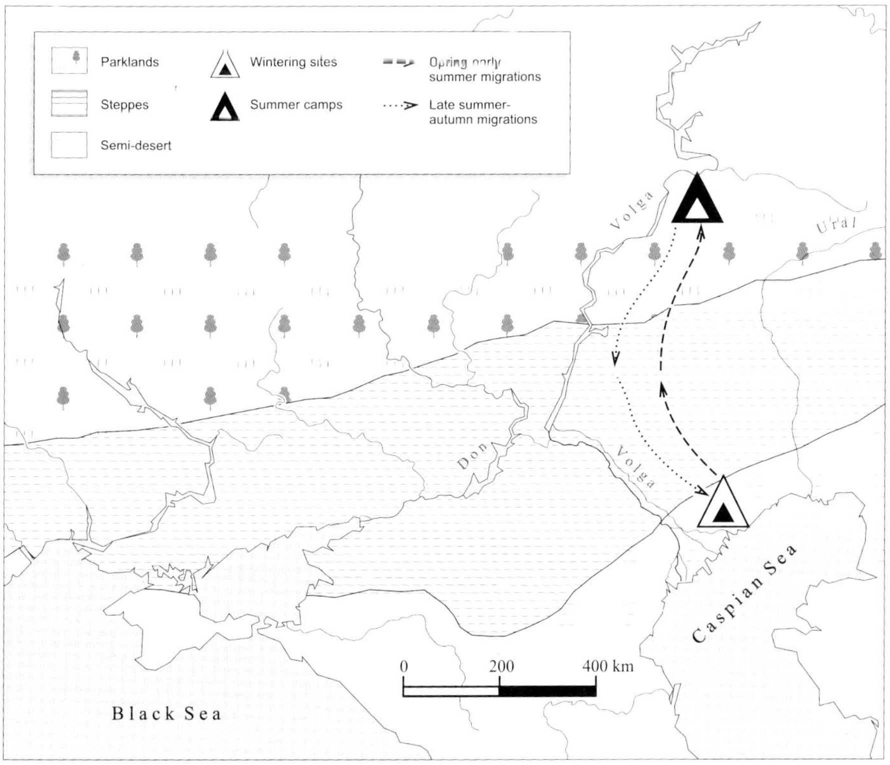


Polovetz annual migrations, 11th century A.D. (Oleksiy Vasilenko, Canadian Museum of Civilization)

Steppe nomads used several means to navigate through the grasslands. One was by reference to the sun, stars and rivers. Another was to move relative to burial mounds, which were placed either at the centre or on the boundaries of tribal territories. Tribal signs (tamga) were marked on prominent stones and on burial mounds. Perhaps the most common means of navigation was to follow well-known routes, which were maintained like roads. Wheeled transport could be used only on tracks with compacted soil. On the softer soils of parklands and forests, a horse-drawn travois was used until recent historic times. In general, the same migratory and trade routes were maintained for thousands of years. Indeed, many modern highways are built on top of ancient roads.

## PRAIRIE NOMADS

Domestic dogs appeared in North America about 11,000 years ago, likely brought with migrants from Eurasia. Dogs were the only domesticated animals used by Plains nomads until the reintroduction of the horse in the seventeenth century. Nomads used dogs to bear and pull burdens, for hunting, and as sources of ceremonial and emergency food until historic times. Two breeds are known from prehistoric sites: large dogs used as draft animals and beasts of burden, and smaller dogs used for hunting. The working dog was about one-and-a-half times as large as the hunting dog.

Dogs were used as beasts of burden by at least 5,000 years ago on the Northern Plains, as confirmed by the discovery of dog bones with wear facets on the shoulders. With dogs, the amount of goods that a family could carry was greatly increased. Large dogs could carry about 10 kilograms in bundles slung along their backs. With a travois, the load could be increased to 15 to 20 kilograms. The travois was a triangular frame constructed of two poles whose front ends converged over the dog's shoulders and whose back ends dragged on the ground. Just beyond the dog's rump, a netted platform, on which the load was secured, was attached to the two poles of the frame. Other devices widely used in the Northern Plains were toboggans (narrow boards with upturned front ends which made a flat platform that could be loaded and dragged over soft snow by humans or dogs) and sleds (small wooden platforms with underlying wooden runners that could be loaded and pulled over ice or hard snow). Goods to be transported were attached to the platforms of these vehicles with leather cords. Transportation equipment that was not needed in a given season (for example, toboggans or sleds) was left at a camp site until the next round of migration.

According to Clark Wissler, an early-twentieth-century ethnographer, the average family of prairie nomads carried the following objects during their travels: a tipi cover and a tipi frame consisting of 12 to 20 poles; a pair of back-rests and tripods for the same, two lengths of tipi lining or back wall, 36 wooden stakes or tipi pins, and four buffalo robes for bedding. A woman's equipment consisted of wood or horn spoons, a few small wooden or horn bowls, two or more leather bottles for water, sewing bags with sinew and bone awl, carrying straps, a knife, a stone maul, an axe, a bag of skin-dressing tools, a toilet bag with a hairbrush made of a porcupine tail, paints, rawhide bags for pemmican and dried meat, a digging stick, a cradleboard, packing gear for several dogs, and a roll of tanned skins for new clothing. The man had a bow, arrows and quiver, a shield, a lance, a stone-headed war club, a knife and sheath, fire-making tools, pipes and tobacco, a bag with paints, a bundle of charms and ceremonial objects, and extra dog gear.

Following Wissler's estimates, the total weight of these objects was approximately 220 kilograms. Extra clothing for a woman and man would weigh over 15 kilograms. Children's possessions, such as extra clothing, robes, toys and games, would add about 9 kilograms for each child. According to these estimates, the goods of a family consisting of a man with one wife and two children would weigh over 270 kilograms. In fact, the average extended family household probably contained about seven persons, but in pre-horse times, their combined baggage likely was less than this amount. Transportation of such a load (not including food supplies) would require about 10 travois pulled by 10 large dogs, plus backpacks on at least two people. During historic times, horse-poor bison nomads averaged 7 to 12 dogs per family, occasionally as many as 20, so that their carrying capacity using only dog travois and human backpacks was certainly near the range of Wissler's estimate.

Plains nomads never developed wheeled transportation. Although possibly known for toys (wheeled toys are known from Mesoamerica), wheeled transport would have been of no use with only the dog as a draft animal. The dog's small size did not allow for effective use of large wheels and small wheels would have been useless in rugged terrain.

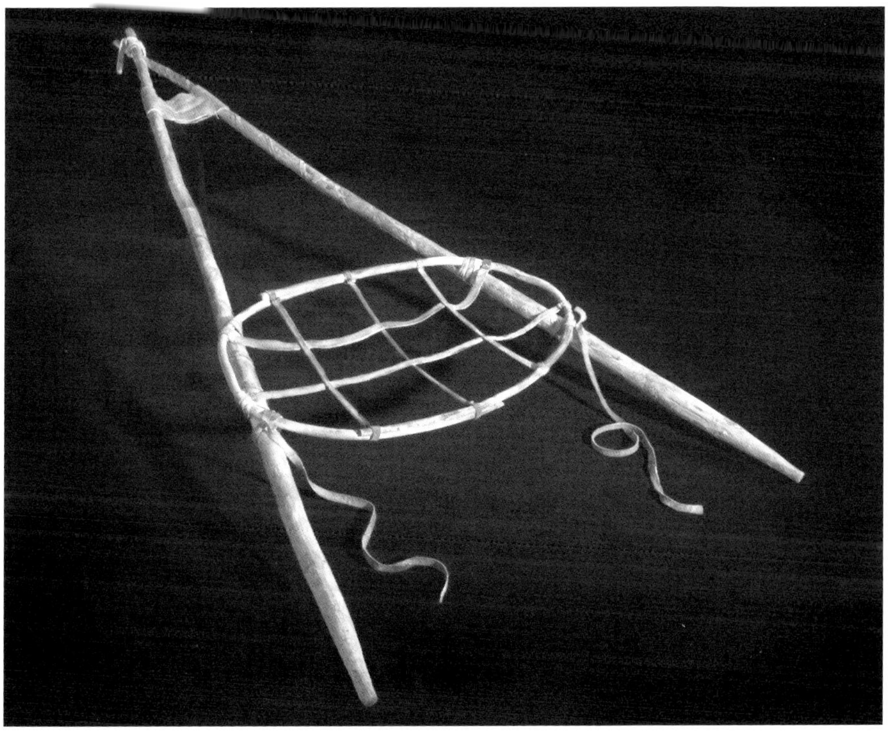

Dog travois, twentieth century (Canadian Museum of Civilization, V-B-409)

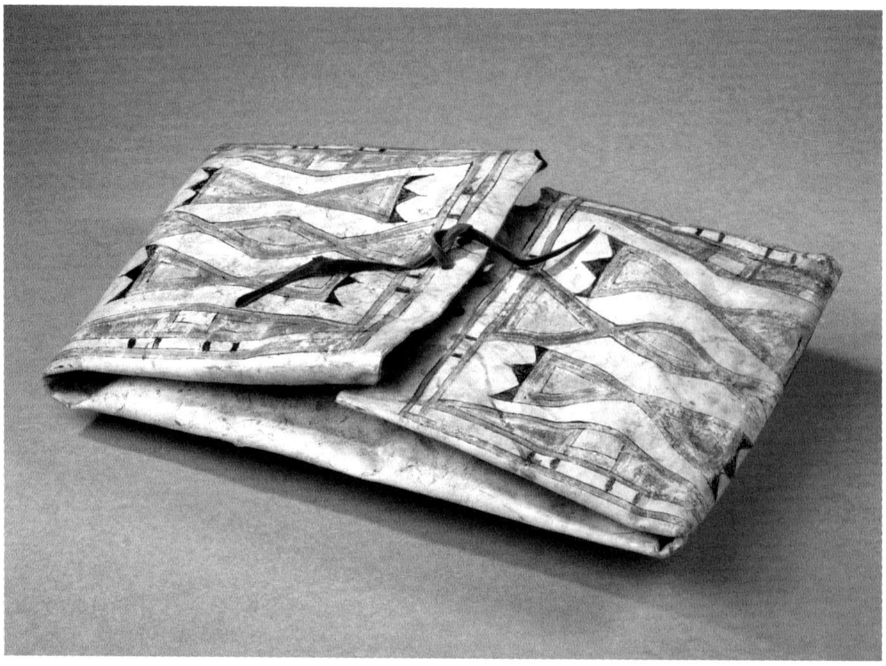

**Above** Rawhide storage container (parfleche), ca. 100 years old (Canadian Museum of Civilization, V-L-2)
**Below** Quill-decorated leather footwear (moccasins), ca. 100 years old (Canadian Museum of Civilization, V-J-4a,b)

Although the dog obviously played a crucial role in the lives of Northern Plains nomads, there is surprisingly little evidence of dogs in the archaeological record. Parts of dog skeletons are sparsely but consistently found in campsites and human burials. In the Head-Smashed-In bison jump, several hundred beads made of dog bones were found. Possibly, dog bones were utilized as intensively as bison bones, leaving few leftovers. Images of dogs are also rare in prairie petroglyphs. According to ethnological records, it seems quite clear that dogs were valuable, but did not receive the same admiration or respect as did horses in the Steppes. On the Steppes, horses belonged to men; on the Northern Plains, dogs belonged to women.

Dogs carried only part of the bison nomads' baggage—the heaviest and most voluminous part, such as tipi poles and tipi covers. People themselves walked and ran great distances carrying and dragging loads. To minimize weight, the heaviest tools, such as hammer stones and even tipi poles, were sometimes left at a camp site, especially when it was known that replacements could be made or would be available in the next camp site. Bundles of goods were wrapped in the tanned hides of bison, moose or elk, and tightened with leather cords or braided bands of leather. Leather bags and rawhide containers were used to store clothing and food. A variety of container shapes was used, taking advantage of various parts of animals, such as a bison stomach or a whole bison fetus. Netted bags made from fine cords of leather (babish) were especially convenient for carrying fresh meat, as they were expandable. Prairie nomads also made use of birchbark baskets. Heavier loads were carried on the back, supported by a tumpline that transferred part of the weight to the forehead or chest.

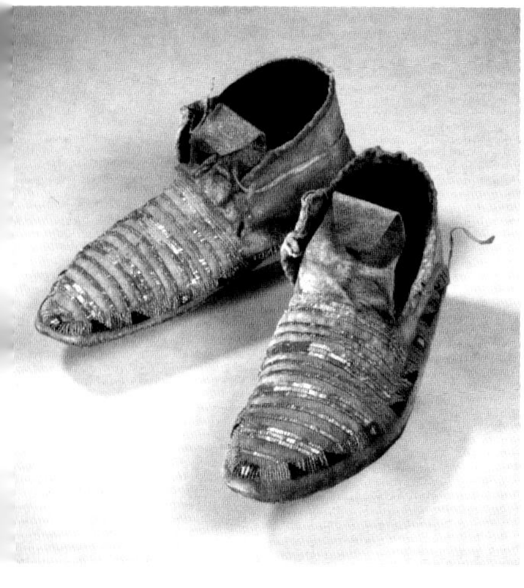

One of the most important parts of the travel equipment for pedestrian nomads was footwear. Moccasins with reinforced (raw-hide) soles were essential for pedestrian travel: they had not only to be comfortable, but also to protect feet, for instance against such common prairie plants as cacti with their long, sharp thorns.

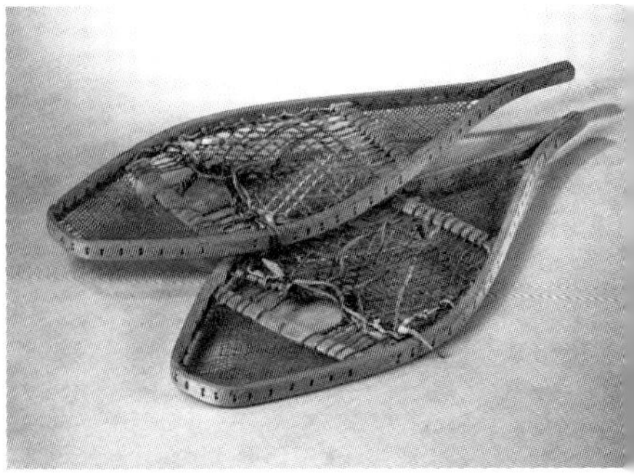

**Above** Snowshoes, ca. 100 years old (Canadian Museum of Civilization, III-L-185 a-b) **Below** Seasonal migrations of Blackfeet, 19th century A.D. (Canadian Museum of Civilization, after Blackfoot Gallery Committee, *Nitsitapiisinni: the Story of the Blackfoot People*, 2001)

Several pairs of moccasins were needed for a long trip, and even more for the annual cycle of a pedestrian nomad. Winter travel was made easier by using snowshoes.

According to ethnological data, annual pedestrian travel commonly reached 1,000 kilometres, with a maximal distance of travel from wintering grounds of about 500 kilometres. Migration routes were decided upon by elders at each major stop and were dependent on experience and current information regarding the availability of resources. In general, movements mimicked those of the bison, from the parkland margins after winter toward the centre of their grassland territory in the summer and then back. The orientation of movement might be roughly north-south in the northern part of the Prairies, and either east-west or west-east in central and southern parts. The migrations were not confined by rivers, as bison are good swimmers and people had to follow. Plains nomads used fords, rafts, and skin boats or simply swam the rivers, depending on their circumstances. On land, their movements covered a large part of the landscape. The many permanent and seasonal bodies of water scattered throughout the Prairies meant that neither people nor animals were closely tied to the river valleys by their need for water.

Northern Plains nomads spent several months in semi-sedentary winter camps among a few dozen to a few hundred people. During mid-summer they gathered into large open grasslands camps containing a few hundred to a few thousand people. The length of stay in these summer camps was on the order of two to three weeks. Aside from the two large extended gatherings and many shorter project-oriented camps, bands spent more than 100 days per year on the move. The distance travelled in a day varied from a few kilometres to a maximum of about 45 kilometres per day, depending on the strategy established by the leaders, the nature of the terrain, weather, game availability, other resource

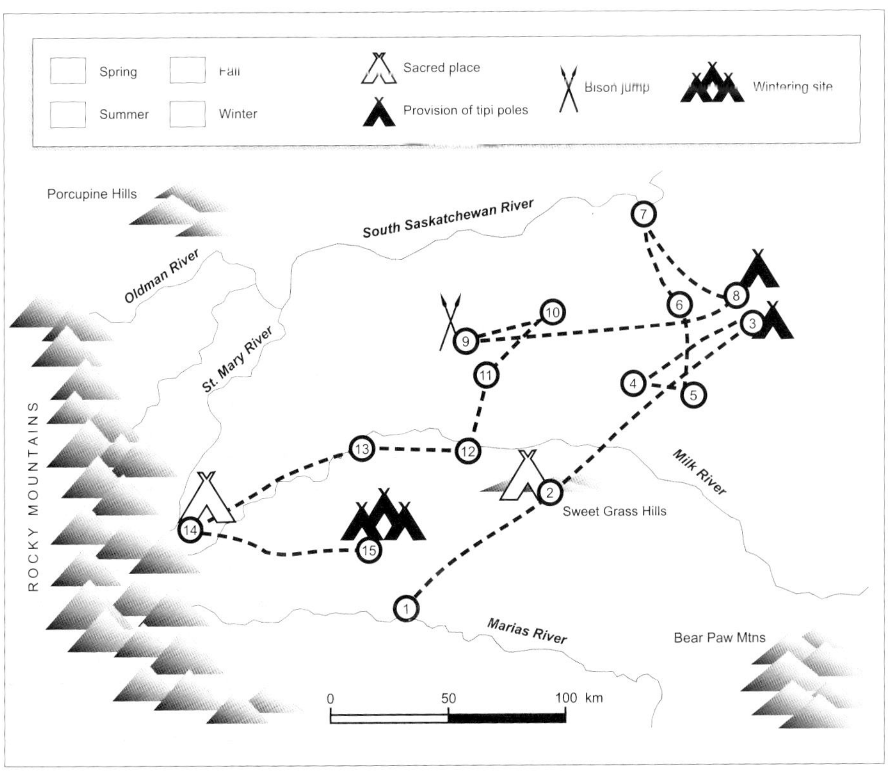

availability, concern about enemies, and so forth. A common distance travelled was about 11 kilometres per day. Tipi camps could be put up and taken down quite quickly, often in about an hour.

Travelling groups normally included about 20 to 50 people (three to five families). Infants were carried in baby bags or cradleboards on women's backs, while young children walked or rode on travois. Women often carried the heaviest loads, while men travelled light, carrying mainly weaponry in order to defend the group against enemies or to hunt for game if the opportunity presented itself. Prairie nomads navigated through the grasslands using the sun, stars, rivers, and their detailed knowledge of local landmarks.

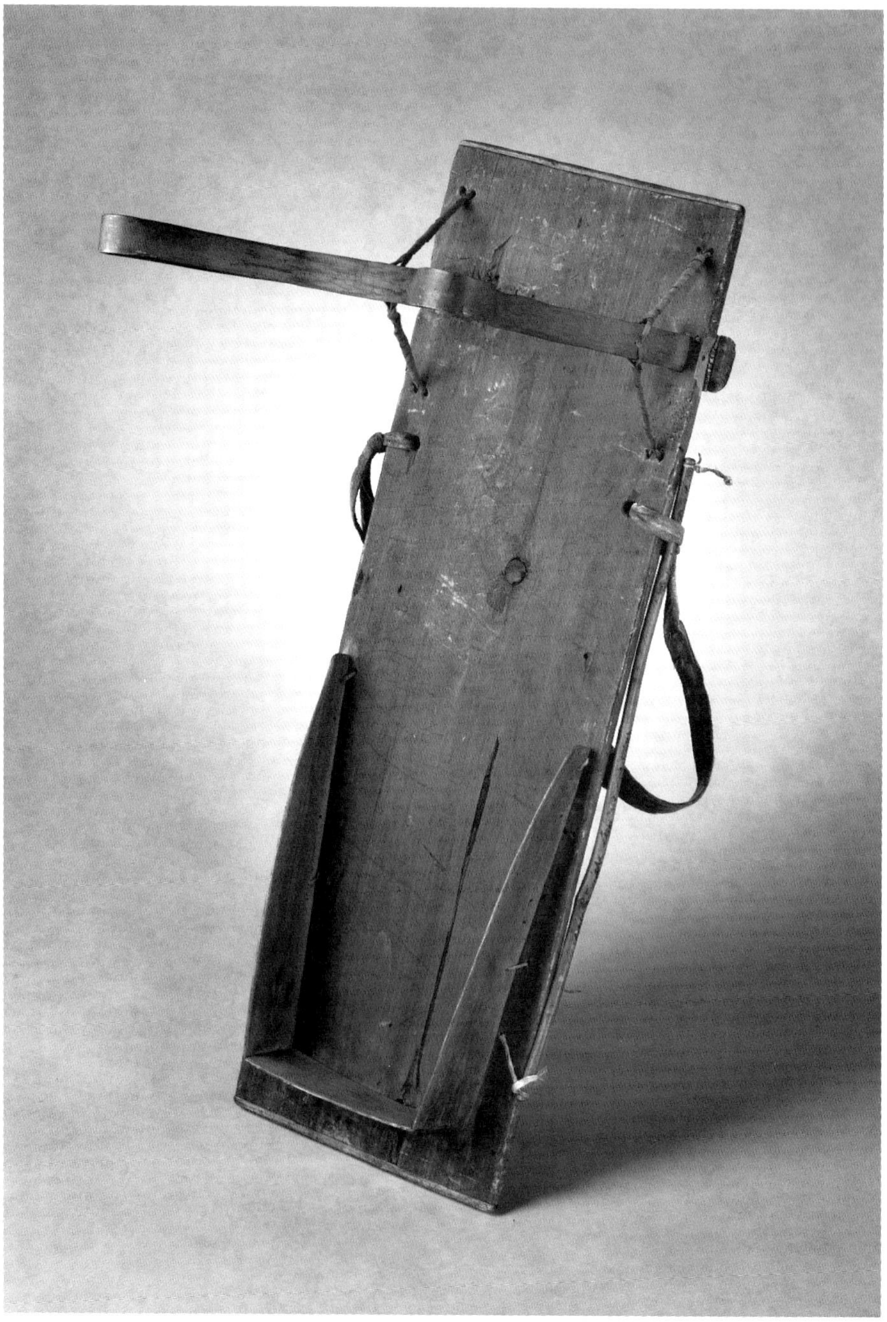

Wooden cradleboard, ca. 100 years old (Canadian Museum of Civilization, III-G-127 a, b)

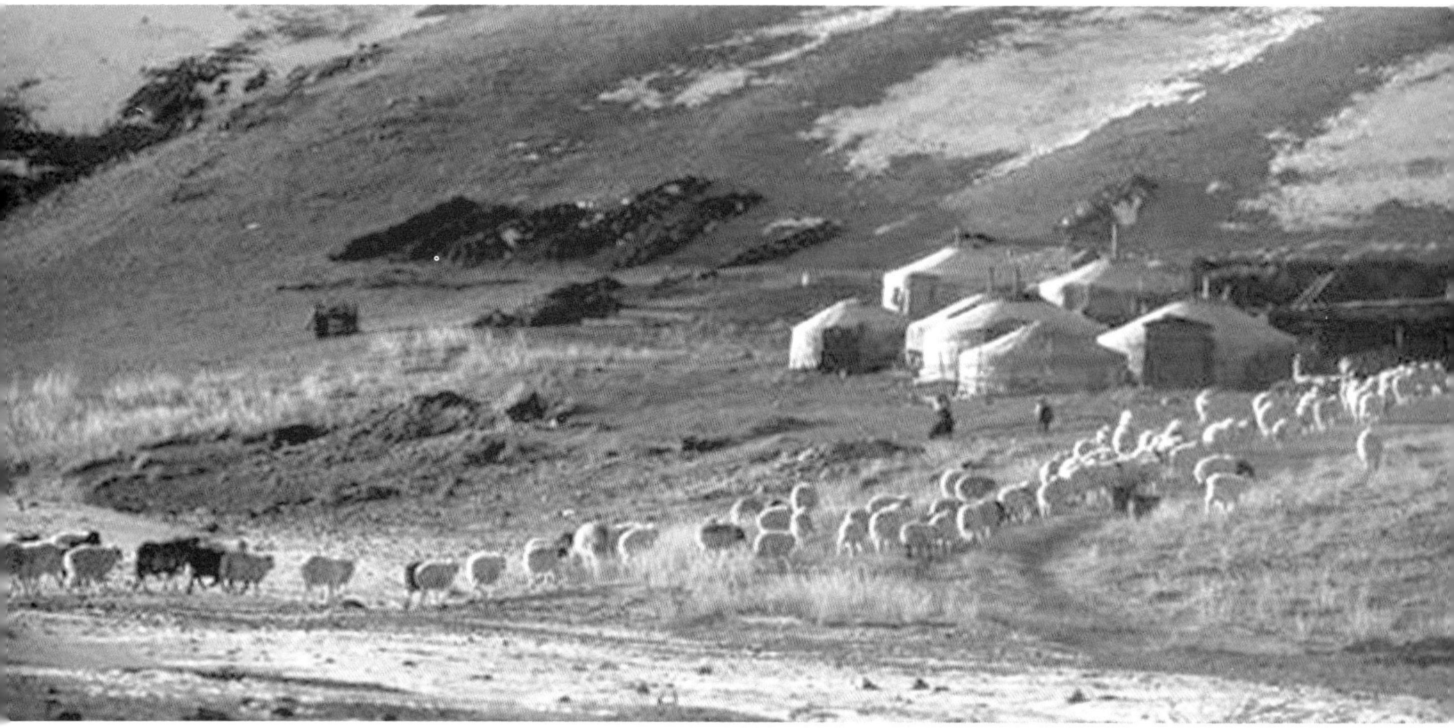

**Above** Nomads' camp, Mongolia, 2004
(courtesy of Ulaantaij Ltd www.ulaantaij.com)
**Below** Tipi camp on the open prairies, September 1871
(note travois set up in storage as tripods) (Charles Horetzky,
1871, Library and Archives Canada C-005181)

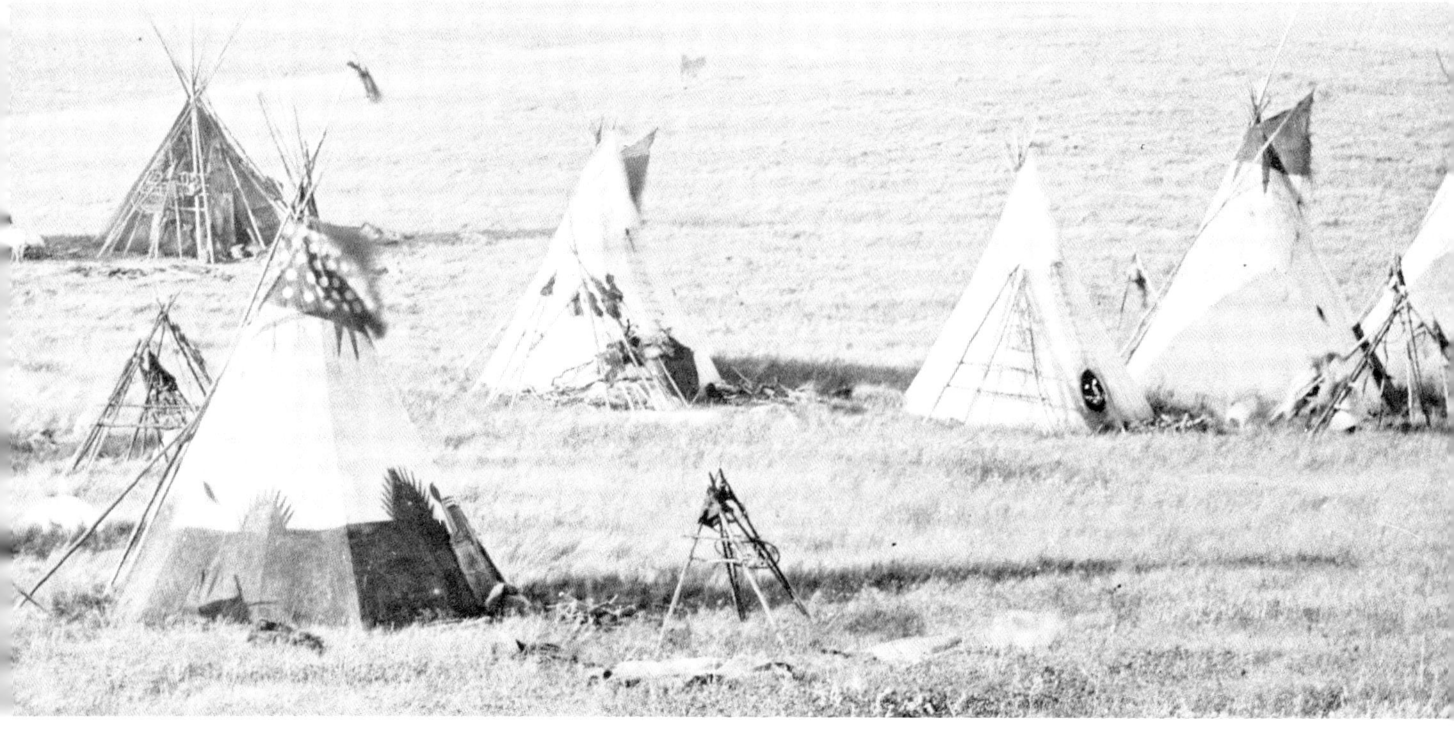

# LIFE IN CAMP

Steppe and prairie nomads lived in temporary settlements using portable, collapsible dwellings, portable furnishings and multifunctional tools. Despite differences in design and materials, the dwellings in both regions shared their most important characteristics: light weight, portability and durability.

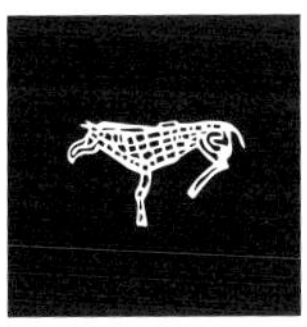

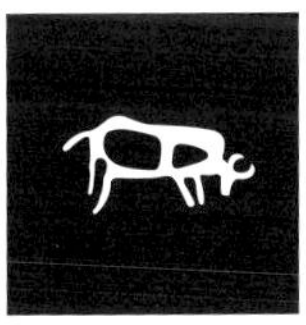

## STEPPE NOMADS

Steppe nomads inherited traditions of building permanent surface dwellings of logs or of wattle and daub, and semi-subterranean dwellings of wood and earth. These are depicted in rock art and in the remains of some early nomadic burials. However, about 3,000 years ago, the collapsible, portable dwelling known as the yurt became their principal habitation. This invention was attuned to the grasslands environment with its lack of wood and to the nomads' need for long migrations. Early historical records describe the transportation of yurts, made of willow saplings laced together with leather thongs and covered by felt, on wagons pulled by oxen or horses. The oldest images of yurts are in Siberian rock art dating to about 2,100 years ago. Historians mention at least two modifications to mobile dwellings, which took place in the Middle Ages: one was a yurt of conical shape supported by one or two poles from inside, and the other was a dome-like yurt without any supporting poles. The first type was more popular among Mongols, the second among Turks. Only the second construction type has survived until recent times. Yurt coverings varied by region, reflecting a combination of tribal traditions and functional modifications.

The domed yurt had several distinctive features. The collapsible construction consisted of a lattice frame, poles, the dome cap and a felt flap entrance (recently replaced with a wooden door). The outside covering consisted of several felt rugs. These were waterproof due to the natural water repellence of the sheep's wool used to produce felt. The dome cap was covered by a separate piece of felt that could be folded open when weather permitted. During historical times, the colour

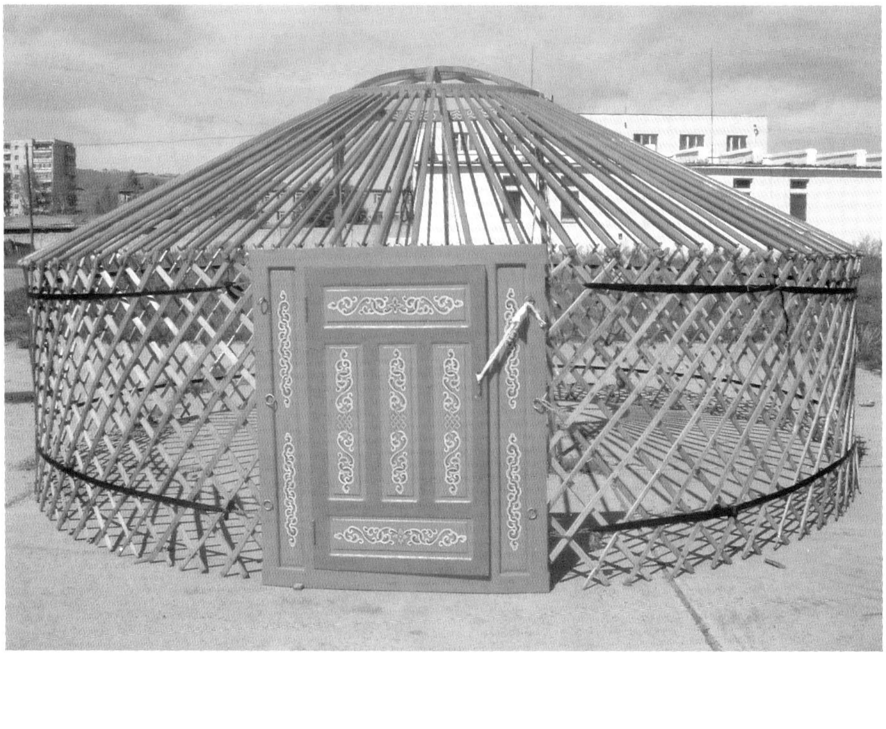

Setting up a yurt, Mongolia (courtesy of Ulaantaij Ltd www.ulaantaij.com)

of the yurt ranged from almost white to different shades of grey, but for special ceremonies the felt was brightly painted.

Traditionally, a yurt was assembled and dismantled by women. Two women could do this job in two hours. The assembled yurt was so sound structurally that it could be transported from place to place without breaking apart. Its advantages were its comparatively small weight (about 300 kilograms), a collapsible frame that could be dismantled into pieces no longer than 2.5 metres, and the perfect protection it provided against every kind of weather. The yurt kept out heat in summer, cold in winter, and precipitation year round. Opening the flap over the roof hole and lifting the lower edges of the wall coverings created a convection current that cooled the yurt in warm weather.

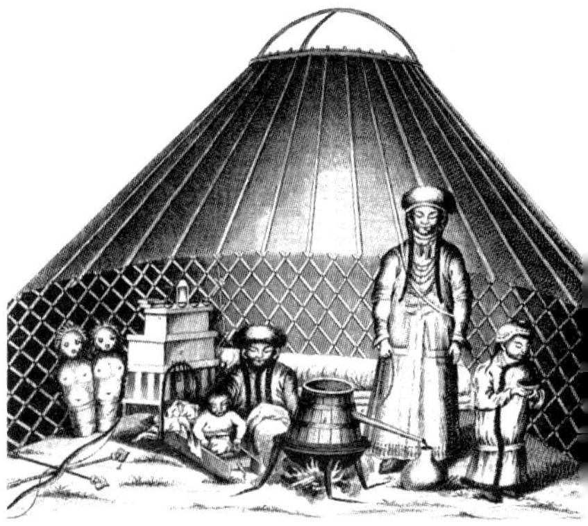

Kalmyk women and children in a yurt, brewing milk liquor. Note Onghons, spirit dolls used as yurt guardians, at the left, and a baby in a cradle with a "sunak," a hollow bird bone which drains urine from the cradle. (Peter Simon Pallas, *Sammlungen historischer Nachrichten über die mongolischen Völkerschaften*, 1776)

Yurts varied from 5 to 12 metres in diameter. An average yurt, designed for a family of five to seven people, was about six metres in diameter. To accommodate larger groups, perhaps for feasting, two yurts could be joined together. Wealthy tribes had special large yurts that were used as places for socializing and ceremonies.

The space within a yurt was divided into male and female parts, separated by reed and wool mats. Children slept in the female side of the yurt, a master and guests in the male side. A pantry was located within the female side as well. Here were stored food supplies, a large leather sack for fermented mare's milk and, closer to the entrance, kitchenware and utensils. On the men's side were placed weapons, horse harness, and other male paraphernalia. Various whips and quirts hung on the walls. The most important furniture was wooden chests that could be used as beds and as places to store valuable possessions, such as clothes, lengths of fabric and jewellery. The floor was covered by rugs, felts and pelts. People sat on the floor with their legs crossed, using pillows for support. They had no stools or chairs; however, from at least 2,500 years ago, they had small wooden tables. A cooking fire was at the centre of the floor with an open smoke hole in the dome cap above to allow the smoke out. Dung, especially goat dung, was widely used for heating the yurt and for indoor cooking.

Steppe nomads had a strong tradition of hospitality. Once inside a yurt, a guest was provided with food and water, and protected from injury. Fights and other manifestations of animosity were not allowed inside the yurt. Storytelling, gambling and feasting took place within the dwellings. Even large numbers of people preferred to feast inside a crowded yurt. Most other household activities, such as sheep shearing, milking, cooking, felt making, and working hides, took place outside.

During summer, there were commonly three to five yurts in a camp. Near the yurts were poles for tying up riding horses, fenced corals for the herd animals, and open hearths for cooking. People stayed at one site for several days or weeks, and could get all their possessions packed and on the move within several hours. During winter, larger aggregations of up to several hundred yurts stayed together for three to four months. In such camps, the yurts were arranged in a circular pattern, with herds kept inside the circle. During longer stays, the outer edges of the yurt were insulated with soil. In some places circles of soil still survive, marking former wintering sites. However, most of the Steppes area has been ploughed, and vestiges of earlier occupations have long been destroyed. Indeed, no archaeological evidence of campsites has been found in the Steppes for the period from 3,000 to 1,500 years ago. Knowledge about nomads for this period comes solely from burials and historical documents.

The location of campsites changed with the season. For summer camps, high grounds adjacent to rivers were preferred, as winds in these elevated locations gave relief from biting insects, which were extremely troublesome nearer the water. In autumn, when there were fewer insects, camps were set right on the riverbanks. During late fall and winter, when pregnant herd animals needed salt as a dietary supplement, salty lowlands were the best locations for establishing a camp.

According to ethnological and historical evidence, steppe nomads rarely undressed in the yurt. The fabric of their clothing protected them well outdoors, and allowed the skin to breathe indoors. However, personal hygiene was an important part of their lives. During the late Bronze Age, Scythian nomads, who were closely connected with northern Greek colonies on the north shore of the Black Sea, used soap to wash their hair and practiced ritual purification through the use of the steam bath. From that time on, small bronze mirrors became an obligatory part of the nomadic outfit, both men's and women's. Bronze mirrors were obtained in trade from Greece, along with cosmetics such as ceruse, recorded archaeologically through findings of small flacons. In respect to costume, silk bands on flaps of sleeves and robes became a popular protection against lice. The silk was imported from China. With the increase in mobility of steppe populations in the Early Iron Age (about 2,500 years ago), the smearing of fat on skin and hair became an important means of protection against the sun and wind. Fats and creams made of whey are still in use by modern steppe nomads.

Metal "Q-tips" appeared among nomads' possessions about 1,500 years ago. At the same time, special tweezers for plucking whiskers came into use. A few bits of archaeological evidence concerning infant toiletry have also been found: for boys, cradle catheters (made of hollow bird bones) called sunaks and for girls, clay pots called toovaks are known from Medieval times (1,100 to 500 years ago). No special hygienic measures were taken to maintain a camp. Special

Bronze mirror, 2nd–3rd century A.D. (Early Iron Age) (P. V. Alabin Museum of History and Regional Studies, Samara, KP-18548/24)

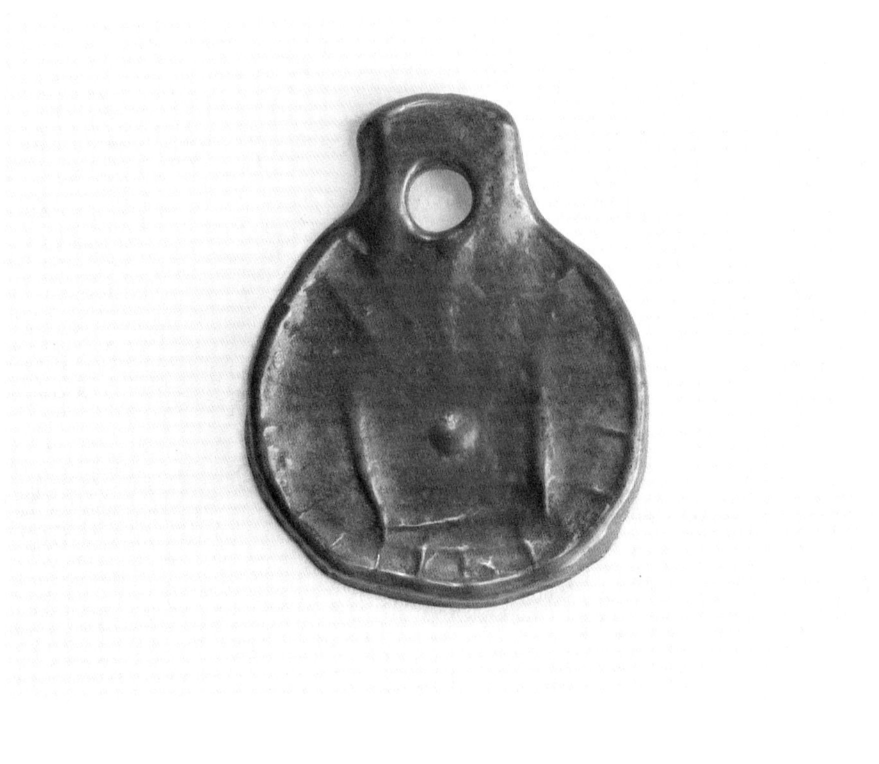

disposal pits and clay films on the floors of dwellings appeared only in towns of the Nomadic Empires, later in nomadic history. The arrival of epidemic diseases was coincident with the appearance of towns.

The towns occupied by later nomads are an intriguing feature of the history of the Steppes, indeed, of World history. Nomadic societies in the Steppes evolved through several stages, from true nomadism toward a lifestyle that combined nomadism and sedentism. These stages were related to increasing specialization in warfare and progressive social stratification. In the first stage, people moved year-round. In the second, the poorest people in a nomadic group stayed at one place, while the others travelled for most of the year, returning for winter. In the third stage, permanent settlements began to appear. Only the grandest people migrated, and the rest stayed in settlements.

From the Early Iron Age on, nomadic states and, later, nomadic empires were repeatedly formed in the Steppes. From the Middle Ages on, nomadic states contained permanent settlements with monumental, long-lasting constructions made of sun-dried and fired bricks, stone, wood and adobe. The towns were located on rivers, their size reaching several hundred hectares and their populations up to 60,000 people. The towns of the Golden Horde were filled with craftsmen, merchants, officials and slaves. The nobles maintained the traditional lifestyle, occupying yurts amongst the permanent houses of these towns. During the reign of the Golden Horde, up to 50 towns, serving as centres of craftsmanship and trade, existed in the Steppes area from the Dnestr to the Tobol Rivers. About ten of these towns minted their own coins.

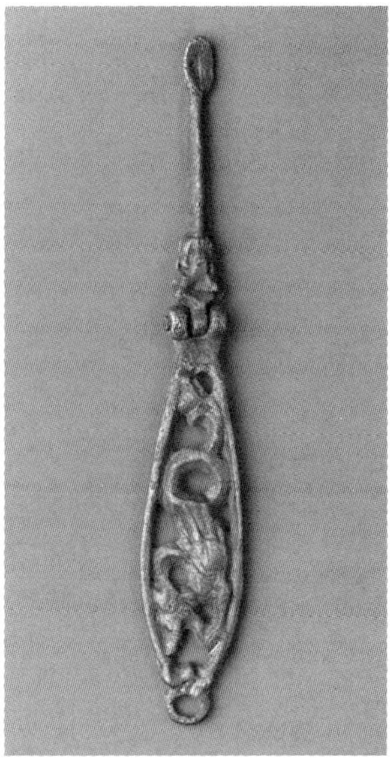

Bronze swab, 8th century A.D. (Early Middle Ages) (P. V. Alabin Museum of History and Regional Studies, Samara, KP-26045/22)

## PRAIRIE NOMADS

According to archaeological evidence, portable circular dwellings seem to have been used in the Northern Plains for at least the last 5,000 years and possibly for 10,000 years. Typically, their archaeological remains are represented by circular rows of stones which once weighted down the lower flaps of tipi coverings. Thousands of these tipi rings still survive in the Prairies on the few remaining unploughed lands.

The Plains tipi was shaped like a tilted cone, with a slightly steeper wall at the back. Its principal components were a framework of poles and a hide covering. The framework included 10 to 16 poles, about four to six metres in length, which were joined near one end. Some tribes began the erection of this framework with three foundation poles. They tied these together near one end, raised the tied "top" ends and spread the bottoms to the edge of what was to be a roughly circular floor about four to six metres in diameter. The rope securing the poles could also be pegged to the ground to give the frame greater rigidity if wind conditions required it. On this foundation, the other poles were laid to complete the conical frame. Other tribes used a four-pole foundation to achieve a similar result. The last pole to be added was at the back of the tipi. The wood

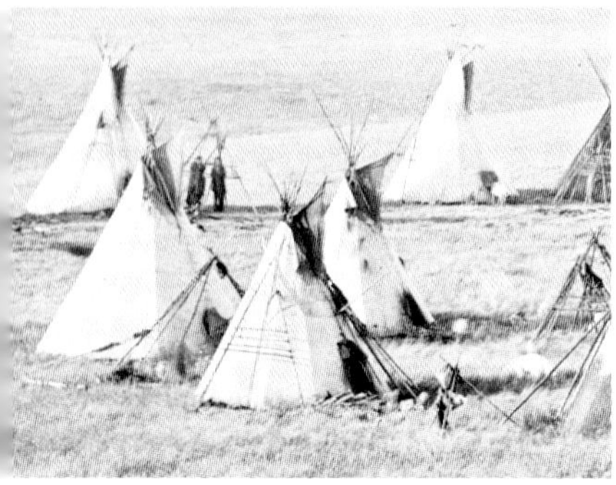

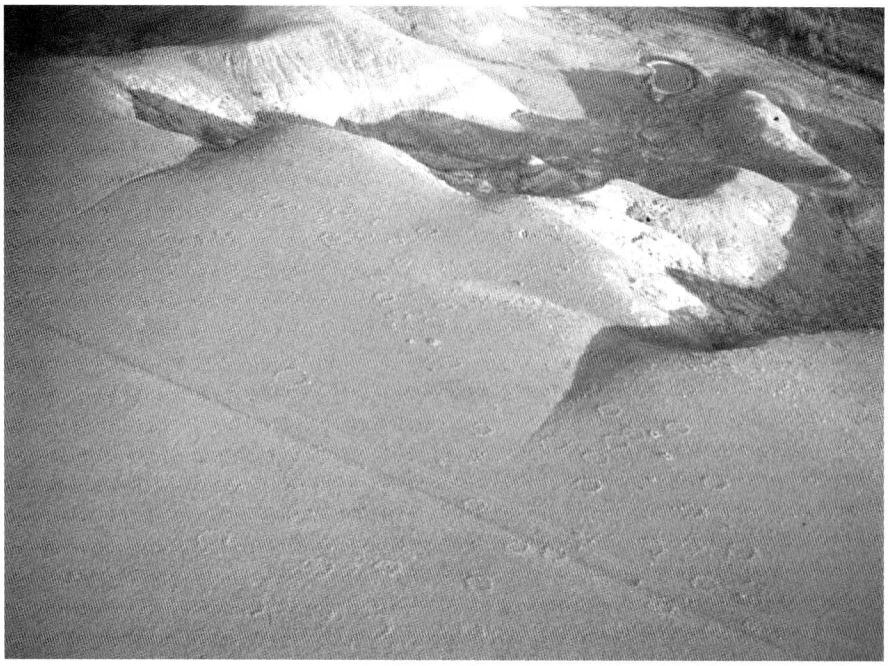

**Above** Tipi camp on the open prairies, September 1871 (note travois set up in storage as tripods) (Charles Horetzky, 1871, Library and Archives Canada C-005181)
**Right** Former tipi camp marked by rings of stone, seen from the air in southern Alberta (Royal Alberta Museum, PN92.1.2900)

chosen for poles was strong, straight and lightweight, such as lodge pole pine or cedar. Since these woods were available only in certain parts of the grassland region, poles were usually moved with camps from place to place.

The tipi cover consisted of from 6 to more than 20 tanned bison hides, depending on the number of people it had to house and the status of the owner. Twelve hides was a common size for a family of seven to eight people and their baggage. The hides were sewn together with sinew and, as part of their preparation, were waterproofed by smoking, which prevented stiffening and cracking after rain. The cover was tied to the last tipi pole and raised to the proper elevation at the back of the tipi. Then it was pulled taut over the frame and closed at the front with transverse wooden pins about 30 to 40 centimetres in length. A low circular opening at the front of the tipi (covered with a hide flap) served as the door. If the weather was cool or windy, the base of the cover would be attached to the ground with wooden pegs or with a row of stones resting on the bottom flap to make the structure more resistant to wind and to reduce drafts.

An important technical feature was the central smoke hole. A gap was left in the top part of the cover extending into the more gently sloping side of the tipi. Two smoke flaps were sewn to the sides of this smoke hole and held in place by two long "guide" poles whose manipulation facilitated the flow of hearth smoke up and out of the tipi. In very inclement weather, the poles could also be used to position the flaps over the smoke hole, in effect closing it. Tipis varied from 4 to 24 metres in basal diameter, depending on their purpose. Larger structures could be constructed by joining tipis together. Tipis more than about 6 metres in diameter and multi-tipi structures were used mainly for ceremonial purposes.

The outsides of some tipi covers were painted using plant and mineral pigments mixed with tallow or glue made of boiled bison hoofs, and melted resin. The paintings reflected the personal experiences of the principal male inhabitant, such as war exploits and the visions he had received. Some tribes, for example the Blackfeet, had obligatory symbolic patterns at the bottom and top of the tipi: a broad dark band at the bottom represented the earth; another dark band at the top represented the sky; and the space between was used for vision painting, usually depicting the warrior's guardian spirit. Continuing the symbolism, tipi poles were said to link the earth to the sky, and to help people's prayers reach the spirits. According to ethnological evidence, the proportion of painted tipis in a camp varied widely among different tribes.

An inner lining, about 150 centimetres in height, was tied to the poles inside the tipi. This served many purposes: to draw smoke upwards, to insulate the tipi, and to reduce the casting of shadows from the central fire onto the outer wall. In winter, the space between the lining and tipi cover could be stuffed with dried grass for insulation.

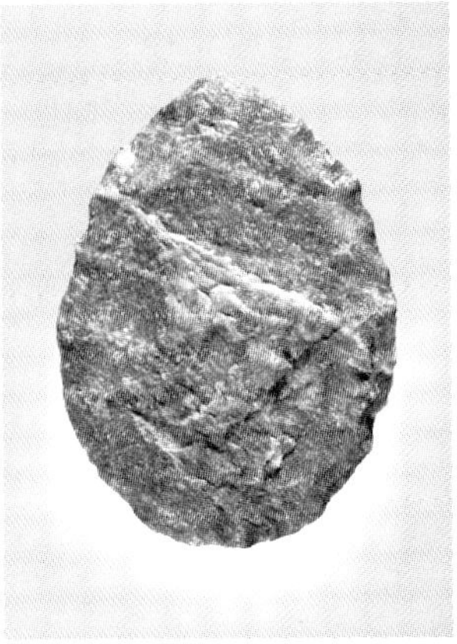

**Above** Chipped stone tool for cutting or chopping (Canadian Museum of Civilization, X-C-124)
**Below** Miniature arrow points used by young boys, ca. 500 years old (Canadian Museum of Civilization, X-B-444j,u,x)

At the centre of the tipi, an open hearth was set, sometimes bordered with stones and sometimes dug out as a shallow pit ranging from 40 to 70 centimetres in diameter. Larger hearths, over 90 centimetres in diameter, were set in ceremonial tipis. Clean-burning firewood that produced neither sparks nor excessive amounts of smoke was preferred for fuel. Common hardwoods that served this purpose included ash, willow and aspen. When no other fuel was available, dried bison dung was used, but mostly outdoors since it yielded a lot of smoke and required wind to burn well. Behind the fireplace, a small patch of bare soil was left as an altar. At this spot, sweet grass or some other sacral incense was burned.

The tipi was generally divided into two parts: men sat to one side of the entrance, women to the other. The oldest man and his wife slept at the back of the tipi, behind the altar. During feasting, that was an honourable place for guests as well. In many tribes, only the head man of the tipi could cross to the rear, passing behind the altar. However, according to ethnological data, the tipi belonged to women. If a man had more than one wife, he would share a bed on the right side of the tipi with his first wife, while the other wives and the children would occupy the left side. Dishes, utensils, food and firewood were kept close to the entrance of the tipi, on the woman's side. Clothing, harness and weaponry were kept at the front and rear, on the men's side. If there were slaves in the household, they slept outside the tipi door.

While in the tipi, men sat cross-legged or with their knees up under the chin and arms folded around their shins. Women sat with both legs folded to one side or on their knees. Elders might have a backrest to lean against, a wooden tripod to which was attached a wooden mat made of willow saplings. Beds consisted of boughs or grass and bison robes, or sometimes just bison robes. Another piece of furniture, which could be used both inside and outside the tipi, was a tripod, usually made of pine saplings. Tripods were used as racks for various possessions, from medicine bundles to leather vessels.

Tipis were easy to assemble and disassemble: it took less than an hour for a couple of women to erect or dismantle one. The disassembled parts were transported separately—the cover on dog travois, and the poles dragged by dogs as they would a travois. A tipi might last for several years, but it eventually wore out. As it did so, it became smaller. The lower parts of the covering, being regularly in contact with the earth, disintegrated first and had to be trimmed. The butt ends of the poles also wore down as the dogs dragged them from camp to camp. Eventually, an old tipi was either given to needy relatives, or the covering

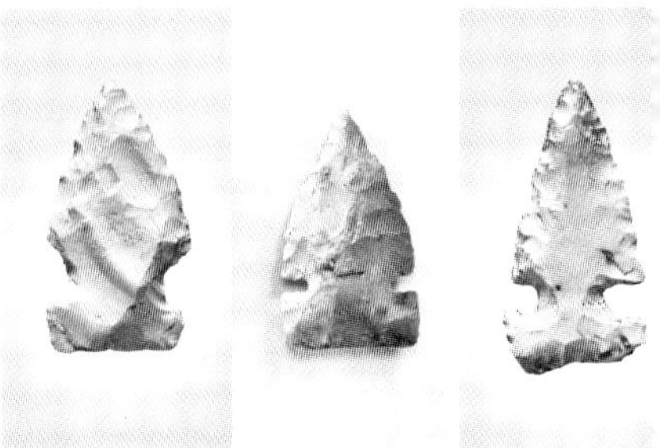

was cut up for use in moccasins, bags and other leather goods while the poles were also recycled or discarded.

In spite of the smoke flap, the tipi could sometimes be a rather smoky dwelling, causing eye irritations for its inhabitants. Therefore, people tried to spend as much time outside as possible. Such activities as hide working, hide tailoring and sewing, tool making and food preparation took place outside whenever weather permitted. However, storytelling and feasting always occurred in the tipi. Leather clothing was highly functional outdoors, but prone to being sweaty when worn indoors. Therefore, inside the tipi, people tended to set aside their robes, shirts and leggings and spent most of their time lightly dressed or almost naked.

Immediately outside the tipi door was a pile of firewood. A short distance farther was an outdoor hearth and work area, often protected from the sun by a temporary sun shelter made of poles covered with hides or leafy branches. Also within longer term camps were sweat lodges, small dome-like structures made of bent saplings covered with hides. Scaffolds or stone cairns for caching meat might also be nearby. If a person died, the scaffold on which he was initially buried would be visible from the camp. The number of tipis in a camp varied from one to hundreds, depending on the season and the circumstances. The largest camps tended to occur in mid-summer during the ceremonial gatherings of regional bands or trade fairs, which might involve more than one tribe. Winter camps and communal bison-hunting camps were next in size, usually involving more than one band and about 10 to 40 tents. During much of the year, however, people lived in band-size or microband-size groups occupying as few as one to as many as ten tipis.

According to ethnographic records, large summer camps were organized into a grand circle, replicating the defensive circle that antelopes formed when attacked by wolves. There is little evidence for this practice in the archaeological record which shows that tipi ring camps were often spread out in much more irregular patterns during ancient times.

The general hygiene of camps was maintained by frequent moves. Even when camps were set in a particular locale for longer periods, people tended to move their tipis to a "fresh" spot within camp from time to time or to change the grass or boughs used for beds. During short stays, accumulated debris from eating and other activities was swept into the central hearth. As to personal hygiene, some ethnologists noted that men took a daily morning plunge into water to toughen themselves and improve their health. The sweat lodge was also a common resort—for pure pleasure, as an offering to a spirit power, for ritualistic cleansing, and as a cure for illness. People used a porcupine tail as a hairbrush and groomed one another to rid themselves of lice. Mothers kept their babies in a bag on a cradleboard. They put moss in the bag as an absorbent for urine and fecal matter and changed the moss several times a day. To baby boys they sometimes attached a kind of conduit so that the moss never became wet.

Tipis were not the only kind of dwelling that prairie nomads used. When on hunting trips, people made expedient shelters with materials at hand. In addition, raiding parties often built defensive dwellings at strategic points along their warpaths. These looked like tipis, but the walls were made almost solid with poles to protect against arrows. Fenced around by a sort of labyrinth of laced saplings, the war tipi also offered protection against entry by enemies.

Unlike steppe nomads, prairie nomads never formed states or empires. Although they lived on the fringes of a great Mississippian period chiefdom centred on the twelfth-century city of Cahokia, the nomads did not adopt their wooden housing styles. Nor did they adopt the earthlodges used by the semi-sedentary agricultural villagers who pushed northwest into the Middle Missouri River region of the Northern Plains about the same time. Instead, the villagers adopted the Plains tipi for use when they were away from their fortified villages.

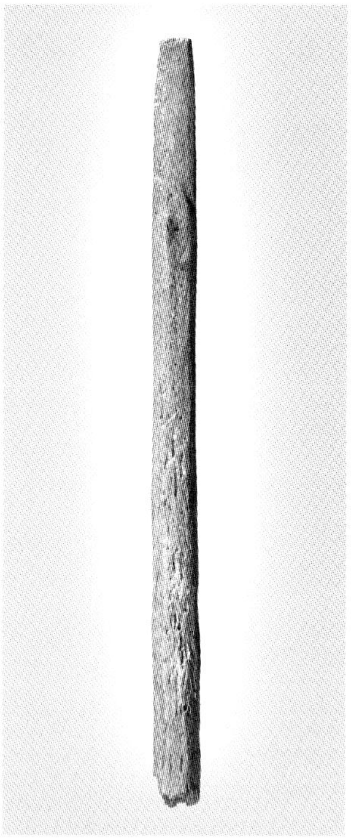

Bone stylus, ca. 500 years old (Canadian Museum of Civilization, X-B-516d)

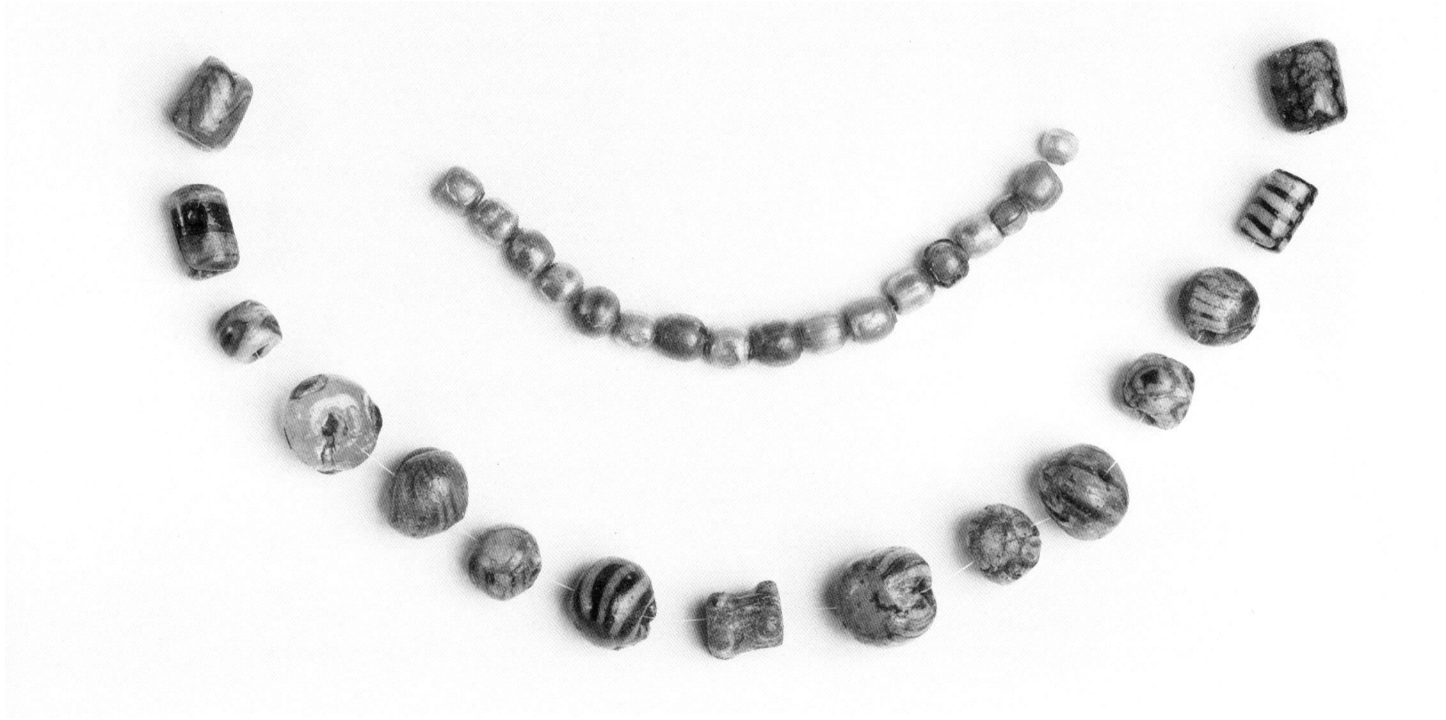

**Above** Necklace with glass beads, 8th century A.D. (Early Middle Ages) (P. V. Alabin Museum of History and Regional Studies, Samara, KP-26045/23, 24)
**Below** Necklace of bison and canid teeth, ca. 500 years old (Canadian Museum of Civilization, X-B-504 a-z)

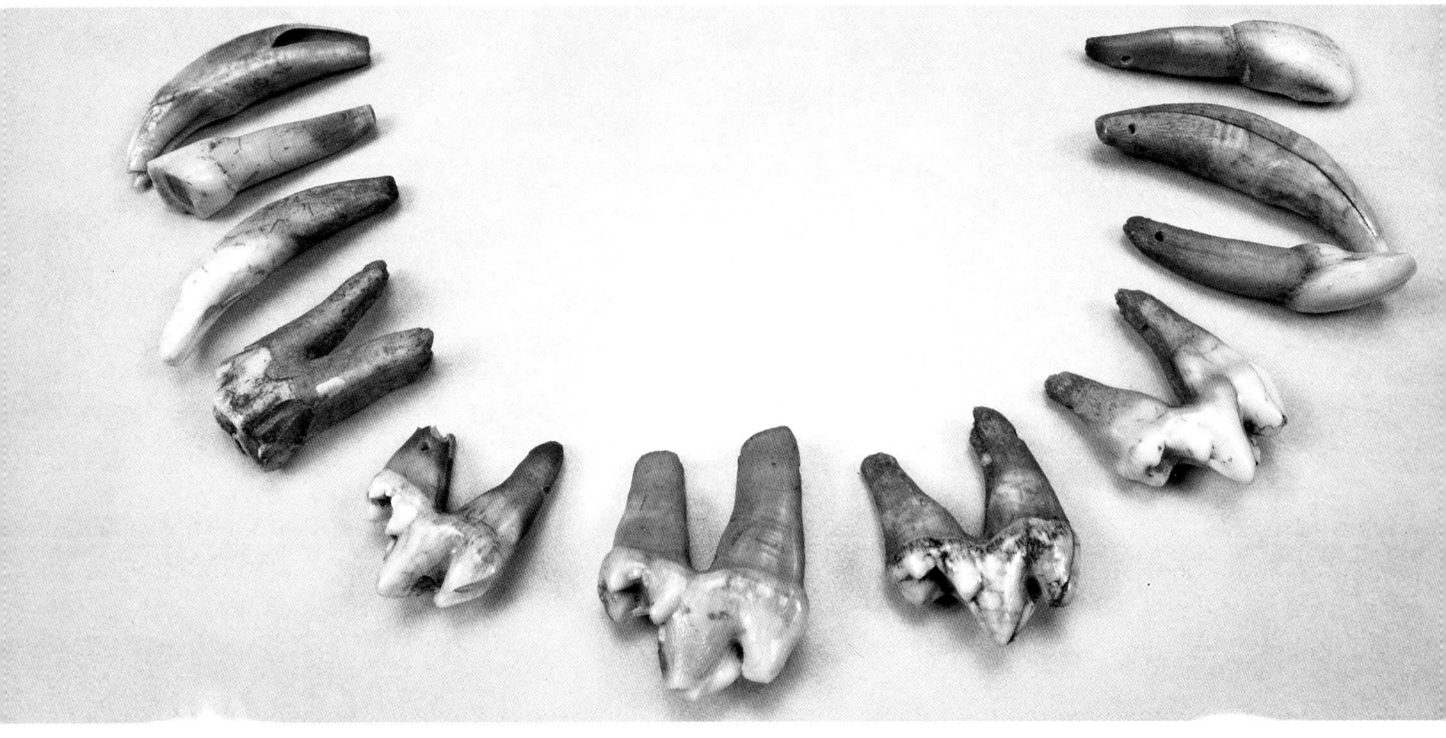

# Clothing and Decorations

Nomads of the Steppes and Prairies made tailored clothing, which was adapted to their lifestyles, but materials and styles differed between the two regions. Tanned hides were the principal clothing material in the Prairies. A combination of hides, woven textiles, and felts were the main clothing materials in the Steppes. In fact, hides and hide products played a large role in the nomadic life of both regions, being used for clothing, shoes, dwellings, cart covers, vessels, and protective weaponry. Decorations were also important in the two regions, serving both aesthetic and protective roles.

# STEPPE NOMADS

In grassland archaeological sites, coverings made of organic materials do not preserve well, unless they are buried under specific conditions that prevent decay. Such conditions exist occasionally in burials in which organic materials lay close to objects made of metals such as bronze or copper, or in cases where organic materials were embalmed.

We presume that the earliest technologies for making coverings involved animal hides. Tools for skin working, such as bone and stone scrapers, knives and perforators, have been found in sites throughout the Northern Hemisphere from Palaeolithic times until recent centuries. In Eurasia, the oldest finds of actual leather products are about 12,000 years old and come from the Gorbunovo site, north of the Steppes. Within the Steppes, the oldest leather artifacts are in Siberian sites dating from the Early Iron Age and in European sites dating from the Middle Ages. The leather working that survives in the Steppes today came to perfection among the medieval artisans of the nomadic empires. Even now, Russian names for hide products are actually Medieval Turkish names (*yufti, safian, bahtarma, mezdra*). Leather was used for winter clothing, leggings, and footwear, as well as for belts, fastenings, bags, and harness.

The oldest evidence for weaving in Eurasia, twisted fibres about 15,000 years old, has been found in the caves of France. In the Steppes, the oldest find of woven clothing, a woman's woolen hat, possibly felt, dates to about 4,500 years ago. From the Bronze Age on, sheep's wool was regularly used for felt making. The process started with the preparation of a thin layer of sheep wool, which was rolled around a cylinder, which in turn was rolled back and forth for several hours while also being beaten. Sheep felt was used for such clothing as

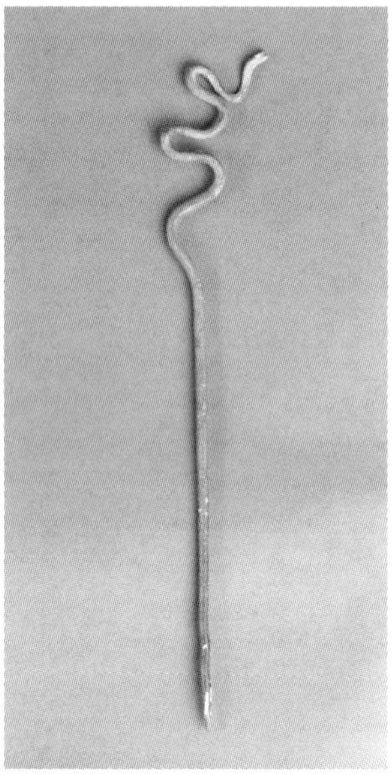

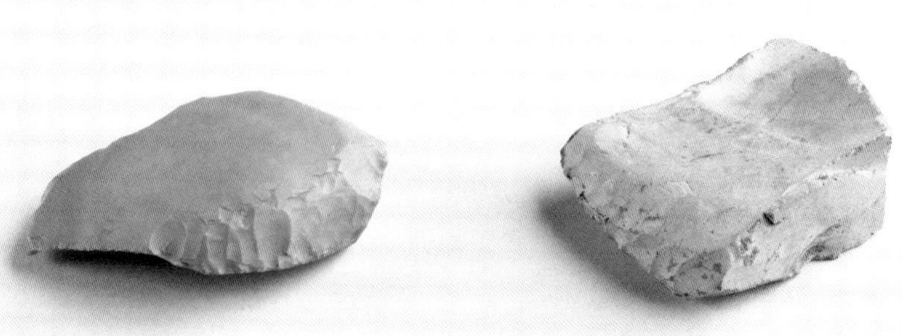

**Above** Bronze awl, ca. 3,500 years old (Bronze Age) (P. V. Alabin Museum of History and Regional Studies, Samara, KP-200/1)
**Right** Flint scrapers, ca. 4,000 years old (Bronze Age) (P. V. Alabin Museum of History and Regional Studies, Samara, KP-25401/4-56)

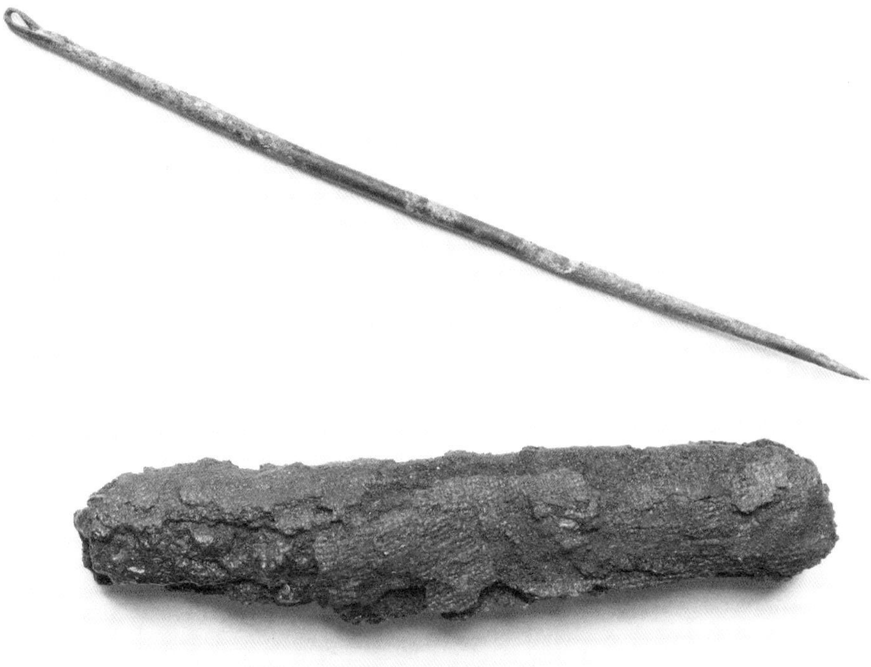

hats, mantles and soft boots. In addition to making felt, wool was spun into yarn, as also were fibres of nettle and hemp. Clay spindle whorls found in Bronze Age burials provide evidence for the importance of this kind of manufacture. Presumably, after the yarn was spun, it was used to make fabric on a loom. Although finds of fabrics are very rare in the Steppes, indirect evidence for the use of twined and woven textiles comes from imprints found on pottery and metal dating as far back as 5,000 years ago. Other indirect evidence for work done on leather and woven materials includes bronze (and later iron) needles and needle holders, which are typical women's sewing tools.

**Above** Bronze needle, ca. 3,500 years old (Bronze Age), and needle case, 8th century A.D. (Early Middle Ages) (P. V. Alabin Museum of History and Regional Studies, Samara, KP-25962/6, KP-26045/90)
**Below** Burning nettle (*Urtica urens* L.) (courtesy of Missouri Botanical Garden, http://www.botanicus.org)

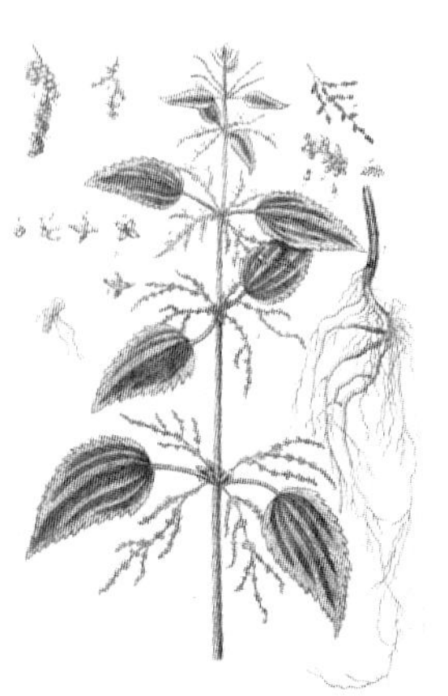

More detailed information about nomads' clothing comes from historical descriptions, the earliest of which date to about 2,500 years ago when Herodotus noted that the Sakas wore a high conical cap (kolpak) and trousers. On bas-reliefs of that period, the following elements of men's costume are visible: kolpaks with flaps covering the ears and nape of the neck, high soft boots with laces, and a short tunic-like robe. The tunic was commonly made of a single piece of material folded in half, covering most of the torso without using shoulder seams. Sleeves were sewn to the straight edge of the body piece. This style has been interpreted as a result of ripping the fabric along the thread, without using a cutting instrument. In 2,500 to 2,300 year old Scythian burials, clothing was made of plain-weave wool and hemp, felt and leather. Leather garments included trousers, stockings and fur coats. Among the burial goods were silks from China, woollen textiles from Iraq, and woollen rugs from Persia.

The Huns (Hunnu–2,300 to 1,600 years ago) were described by Chinese historians as wearing clothes of hide and wraps made of felt and fur. According to archaeological finds in the Noin-Ula burial mounds of Siberia, men wore robes made of hide, lined with felt and edged with fur, and trousers consisting of two wide leggings that ended in footwear. The leggings were put on separately and fastened to the waist. Footwear consisted of felt half-boots covered with leather and decorated with embroidery. Men wore kolpaks on their heads. Women wore cylindrical, flat-top caps. Their hair was plaited in two or three braids and covered with a sheath. Men and women wore wide belts with bronze buckles, and bronze pins ("fibula") fastened to the breast.

From 1,600 years ago, the Steppes were dominated by Turkic tribes. Nomads of this era were described as wearing long dresses made from skins, felt and coarse wool cloth. The robe-like garments were wrapped with the right side over the left. In fall and winter, nomads wore waterproof robes made of camel or sheep hair, and a sheepskin coat. One winter garment required about forty lamb skins. Rich people covered their sheepskin coats with imported fabric. Both men and women braided their hair and wore earrings. Men wore a kolpak and a small skullcap under it. Winter hats could be made of lamb and kid skins, but furs of animals such as wolf or fox were preferred. The men's costume always included a leather belt decorated with bronze or gold overlays, the number and material of which distinguished the warrior's bravery.

Women wore a hat, pants and a robe with a belt. The hat was one of the most important elements: ritual changes in hats during initiation, wedding, and childbirth symbolized a change in social status. Many elements of women's clothing had spiritually protective functions, for example, jewellery and attachments to clothing and hair. One such component was a covering for braids. This ritualistic covering on hair or braids is recorded repeatedly in archaeological sites for at least the last 3,000 years. About the same time, steppe nomads began combing their hair with bone, bronze and gold combs. Bronze mirrors, traded from Olbia, a Greek colony on the Black Sea, and later from China, also became an important part of men's and women's accoutrement. Women kept their bone combs, together with their bone-handled mirrors, in a pouch. Warriors attached their mirrors to their belts through a hole in the mirror.

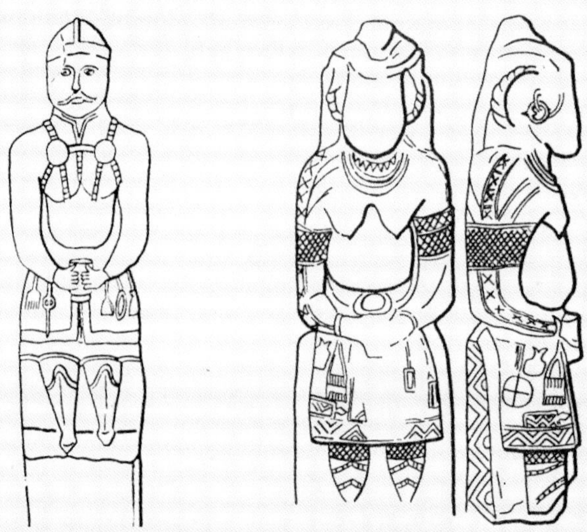

**Left** Stone statue of a Polovetz man, 10th–13th century A.D. Note tools suspended from man's belt (left to right): comb, quirt, strike-a-light, mirror and pouch (*Archaeology of the U.S.S.R.: Eurasian Steppes in the Middle Ages*, Moscow, 1981, p. 265)
**Right** Polovetz woman's costume and hairdo, 10th–13th century A.D., depicting various decorations: necklace, earrings and headdress. Attached to her belt are (left to right) a mirror, a small cosmetic bottle and a comb (*Archaeology of the U.S.S.R.: Eurasian Steppes in the Middle Ages*, Moscow, ed. S. Pletneva, 1981, p. 266)

Steppe nomads were fond of rich decoration for their costumes. They used patterned felts for bags, hats and rugs. To make a patterned felt, they laid a pattern of coloured wool on a base of non-dyed wool (mineral and plant dyes were used to make the coloured wool). Then, they poured hot water over the pattern, rolled the coloured and uncoloured wool into a bolt, and rolled it back and forth for several hours to compress the felt. The patterns also could be applied with coloured cord, which was sewn to the uncoloured wool base. Among the design patterns described by ethnologists, the "ram's horn" motif seems to have been quite common. All clothing, headgear, and even footwear could be embroidered with coloured woollen yarn and small beads. Sarmatians of about 2,100 years ago commonly attached metal trim, including small golden studs, to the collars and lapels of their robes. Children's costumes of the Middle Ages were adorned with many kinds of protective amulets—hare bones, cowry shells, large beads and pendants.

Both males and females enhanced their appearance and demonstrated their status with jewellery. Men wore earrings, rings, and complex decorations on their belts. Women wore earrings, bracelets, necklaces, gorgets, temporal pendants and hair decorations. In early Bronze Age burials, jewellery made of bone and copper was common, while gold and silver artifacts were rather rare.

With the development of trade networks during the first millennium B.C., glass beads came into the Steppes from Greece and Rome. Indeed, glass of all kinds was imported into the Steppes until about 600 years ago when craftsmen from many former external centres were forced to move into steppe towns by the conquering Golden Horde. At that time, production of glass jewellery became possible in the Steppes. More exotic jewellery, such as scarabs, came from Egypt. The burial costumes of the steppe aristocracy of 2,500 years ago were richly decorated with gold: plaques, platelets and other kinds of gold embellishments sewn to all pieces of clothing, including footwear and headdresses. Golden jewellery included massive diadems, bracelets, temple pendants, and rings. Gemstones were also part of some pieces of jewellery, but most were made only of gold. Precious

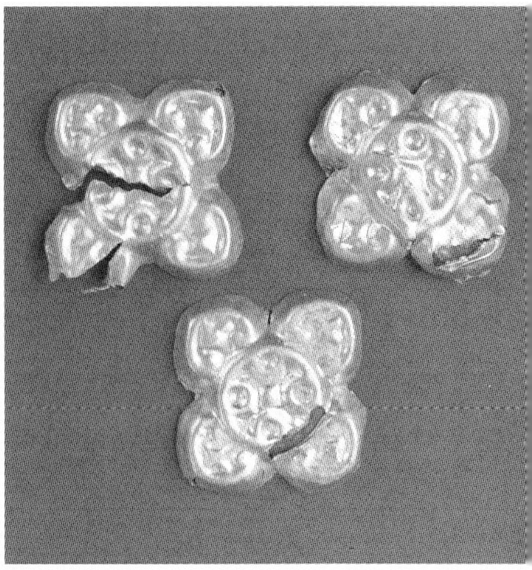

**Above** Golden inlays for a belt, 8th century A.D. (Early Middle Ages) (P. V. Alabin Museum of History and Regional Studies, Samara, KP-23249/46 to 48)
**Below** Gold earrings, 9th century A.D. (Early Middle Ages) (P. V. Alabin Museum of History and Regional Studies, Samara, KP-26132/1, 2)

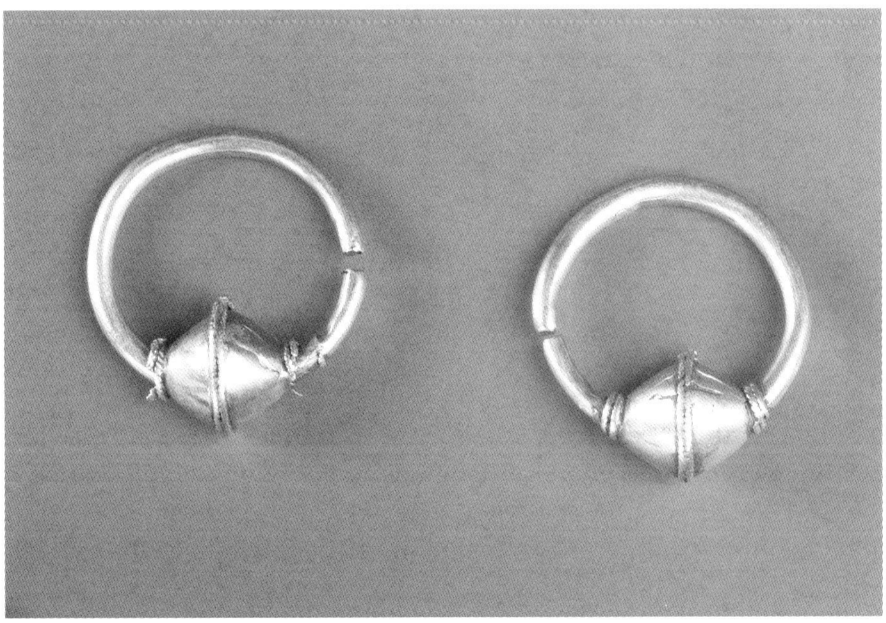

and semi-precious stones were traded into the Steppes from Pakistan along the Great Silk Road, but the use of stones in jewellery became common only during the Middle Ages, after the invasion of the Steppes by Huns.

Tattooing was very uncommon among steppe nomads. The practice is recorded archaeologically for only one Siberian group, the Pazyryk culture (2,500 to 2,200 years ago), in whose burial mounds the male mummies were almost completely covered with tattoos depicting fabulous animals.

## PRAIRIE NOMADS

Mummified human remains found in Spirit Cave, Nevada (Southern Plains) and dating to about 10,600 years ago are among the oldest in North America. These were wrapped in two plain-weave (plaited) reed mats, and dressed in a skin robe, with moccasins made of three different kinds of animal skin. Near the mummy were woven bags, likely made on a loom. The next evidence of woven textiles, made of plant fibres, appeared in the Southern Plains about 1,800 years ago. However, this tradition left scant woven evidence in Northern Plains prehistory—occasional impressions on exterior surfaces of some types of pottery give a glimpse of twined, knotted or woven materials. Our best knowledge about prairie textiles comes from ethnological data, but even there, information about textiles is sparse. Simple finger weaving was very limited. Early observers noted only a few woven items, such as blankets of woven strips of rabbit fur, covers for ceremonial bundles woven from thick strands of bison hair and babish bags, soft expandable bags made from fine cords of bison hide.

According to ethnological descriptions, the clothing of prairie nomads was made exclusively from animal skins. The types of animals and techniques of hide working were different for different parts of clothing. Shirts, leggings, dresses and breech clouts were made of deer or antelope skin; robes and coats were made of tanned bison hides; moccasins were made of bison hides; winter caps and mittens were made of wolf, bison, muskrat and other furs.

A man's summer outfit consisted of a bison robe with thin hair; a deerskin shirt; a pair of deer skin or antelope skin hip-length leggings; a deer skin breech flap; and moccasins. The shirt and leggings might be fringed and garnished with beads and porcupine quills. A woman's summer outfit consisted of an elk skin robe, an elk skin or bighorn skin dress, a pair of antelope skin knee-length leggings, and moccasins.

A man's winter outfit included a bison robe; a fur hat and mittens with hair inside; a shirt; leggings; a breech flap; moccasins; snowshoes; a belt and belt knife; and a bag containing fire-making apparatus. A woman's winter outfit was similar to that of a man, including a bison robe, a bison dress, bison or elk skin leggings, and bison skin moccasins. Young girls and children sometimes had coats made of strips of rabbit fur.

During summer, men wore only their breech flap while inside the tipi; women removed their leggings and moccasins for summer nights. During winter, or while

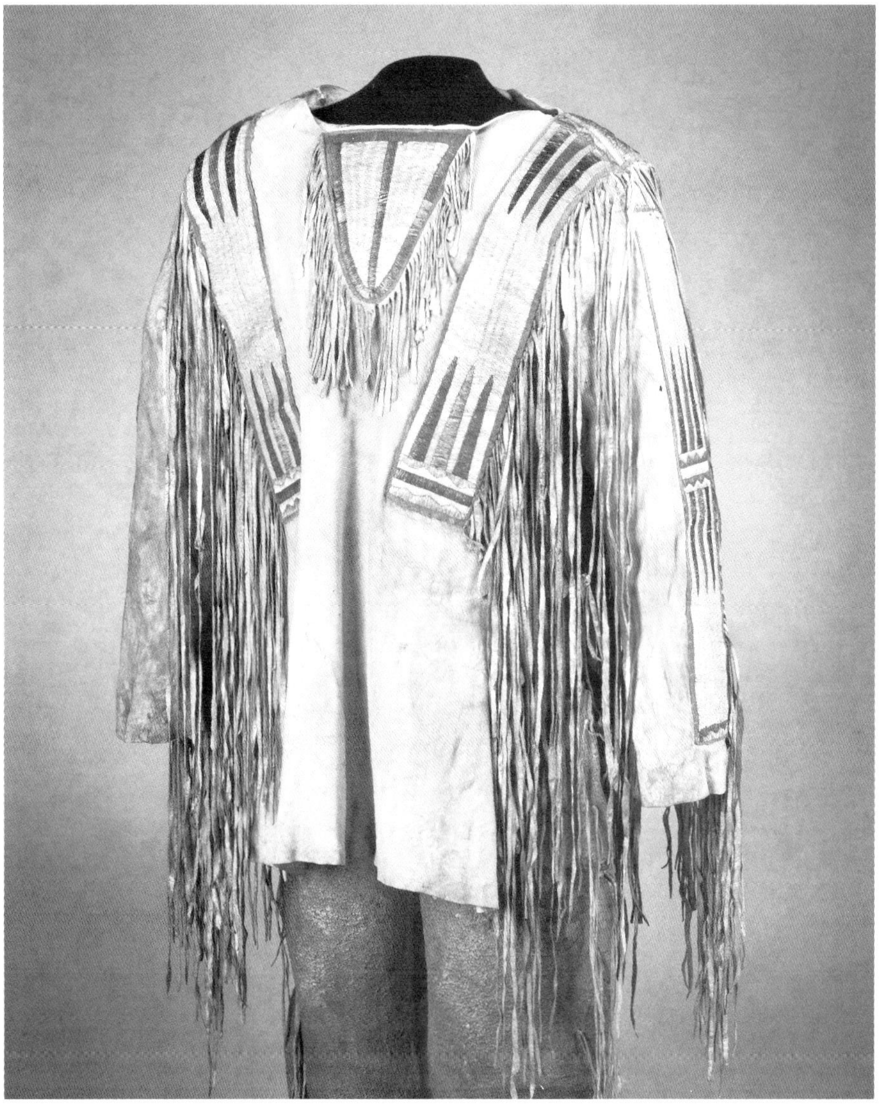

Men's leather shirt with leather fringes and porcupine-quill appliqué, ca. 100 years old (Canadian Museum of Civilization, V-X-125)

travelling, people kept their clothing on all the time, even at night. Skin clothing would last for approximately a year, but by spring it became saturated with grease and vermin due to continual wear. Consequently, people replaced winter clothing with lighter apparel during spring and summer.

Women did the work of converting hides into leather. Indeed, women were judged by the quantity and quality of dressed skins they produced. So important were these products to prairie nomads that a bison robe was a standard unit of trade. Hides taken in spring and summer had short, thin hair. These were dipilated and used for shields, masks, bags and lighter clothing. Animal hides taken in the fall had thick heavy hair. These were used for robes and other articles on which the hair was retained.

Hide working was a complex process. Once the hide was removed from the animal, it was stretched on the ground, hair side down, using wooden pegs. Then, flesh, fat and muscular tissues were removed with a stone or bone flesher. At this point, the hide could be set aside until further work was convenient. The stone endscrapers used for this work are common in Northern Plains archaeological assemblages. Variation in length, from several centimetres to a fraction of a centimetre, reflects the life cycle of these tools from initial manufacture through several stages of wear and resharpening, to eventual discard. If rawhide was needed, the next steps were to thin the skin to an even thickness using a stone scraper and to remove the hair from the exterior surface using the same tool. The skin was then left to dry.

To make a soft skin, the same process of thinning and removal of hair was followed. In the case of smaller animals, such as deer and antelope, some groups used a beaming tool, made of split leg bones or ribs, to thin the hide and remove the hair. This was done by throwing the hide over a log and drawing the tool over the hide like a spoke shave. Once the hide was thinned and depilated, it was rubbed thoroughly with a mixture of animal brains, fat and liver. After leaving it to dry for a night, the skin was soaked in water, then wrung dry and rolled into a bundle to cure. Next, it was stretched again, and rubbed on both sides with a rough gritty stone to break the surface fibres while removing any remaining water. Finally, it was pulled back and forth over a taut rope until it was soft and pliable. It took several days of fairly steady work to tan one large skin.

After tanning, some pieces of leather were smoked over smudge pits to make them waterproof. The smudge pit was about 35 centimetres in diameter by about 20 centimetres in depth and contained a smoky punk-wood fire. The hide was sewn into the shape of a bag, inverted, and attached by its bottom to a tripod or some other support. This was suspended over the smudge pit and the top edges of the "bag" were pegged to the ground to confine the smoke. Smoked hides not only repelled water but remained supple after drying. They were excellent for such things as tent covers, clothing and bags. By comparison, unsmoked hides shrank while drying, a property that make them useful as hafting materials. Smoking also was used to give hides desirable shades of colour, from light tan to dark orange-brown.

Partially manufactured bone beads, ca. 500 years old (Canadian Museum of Civilization, X-B-533 a, b)

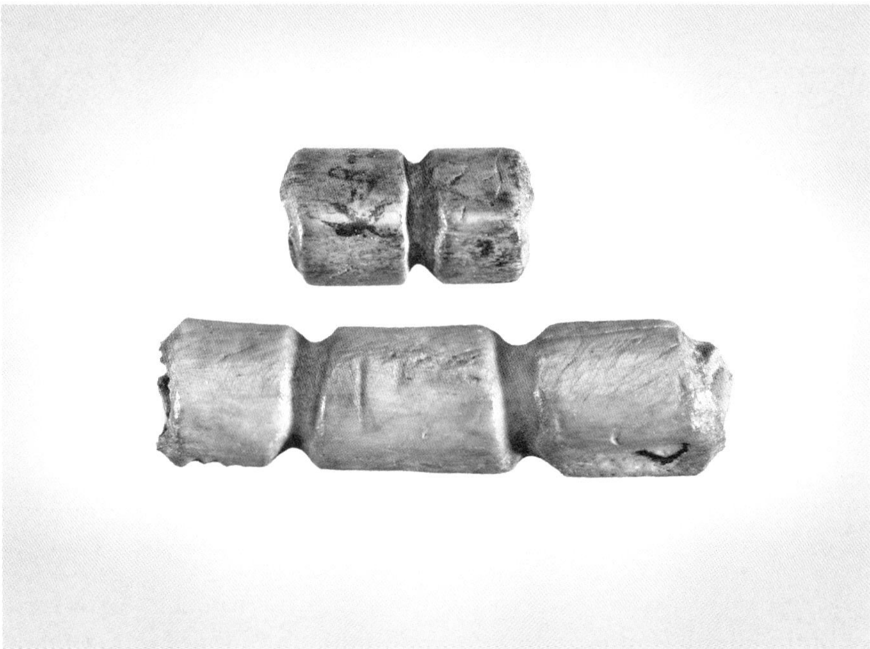

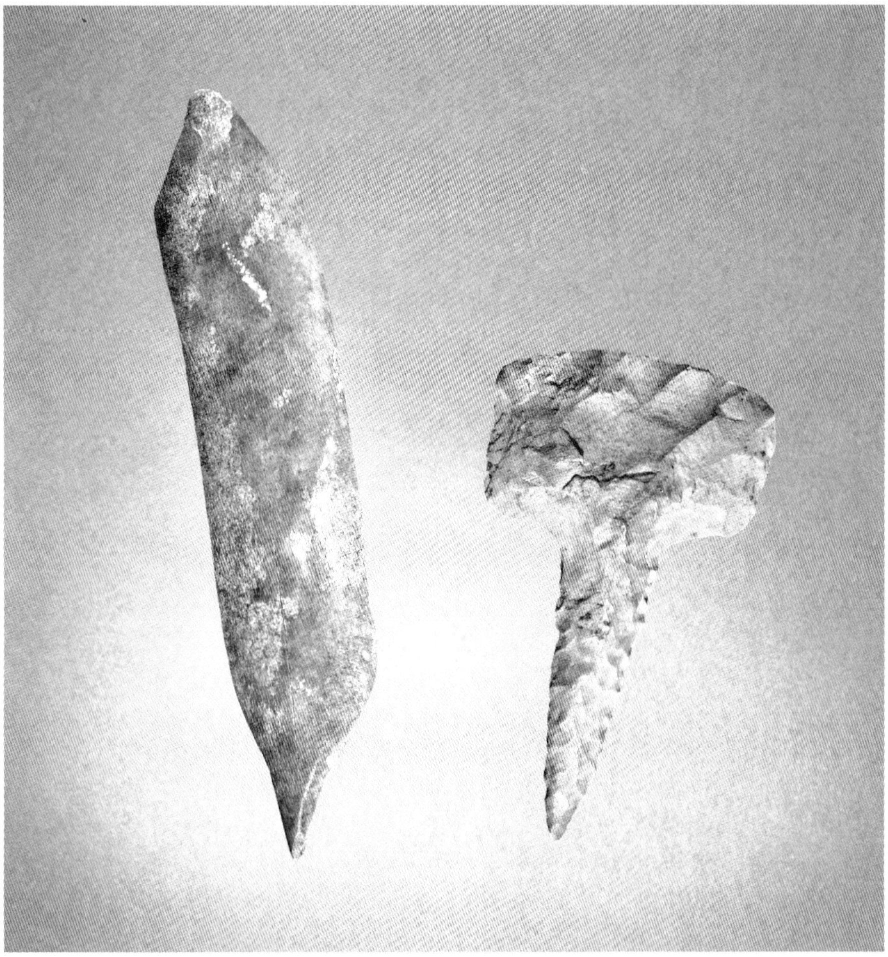

Bone drill, ca. 4,100–3,600 years old, and chipped stone drill (Canadian Museum of Civilization, EbOp-16-250, X-B-304)

Once the skins were tanned, women could make clothing. A woman's sewing kit included sharp-edged flakes that served as cutting tools, stone perforators and bone awls for making holes, and sinew that was used as thread. Sinews were moistened in the mouth before use, as they stretch when wet and hold the seam tighter after drying. Prairie nomads made tailored clothing, but attempted, as much as possible, to retain the natural shape of a hide to minimize waste and the number of seams. For example, a woman's dress could be made of two or, in some tribes, three skins. Two skins, matched in size and shape, made the front and back of a dress that hung from upper chest to midway below the knees. The dress was laced up the sides, belted at the waist, and suspended from the shoulders by two straps of leather that passed from front to back. The shoulders might also be covered with a sort of flap or cape that extended down the arms to the elbows.

Ornaments were an important part of clothing, serving as both decoration and charms. Tufts of hair, scalp locks, furs, feathers, shells and animal teeth were used for trimmings. For example, eagle feathers and ermine skins were valued decorations on men's clothing, symbolizing bravery and ferocity, whereas elk "eye" teeth on women's dresses symbolized fertility. Appliqués with dyed porcupine-quill embroidery were common on all fancy dress. Many manufactured articles, including clothing, but especially robes, were decorated with paint. Some people daubed the whole robe in one colour, for example white or

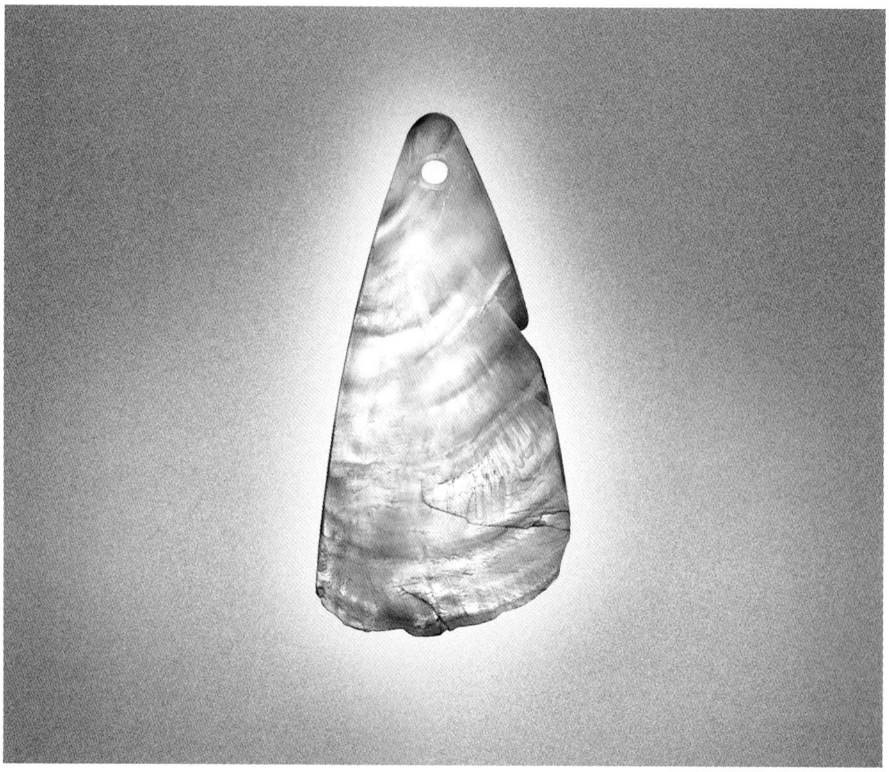

Shell pendant, ca. 500 years old (Canadian Museum of Civilization, X-B-530 a)

blue; others painted them with biographic icons, spiritual visions, or geometric designs with symbolic meanings. Geometric designs with circles, rhomboids, squares or dots, organized in rows or incorporated in stripes (preferably horizontal), were common. Polished deer hooves could be attached to robes, leggings and dresses to make a musical tinkling sound.

Several types of jewellery have been recorded by archaeologists and ethnologists, such as flat circular shell beads; tubular shell and bone beads; pendant teeth, shells and claws; and, more rarely, stone beads and gorgets. Presumably, many of these were worn as necklaces. Others were parts of earrings or ear pendants made of sinew, feathers, porcupine quills, shells and bones. Bone and copper bracelets have been recorded in prehistoric burials of prairie nomads, although these objects are uncommon.

Prairie nomads exhibited both individual variation and changing fashion in their hairstyles. Women tended to divide their hair along the crown and combine it into braids, which were either decorated with encasing fur, feathers and beads and hung free behind the ears, or gathered into clumps behind each ear, from which decorations were suspended. Women often daubed vermilion down the part in their hair. Men wore their hair in many forms: sometimes gathered into a single "tail" which hung far down their back and was wrapped in skins; sometimes gathered in two or more braids; sometimes bunched into a small clump on the crown of the head; sometimes with bangs cut square on the forehead and brushed to stand up; and sometimes with a lock of hair cut square and allowed to cover the nose. Whatever the style, men added feathers, furs, shell quills and other decorations to make their coiffure distinct. For combs, they used porcupine-quill or buffalo-tongue brushes.

Face and body painting was another form of personal decoration used by prairie nomads. During historic times, the colours they preferred were pale and dark red, yellow, blue, glossy grey, white, black and green. One other type of decoration was tattooing which, according to ethnological evidence, was common among prairie nomads. For men, tattooing was a mark of rank that distinguished the warrior. Men were tattooed with a variety of figures over the cheeks, chin, arms and breast after having struck their first enemy. For women, tattoos were less extensive, comprising a round spot in the middle of the forehead, lines from the corners and middle of the mouth down the chin and occasionally transversely across the cheek, and rings around the wrists and around the upper parts of the arms. These were usually applied to girls between 12 and 14 years of age.

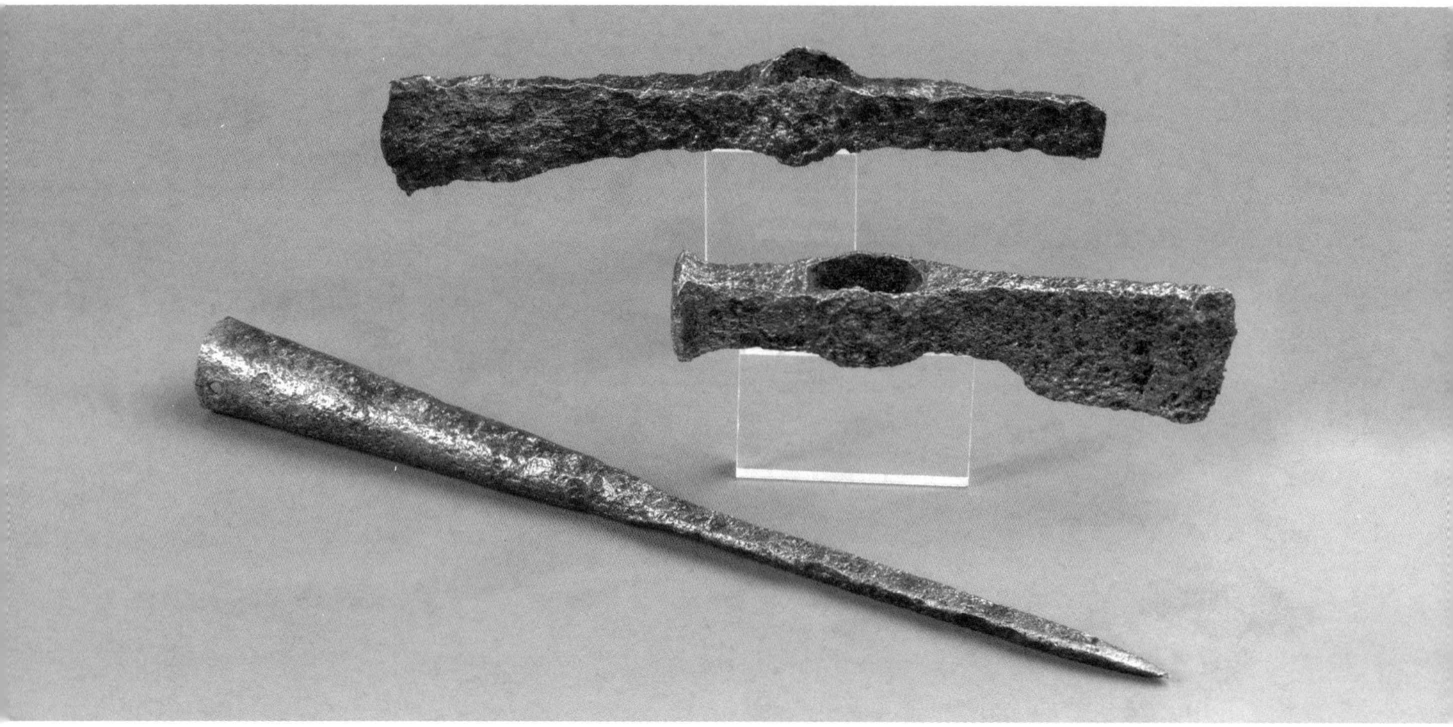

**Above** Iron axes (top) and spear (bottom), 7th–8th century A.D. (Early Middle Ages) (P. V. Alabin Museum of History and Regional Studies, Samara, KP-26045/3, 4, 5)
**Below** Copper spear point, ca. 3,500 years old (Canadian Museum of Civilization, X-A-438)

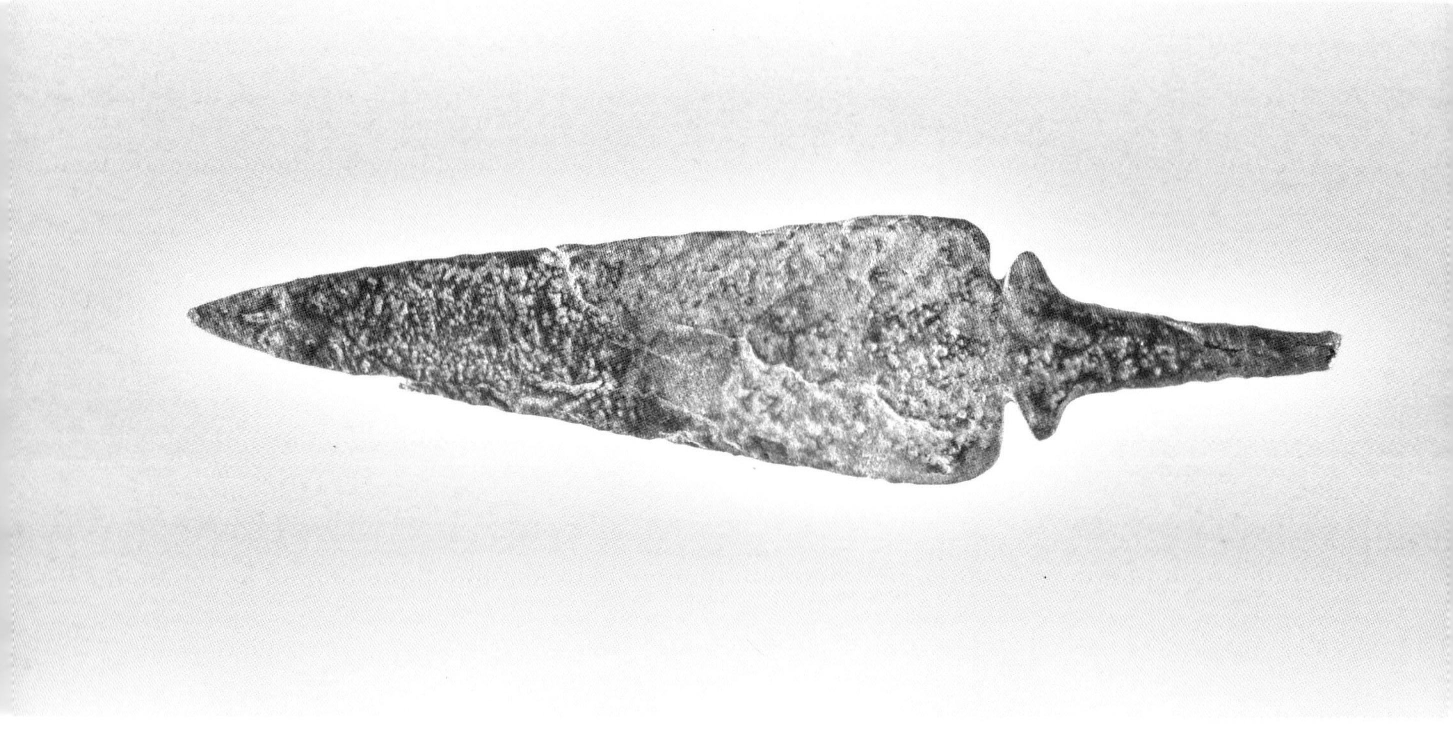

# The Role of Metals

The availability of metallic ores is similar in the Steppes and the Prairies—both regions are metal poor, having access to such ores only in peripheral regions, such as bordering foothills and mountain ranges, or by import from more distant sources. However, the availability of stone materials is quite different.

In the Prairies, stones of low, medium and even high quality for tool-making are abundant (although unevenly distributed) in surface deposits left across the region by continental glaciers. Thus, it is not surprising that chipped, pecked and ground stone tools of many kinds were made and used throughout the ancient history of the Prairies. In the Steppes, however, surface deposits are predominantly silty and contain few rock fragments of suitable size and quality for the manufacture of stone tools. People had access only to very limited regional stone resources. This difference in stone availability was one reason why metal tools played very different roles in the nomadic lifestyles of the two grassland regions.

In both regions, the earliest use of metal was for spiritual/sacral purposes, such as the use of iron oxides (ochre) in burial ritualism. The tradition appeared as early as the Upper Palaeolithic in Eurasia, from which it was carried to North America and maintained until historic times. The use of meteoritic iron in ceremonial objects was also recorded in both regions. Copper came into use as a sacral material at about the same time in Eurasia and North America—about 6,000 years ago in the Steppes and about 7,000 years ago east of the Prairies around Lake Superior. In both the Steppes and the Prairies, copper was imported as already manufactured objects for sacral, symbolic, or high status use. In the Prairies, copper never became an important tool-making material. However, its symbolic role persisted through time. Until European contact, copper objects were made solely by the cold hammering technique, which produced edges that were softer than those made of high quality chipped stone. The development of bronze production in Mesoamerica occurred so late that there was no time to develop continental trade of bronze objects into the Prairies, or to test their qualities against the proven capabilities of stone tools.

Steppe nomads adopted technologies of bronze production shortly after their invention in the Near East. This allowed the local production of bronze tools and, particularly weaponry, from regional copper-bearing sandstone deposits. Sources of copper ores were not any closer than sources of a high-quality stone, but the bronze was lighter and more durable than stone and its malleability encouraged experimentation with shapes, which was especially effective in weaponry and jewellery. The increasing priority that metals played in the production and development of weaponry in the Steppes persisted from the mid-Bronze Age on. With improved weaponry came increasing militarization of nomadic communities which, in turn, stimulated constant modernization of weapons and techniques of warfare.

About 2,500 years ago, steppe nomads began to produce iron weapons, which provided a vitally important improvement to their military capabilities. Indeed, out of the two main groups of iron objects—weaponry and agricultural implements—weaponry was by far the more important until the formation of nomadic empires. Meanwhile, without smelting technology, the use of iron in the Prairies was limited to the veneration of meteoritic iron as sacral objects.

# STEPPE NOMADS

Metal deposits are located on the margins of the Steppes. The Ural Mountains and their foothills are major sources of copper ores, but there are also several locales within the Steppes where copper ores can be found interbedded in sandstone. Iron ores are available in the Black Sea lowlands and in the Kursk region (the western part of the European Steppes/Parklands). There are major sources of gold in the Ural Mountains and in the North Kazakhstan Steppes northeast of the Ural Mountains, however, the nearest silver deposits are in the Caucasus and Greece.

## Copper

The first attempts at metallurgy were associated with copper. The oldest copper objects, made of cold-hammered native copper, are about 9,000 years of age and have been found in the Near East. Copper could not compete with stone tools in hardness, but its malleability, lustre, and beautiful, bright colour made it highly attractive for spiritual purposes, partly as a sacral material that seemed capable of deflecting evil spirits. By 7,500 years ago, methods of smelting copper from copper ores had been discovered in the same region. Smelting required heating the ore to 700 to 800° C, which was achieved by pumping air through ceramic tubes into special furnaces fuelled with charcoal. About 300

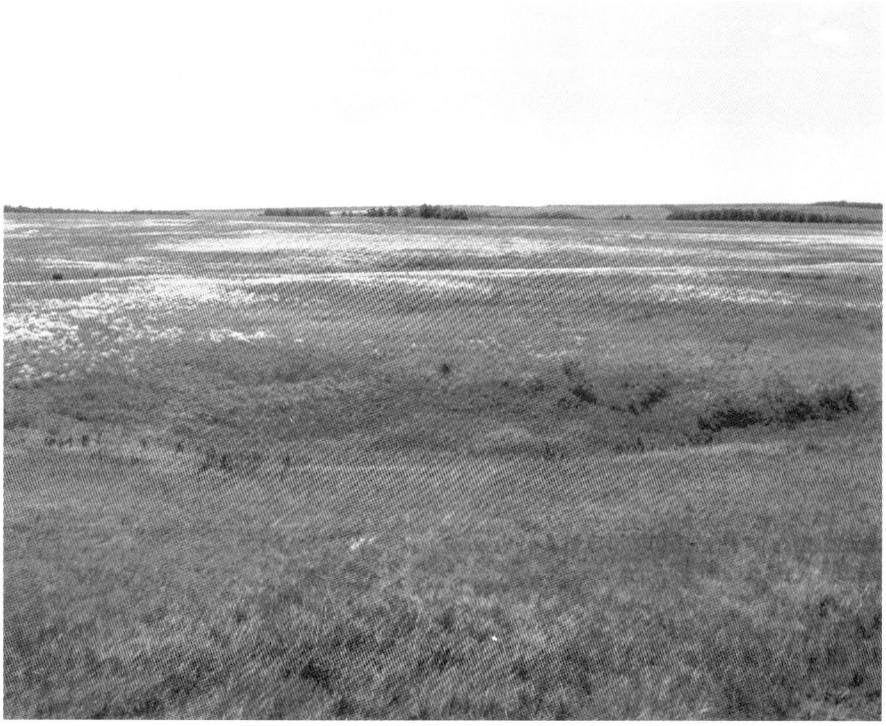

Bronze Age copper mine, ca. 3,500 years old, Mikhailo-Ovsianka, Samara Region, Russia (courtesy of Boris Aguzarov)

kilograms of charcoal is needed to produce one kg of copper from ore. As a result, copper smelting had to take place in fuel-rich areas.

Between 7,000 and 6,000 years ago, copper smelting flourished in the sedentary villages of the Balkan-Carpathian cultures southwest of the Steppes. These early copper industries produced not only to satisfy their own needs, but also for trade. The first copper objects reached the Steppes during this period and were mainly cult objects, symbols of power, and adornments—items such as sceptres, mace heads, axes, rings, earrings and bracelets. Smelted and annealed copper was harder than cold-hammered native copper, especially if it contained certain admixtures, but its hardness was still much lower than that of quartz (hardnesses of 3.5 and 7.0 respectively) and insufficient for practical use in most types of tools.

The subsequent discovery, in Mesopotamia, of copper alloys (bronze) enabled the production of metal objects that were useful for practical purposes. The earliest copper alloy was made with arsenic (arsenic bronze), likely produced as a by-product of smelting copper sulphide ores. Later alloys were lead, tin and zinc. The relative hardness of the bronze, depending on the alloys, varies from 5 to 7 and is close to that of quartz.

Smelted and cast copper first appeared in the Steppes as ready-made imported objects—sickles, single-bladed knives, dagger-like knives, cutters, sleeve and wedge-like chisels and flat adzes. The discovery about 4,500 years ago of major deposits of copper ore in sandstone near the mid-Volga region and in the central Ural foothills brought opportunities to produce cast tools within the Steppes using local minerals. Nomadic populations of the Steppes are believed to have adopted tool forms developed in the Caucasus region—knives, axes, adzes, chisels, awls, and so forth. However, instead of the copper-arsenic alloys (arsenic bronze) typical of Caucasian products, the steppe nomads of the Early Bronze Age cast their metal objects with pure copper. Metal objects in burials reflected the high social status of the deceased. In addition, some burials of this period contained casting moulds, suggesting the formation of professional metallurgists within nomadic society. These specialized groups seem to have focused on metallurgical activities year-round and to have segregated themselves from the annual migrations of pastoralist populations.

Experiments with artificial alloys began in the Steppes about 4,000 years ago, with the arrival of new, highly specialized metallurgical groups. Year-round metallurgical settlements began to appear near the copper mines of the southern Ural area at that time. The settlements were actually circular militarized forts with dwellings built into the walls and with copper smelting ovens in each dwelling. The copper-bearing deposits south of the Ural Mountains were divided into 70-kilometre segments, each controlled by a fort. About 19 such forts are known. The mines controlled by the settlements had elaborate networks of mining pits that reached up to 40 metres in depth. Among the equipment used in these mines were various hammer stones, chisels, pestles, abrasive stones, anvils and picks. The metallurgical forts specialized in the manufacture of certain objects intended for trade: knives, sickles, cast and cold-hammered spearheads, celts, adzes and jewellery. These were made of arsenic bronze. In the dry Steppes, ore processing was not easy due to the lack of fuel. Therefore, mined ore was also traded to peoples

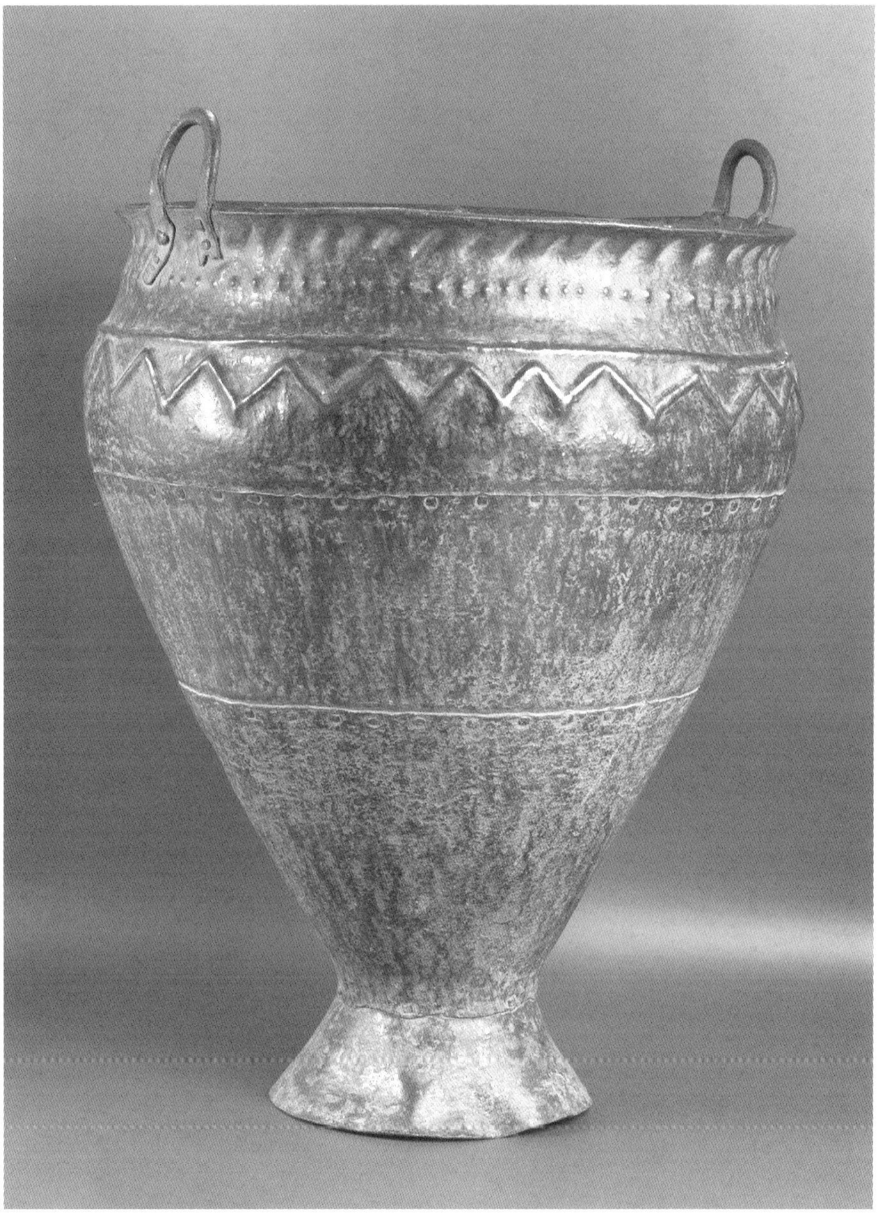

**Left** Bronze cauldron, ca. 4,000 years old (Bronze Age) (P. V. Alabin Museum of History and Regional Studies, Samara, KP-210)
**Below** Bronze bracelets and ring, 8th century A.D. (Early Middle Ages) (P. V. Alabin Museum of History and Regional Studies, Samara, KP-26045/1, 19, 20)

living south and southwest of the mines. Since pastures around the forts were insufficient as year-round sources of food for animals, it is likely that cattle were traded to people in the forts in return for bronze objects and ore.

By the end of the Bronze Age (about 3,000 years ago), copper-tin alloys had replaced arsenic alloys. However, even by that time, in areas such as the Lower and Middle Volga regions and the South Ural, metallurgists were still casting objects of pure copper. Copper-working technologies of that time included cold hammering, smelting and casting with annealing, and cold hammering of smelted bronze foil. Still, only 15% of the metal objects produced were everyday tools; the majority were symbolic objects, produced specifically as burial goods, and weaponry. Production of symbolic objects was especially sophisticated, including almost all known techniques, such as pressing, impressing, drawing, granulation and incrustation. These techniques allowed the creation of very dynamic

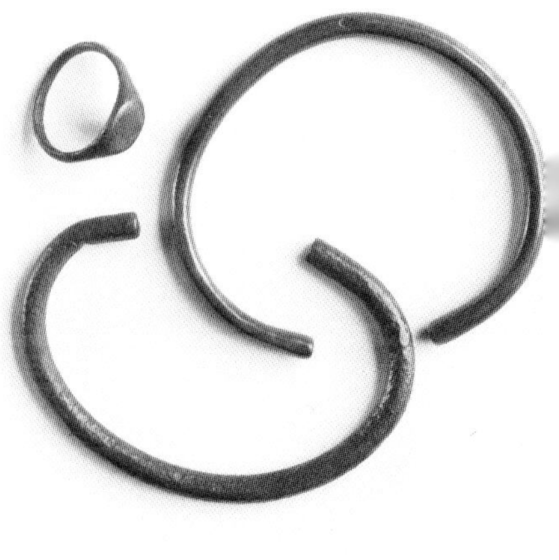

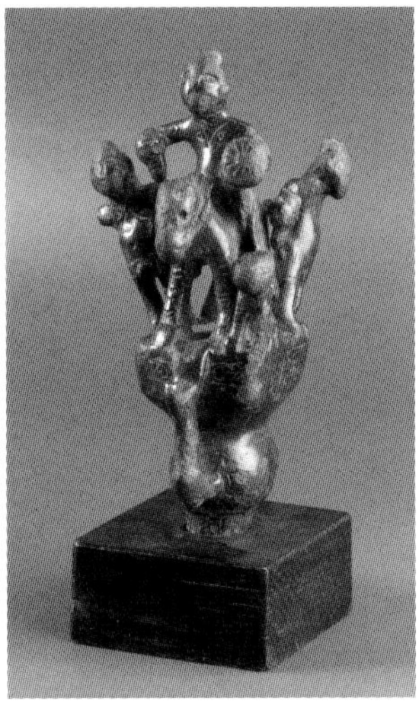

Bronze sculpture, Early Middle Ages (P. V. Alabin Museum of History and Regional Studies, Samara, KP-24640)

images in art, the so-called animal style, and further advances in weaponry, such as bronze daggers, elongated bronze pike heads and, possibly, shields.

It must be said that, until the Late Bronze Age, stone was still used for arrowheads, scrapers and knives (probably for hide working). In some Late Bronze Age cultures, such as Catacombnaja and, especially, Sintashta-Potapov, flint arrowheads designed for use with a composite bow were still common artifacts in occupational sites, as well as in burials. Such weaponry and tools were found along with a variety of bronze tools, weaponry and jewellery.

## Iron

Iron occurs rarely in elemental form (iron-nickel crystals) as meteorites and as inclusions in basalts, and commonly in ores, such as hematite, limonite and magnetite. The first use of iron was associated with the reddish colour that could be achieved through heating common iron ores in an open fire. Sprinkling the reddened iron ore powder (ochre) over interments, imitating the life-giving qualities of blood, was widely used in burial ritualism from at least 20,000 years ago until the end of the Bronze Age (3,000 years ago). One of the earliest uses of pestles and mortars/palettes was for grinding ochre.

The earliest iron to be forged was meteoritic. Cold-hammered meteoritic iron was known since about 6,000 years ago, long before the discovery of iron smelting. Among the artifacts made of cold-hammered meteoritic iron, most are luxury objects: swords and daggers made entirely of iron, and cast-in edges of meteoritic iron in bronze or gold axes and other edged weapons.

Iron ore can be reduced at 1100° C, but its melting point is about 1540° C. Neither of these temperatures can be achieved with open fires or even in a primitive furnace. The earliest iron was likely a by-product of copper smelting, as some copper ores contain up as much as 30% iron (e.g., chalcopyrite). The process of smelting iron from ores differs from smelting copper. Iron remains solid at temperatures that melt copper and bronze. However, heating iron ore to 1100° C produces a spongy mass which, with repeated hammering and quenching in water, creates a tough metal called wrought iron.

It is unknown where iron working was invented. Scholars place its beginning somewhere between northern Anatolia and the Levant. Iron smelting technology was known from about 5,000 years ago, but became important only about 1,800 years later. Since wrought iron was inferior to bronze until the discovery of steel, it has been suggested that iron came into use only because of a disruption in the international trade of copper and tin within the Mediterranean world about 3,200 years ago. Steel, or carburized iron, is an iron-carbon alloy, containing 0.7 to 2.0% carbon. Discovered around 3,100 years ago, steel (hardness between 6 and 7) is harder than bronze and can hold a sharper edge. It was refined by re-heating and annealing. However, carburization was hard to control and, if more than 1% carbon was added, the steel became brittle. Both iron and steel working were non-intuitive processes, which required great personal experience from a master. Thus, the quality of products varied greatly from one blacksmith to another. Interestingly, "magic swords" produced by wizard-blacksmiths were an important part of Early Iron Age mythology. No such mythology surrounded bronze weaponry.

About 2,800 years ago, the technology of iron forging penetrated the Steppes, brought there by new groups of people called Scythians. This created the opportunity to produce metal objects from cheap local sources—bog ores. Within the Steppes, blacksmith shops could be established only in sites adjacent to water and fuel sources, such as river valleys and their tributaries. To achieve temperatures high enough for iron reduction, charcoal was used in forested areas, but steppe blacksmiths likely had to use twigs, shrubs and straw instead of charcoal. Bronze was converted to utilitarian uses after the discovery of iron, while iron became increasingly important for the production of weaponry. Among the iron objects of the Early Iron Age Steppes are swords, daggers, knives, arrowheads, and some utilitarian objects such as axes, locks and needles. However, until the formation of towns and the introduction of agriculture by the medieval nomadic empires, the production and diversity of weaponry was much greater than that of utilitarian objects.

Iron casting became possible only with the invention of the blast furnace about 2,100 years ago in China and about 600 years ago in Europe. Before that, all casts were made of bronze. After the introduction of iron, bronze casting remained important for producing objects of complex shape, such as cauldrons, goblets and kettles, and for objects, such as arrowheads, that were needed in large numbers.

## Prairie Nomads

The Prairies are not rich in metal ores. The closest sources of copper are to the northeast in the boreal forest of northern Manitoba. To the east, native copper is abundant around Lake Superior. Iron deposits are also abundant around Lake Superior, which supplies 85% of modern requirements for the U.S. steel industry. Small quantities of gold have been found along the North Saskatchewan River, but there is no evidence that these were exploited until the early twentieth century. The closest sources of silver are far to the north of the Prairies, on the eastern slopes of the northern Rocky Mountains. These, too, appear not to have been exploited during ancient times.

### Copper

The earliest metal objects found in the Prairies are made of copper. These were likely obtained from the Great Lakes region, which is the closest source. The Lake Superior area contains the largest concentration of native (elemental) copper in the world. The copper is close to the surface, and is over 80% pure. This source was freed of ice and melt water, and available for exploration by about 9,500 years ago. South of Lake Superior, glacial transport left a surface scatter of copper nuggets ranging in size from peas to boulders, which were clearly visible on the postglacial landscape of the American Midwest. The oldest copper object discovered in stratigraphic context is an approximately 8,000 year-old fragment of cold-hammered native copper found in the Keweenaw Peninsula of Michigan. More reliable dates of about 7,000 years come from the South Fowl Lake sites in Minnesota.

Due to its high quality, native copper did not require smelting, and for most of the prehistoric period in the Americas, copper was cold-hammered. By 7,000 years ago, copper working technologies included cold hammering, stretch-hammering, drawing (through drawplate perforations lubricated by fat) and annealing. The oldest techniques included riveting—fastening a copper object to a shaft by hammering a copper rivet through the tool into the handle. Edge bevelling and sharpening were achieved by grinding with various sandstones, whereas polishing and burnishing were done with fine sand and wood ash. Antler tines were likely used as embossing tools.

Technologies of copper working were further developed about 2,500 years ago by Hopewellian cultures southeast of the Prairies region. Definite evidence for copper mining is associated with this period. To detach workable pieces, the mine pits were fired to cause facial cracking, and cracked ore was detached from the walls using hammerstones. During that period, people learned to produce sheet copper and copper foil by cold hammering. They also developed sinking, moulding and forming technologies by which copper foil was pushed and gently hammered into or around carved wooden and stone forms, then extracted to produce a three-dimensional object. Another process, cladding, involved, for example, putting copper foil over a wooden mould to make beads. This process became common in Mississippian times after about 1,000 years ago. Copper objects tended to replicate stone or bone objects of the same period.

The range of copper-made objects included: adzes, chisels and axes (at least some of them for woodworking); wedges and gouges for flaking; awls, punches, pikes, drills and needles for perforation; spatulas and spuds (for digging), fishhooks and gaff hooks; mortuary masks; beads, ear spools and bracelets; embossed cut-outs in the form of crescents and spirals, believed to have been ornamental; and crescents that have been interpreted by different researchers as knives, gorgets, or hair decorations. The most common artifact by late prehistoric times was beads. Among the more unique objects were mortuary masks, such as overlaid "copper noses." Some objects were rather regional in distribution, for example, pikes, semi-lunar knives and spuds used in the agricultural parts of southeastern North America. Others were traded far afield.

Interpreting the function of copper artifacts that resemble stone and bone models is problematic, since we know that cold-hammered copper is soft and cannot adequately be substituted for stone in most types of tools. Yet, studies of wear marks on some types of copper artifacts suggest that these were, indeed, used for woodworking, piercing, fishing and, probably, hide working. The proportion of such artifacts was much higher in areas that were poorly supplied with workable stone, particularly in the American Midwest. However, many copper artifacts were used as mortuary goods and served as means of protection and symbols of power. Some objects, such as mortuary masks and axes, reflect the status of the deceased. Others, such as the celts and projectile points found in children's and women's burials, correlate with a belief in the protective function of copper and copper objects.

Copper objects were among the oldest trade items. By 4,500 years ago, raw copper or ready-made copper objects had reached most of Eastern North America and, to a lesser extent, the grasslands at the centre of the continent. Trends in geographic distribution of traded copper artifacts include a higher occurrence of ornaments, knives and projectile points close to the source area; of awls and gorgets in areas south and east of the source area, and of celts, axes and adzes in the most distant reaches of the copper trade network.

Among the oldest copper objects that reached the Prairies were copper projectile points that replicated large lanceolate stone spear points of the Late Palaeoindian period (e.g., Agate Basin culture). The age of the copper lanceolate projectile points from western Manitoba has been estimated as 8,500 to 8,000 years according to the geomorphological position and typology of the finds (direct dating was not possible). However, the Prairies always remained

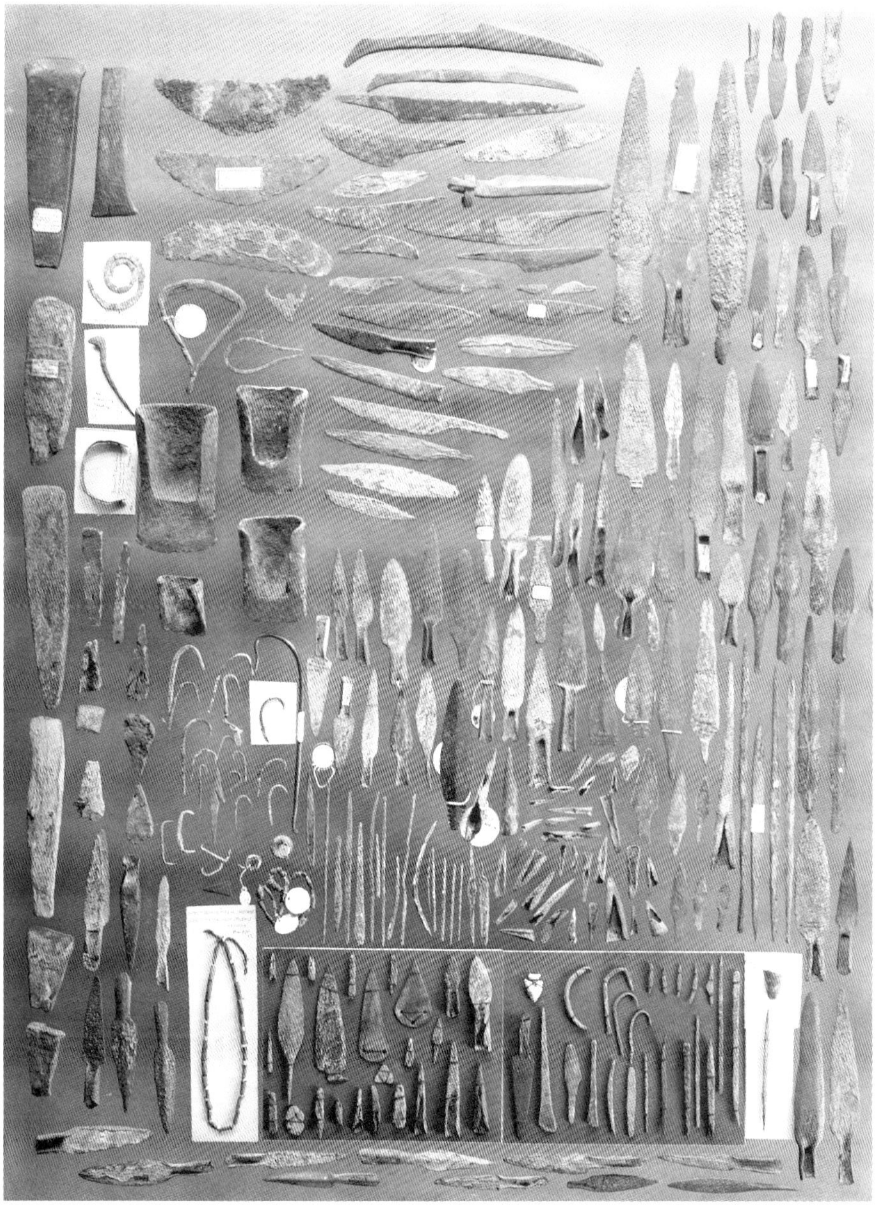

Range of copper objects made in the Lake Superior region and traded into the Prairie region (MTU Archives and Copper Country Historical Collections, Michigan Technological University, Reeder Photographic Collection)

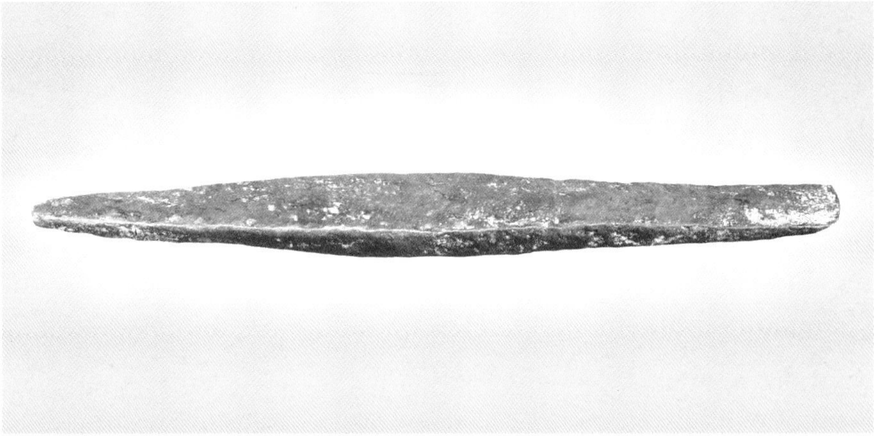

Copper pick, ca. 3,500 years old (Canadian Museum of Civilization, X-A-440)

at the periphery of the copper trade network, and copper artifacts were neither common nor numerous in nomads' households. On stylistic grounds, most copper objects found in the Prairies date to less than 5,000 years ago. Copper tools for everyday use remained rare, because stone was a proven and far more abundant tool-making material in that region. Copper artifacts that have been found in the Prairies include stemmed projectile points, socketed projectile points, axes, copper bars, a crescent-shaped blade, sheet copper and beads made of rolled sheet copper, most of which were found in burials.

Smelting of native copper can be achieved at temperatures near 1000° C, unlike impure copper ores which melt at about 800° C. Copper smelting must be done in fire-resistant vessels and, therefore, it could not be performed before fired ceramics came into use about 2,000 years ago in the North American Midwest. The development of copper smelting metallurgy in the Western Hemisphere first appeared in the mountainous regions of South America about 3,500 years ago. By 800 to 600 years ago, that technology had been adopted in Mesoamerica where bronze was being produced using copper-arsenic and, to a lesser extent, copper-strontium and copper-lead alloys. However, according to present knowledge, bronze objects did not reach North America and its prairie communities before the arrival of Europeans.

## Iron

The earliest use of iron in the Prairies was the same as that in the Steppes: as an element of ritualism. Powdered ochre was sprinkled in burials over or below the deceased and burial goods such as ovate stone knives and projectile points were smeared with ochre from at least the time of the Clovis culture (11,500 years ago) onward. A thousand years later, bison skulls in mass kill sites were painted with red ochre as part of hunting ritualism. For at least the last 1,500 years, red iron oxides have been painted on weapons, shields, and human bodies as part of the ritual of warfare. In addition, ochre mixed with some sort of binder has been used as paint in rock art for thousands of years in and around the Prairies. The hematite used for these various purposes was obtained by baking and powdering iron-rich earth found in certain locales in the Prairies, such as mineral springs, or by trade from adjoining regions.

The prairie nomads never practiced iron metallurgy. However, meteoritic iron was in demand for ceremonial purposes. According to historic descriptions, large meteorites such the Iron Creek meteorite in Alberta were venerated as shrines. Where meteoric boulders were not available, they were sometimes replicated by pecking a granulated pattern of shallow holes over the exposed surface of stone boulders. These boulders were central features in bison hunting ritualism, which was aimed at ensuring successful hunts. Pieces of meteorites were traded long distances. Fragments from the Brenham fall in Kansas have been recorded in archaeological sites thousands of kilometres away. Evidence for trade in meteorites is recorded archaeologically from Early Woodland times (2,500 years ago) on. Southeast of the Prairies, fragments of meteoritic iron were cold-hammered into celts, axes and adzes as much as 3,000 years ago. These were reserved for ceremonial purposes, their edges apparently never having been used. Iron was used in amulets, such as a canine tooth with a small ball of iron set into it and chisels mimicking beaver teeth. It was also used in jewellery, such as the copper ear spools with an overlay of iron foil and iron beads discovered in Illinois, at the eastern edge of the North American grasslands. Iron meteorites, cut or pounded into foil, were used as divining mirrors in Mesoamerica, and as a backplate inset for mica mirrors at the southernmost edge of the North American Great Plains. In the Arctic, people used meteoritic iron only for practical purposes, such as cold-hammered knife blades, harpoon points and engraving tools. Yet, very few of the iron products made elsewhere in ancient North America found their way into the Prairies.

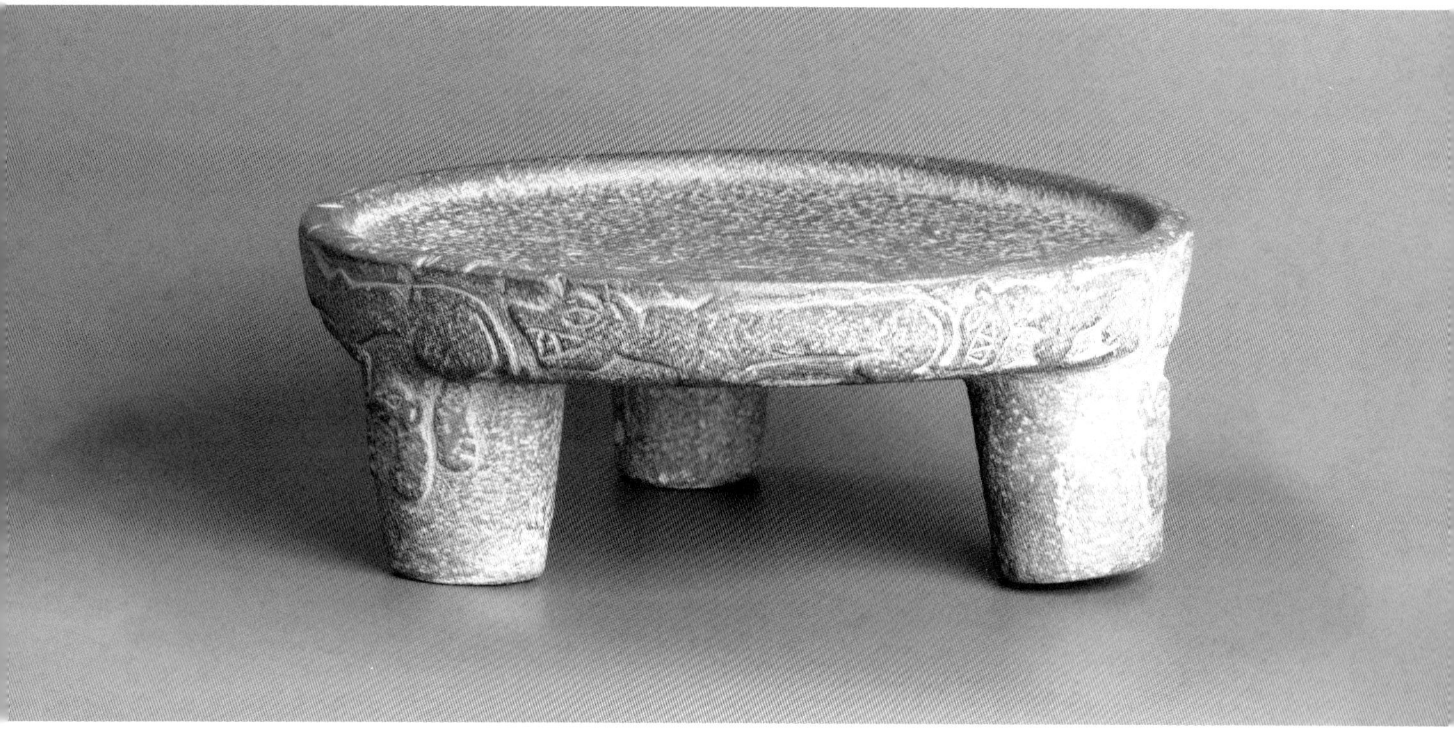

**Above** Stone dish or credence, ca. 2,500 years old (Early Iron Age) (P. V. Alabin Museum of History and Regional Studies, Samara, KP-209/19)
**Below** Calumet pipe, ca. 200 years old (Canadian Museum of Civilization, V-E-278 a, b)

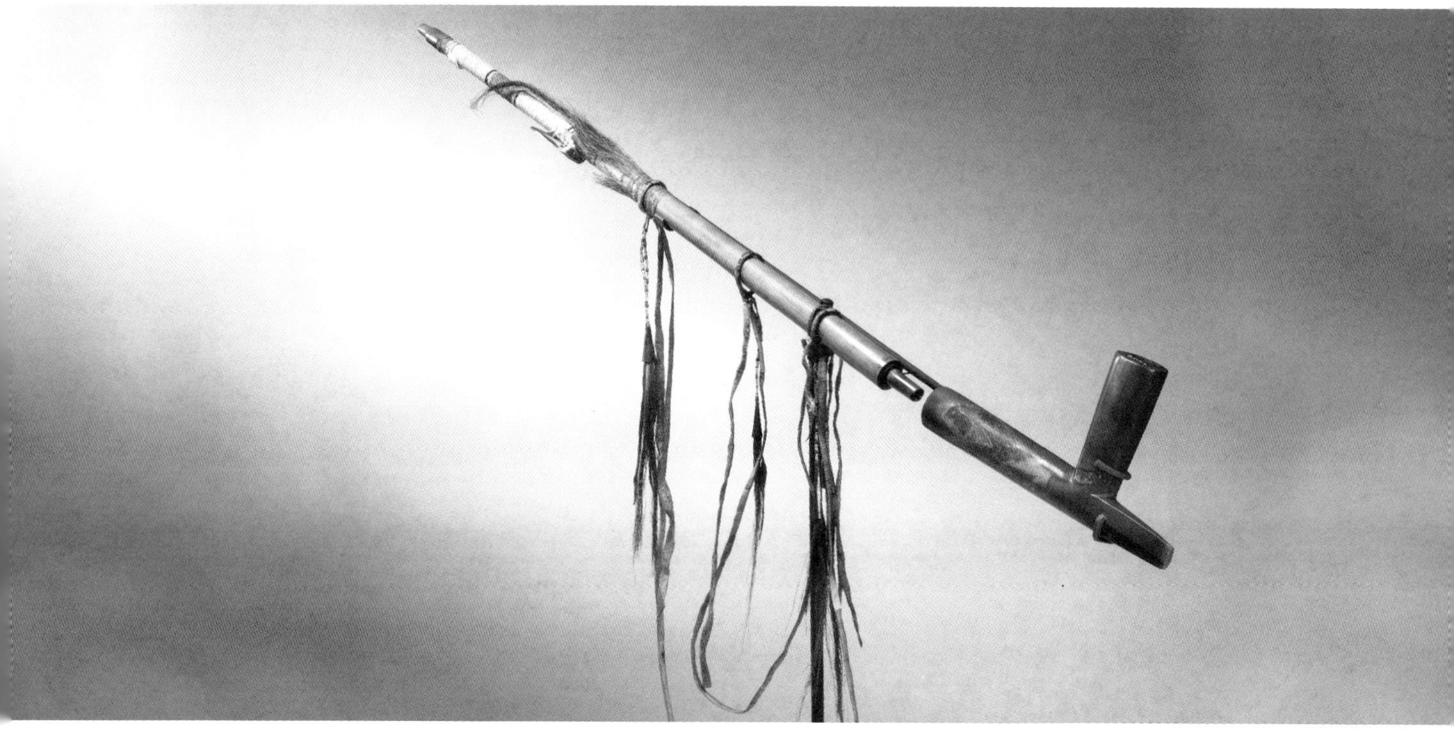

# SPIRITUAL LIFE

For a large part of the nomadic period, the central religious concept in both regions could be described as animism: the belief that a supernatural power organizes and animates the material universe. For many believers, this power was omnipresent, disembodied and unknowable. For some, it resided in the sun. Its effects on the universe, however, were thought to be embodied in many forms, all of which had spirit powers.

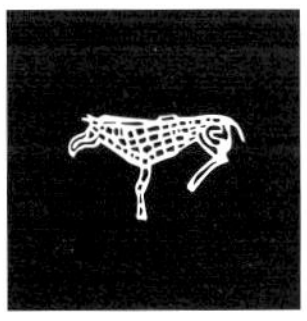

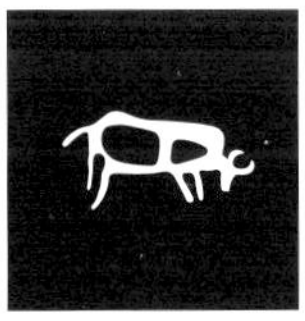

The range of things having such powers was very wide—animals, plants, the sun, sky, thunder and lightning, wind, earth, rocks, unusual landscape features and many other natural phenomena. Each of these had the power to do good or evil for humans. However, people believed that these spirits could be influenced to bring benefit rather harm—if the proper ceremonies, sacrifices, prayers and fasts were observed. Thus, steppe and prairie nomads were careful to appease the appropriate spirit powers before and after every important endeavour. These beliefs are recorded in sacred texts in the Steppes, as well as in oral mythologies, traditions, burial rites, and the sacral imagery of both regions.

It has been said by experts that there is a world of difference between Eurasian and North American mythologies. Nevertheless, the mythologies of prairie and steppe nomads contain a high number of corresponding motifs, even though the two areas are separated by large territories where such motifs have not been recorded. Images of animals played a central part in sacral and decorative art. In both areas, real animals were depicted along with fabulous creatures, but in the Prairies, images of real animals predominated. In the Steppes, an animal was usually depicted in action, for instance in a scene showing a carnivore chasing or tormenting a herbivore. In the Prairies, each animal tended to be depicted alone.

Incense and hallucinogens (cannabis in the Steppes; tobacco in the Prairies) were an important part of ceremonialism in both regions. Hallucinogenic ceremonial plants were the only crops planted by the nomads.

In both nomadic societies, ceremonies and gatherings were accompanied by music and dancing. The human voice was central, and musical instruments tended to be small and portable. In both areas the oldest instruments were flutes and whistles. A major difference, however, was the presence and great diversity of stringed instruments in the Steppes. No such instruments were used in the Prairies. Different kinds of percussion instruments—rattles and drums in the Prairies and tambourines in the Steppes—often played the same role, such as their use by shamans during special ceremonies.

Nomads believed in an afterlife and took care of their dead by following certain burial rituals and supplying objects that were needed in the afterlife. Despite their migratory lifestyle, nomads had preferred burial grounds. After a temporary burial in one location, people in both regions often collected the remains for secondary burial in a group cemetery. Creation of rather spectacular tombs by erecting burial mounds over inhumations was part of the burial ritualism in both grasslands. However, the period of mound building in the Steppes was much longer than in the Prairies.

Mortuary goods might be everyday items, valuable objects, or objects produced specifically for burials and, in the Steppes, even antiquities. In both areas, sacred materials were put into burials. Ochre and white-coloured materials were common in both regions: in the Steppes, they were used separately in different periods, whereas in the Prairies, they were used together, representing parts of the same mythological concept.

Extensive study of steppe burials has determined that the Steppes were dominated by Europeoids of Indo-Iranian origin between 5,000 and 2,500 years ago and by people of mixed Europeoid and Mongoloid origins between 2,500 and

1,500 years ago, and that since about 1,500 years ago, the proportion of Mongoloids of mixed Asian origin has increased. In the Prairies, the study of human remains has been too limited to make such determinations, although it does appear that there may have been inward migrations of people from the Great Basin about 4,500 years ago, bringing different physical and cultural features.

## STEPPE NOMADS

**Systems of Religious Belief.** Since the Bronze Age, religious beliefs of the steppe populations were influenced by the polytheistic concept of Indo-Iranian tribes, as described in one of the most ancient religious scripts in the world, the *Rigveda*. The earliest hymns of the *Rigveda*, composed about 3,200 years ago, are concerned mostly with propitiation of gods. Indo-Iranian mythology followed themes of life, regeneration, light and the sun. In their pantheon of gods, the highest deity was associated with the sun and fertility, the next deity in the hierarchy being associated with thunder and war. The cosmos consisted of an Underworld, Middle World and Upper World, each governed by specific deities. People worshipped fire and water as a universal means of purification. Fire was considered a messenger and mediator between gods and people and, in this capacity, was used during burial rites, such as cremation. People also idolized some animals, especially horses and cattle. The sacred bull, for example, personified the vault of heaven and symbolized male fecundity. An important component of religious practices was the offering of sacrifices—particularly animals, such as horses, oxen or sheep—to the gods.

The militarization of nomadic societies in the Early Iron Age was marked by the growth of a cult of the hero-ancestor. The leader of each tribe was considered to be the living embodiment of a mythical tribal hero-ancestor, who, through his successor, continued to protect the tribal territory even after death.

Not much is known about the religious concepts of steppe nomads during the Early Iron Age. In one of the few descriptions, Herodotus wrote that Scythian rites included the worship and offering of sacrifices to golden objects—a yoked plough, a battleaxe and a bowl—that, according to their creation myth, had fallen from the sky. The Scythians were influenced by the Greeks, and, according to Herodotus, worshipped the same gods as did the Greeks, although the Scythians erected neither stationary altars nor temples.

At the beginning of the Middle Ages, about 1,500 years ago, nomadic tribes of Turkic origin brought to the Steppes a new religious system and a new hierarchy of gods led by the warlike Tengri Khan (God of Sky). The advent of this new religion is recorded in runic scripts carved in rock in the Altai region. This religion persisted until the acceptance of monotheistic religions about 1,000 years ago.

**Imagery.** During the Bronze Age, geometric images were the dominant decorations on pottery, whereas animal depictions dominated rock art, especially in the Siberian Steppes. The geometric forms included rhomboids and triangles

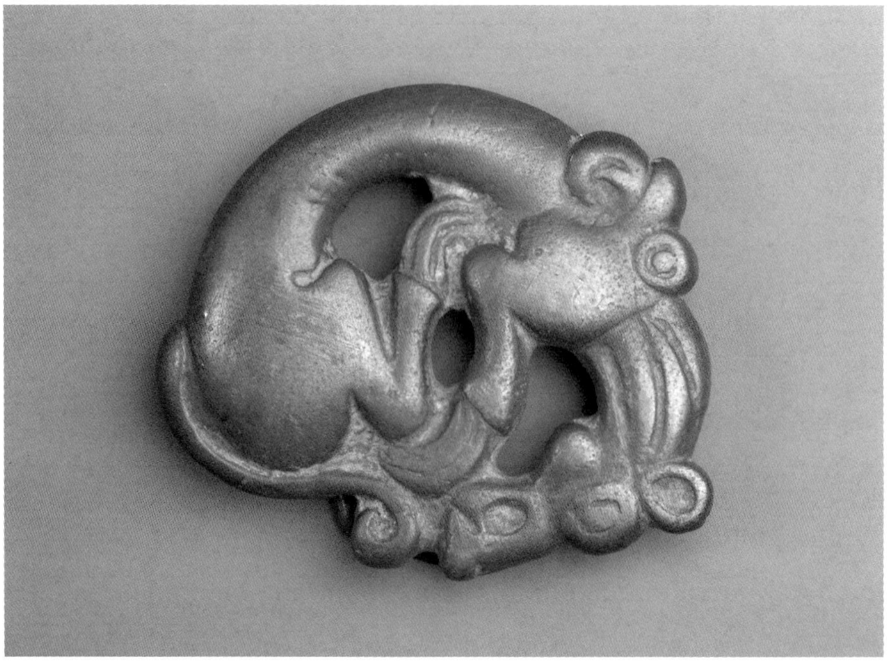

Bronze badge, ca. 2,500 years old (Early Iron Age) (P. V. Alabin Museum of History and Regional Studies, Samara, KP-24639)

carved on stone slabs in burials, and zigzags, swastikas and solar wheels, symbols of the Universe, on pottery. Images of animals were rare in the European part of the Steppes, but horses did appear in Siberian rock art of the period along with chariots reflecting mythological sun chariots.

During the Early Iron Age, a specific "animal style" flourished in the Steppes. It depicted real animals, such as deer, antelopes, wolves, lions and rams, and fabulous winged animals—all in dynamic, often flexed, positions. The animals were often shown interacting with other animals, for example a predator tormenting a herbivore. Most of the realistic animals were wild, which reflects the influence of southwest Asian cultures. However, the steppe populations developed some new compositional devices, such as paired animals, and animals coiled into a ring. They also added some new creatures to the pantheon, such as the panther, griffin and camel. The latter was worshipped by all Indo-Iranian tribes of the Iron Age Steppes, camel images likely being used in the New Year fertility ritual.

The Sarmatians and, later (about 1,700 years ago) the Huns, adapted the animal style to their own worldview, depicting mostly familiar animals and, to a much lesser extent, fabulous creatures. Domesticated animals, such as goats, rams, yaks, horses and camels, were illustrated along with elk and eagles in static, tranquil poses, sometimes with trees in the background. Images of people were more common among the Huns than among the previous peoples.

The imagery of Turkic tribes in the Altai (about 1,400 to 1,200 years ago) was even more realistic than that of the Huns. Rock art and carvings on bone and wood objects depicted people in scenes of battle and prayer, along with animals. However, the animals differed from those depicted in previous epochs: horses, tigers, and roe deer (*kosulia*) became common, marking the influences from Central Asia and Siberia. The importance of rock art decreased over the Early Iron Age, and by the Middle Ages, drawings were being made rather casually and often crudely. During the Middle Ages, images (*tamgi*) such as animals or birds representing specific tribes, and later runic scripts having the same purpose, were depicted on pottery and on rocks used as territorial markers.

**Personal protection.** Worship of weaponry was a part of the Indo-Iranian ritualism described in the Rigveda. For males, weapons were the most important means of personal protection, both physically and sacrally. The finials of their swords, for example, might bear magic symbols, such as a bird of prey. Weapons could be made of, or adorned with, materials that were ascribed protective properties—mainly copper and bronze during the Bronze Age, and precious metals during and after the Iron Age. Later, the best steel swords were believed to have been made by magical blacksmiths. In the Steppes, amulets were an important means of personal protection for women and children. Burials of children always contained amulets that appealed to various goddesses.

**Sanctuaries.** Unusual components of the landscape, such as caves, grottos, and prominent places along migration routes were used as sanctuaries where offerings were made and sacred ceremonies were held. Some such shrines were used by different groups of people over thousands of years, for example, the Greve Brothers Cave and the Tzarev Mound in the Samara region. During the Early Iron Age, the Scythians constructed special shrines out of piles of branches. On top of an artificial hillock of branches, they erected a wooden platform on which they placed an ancient iron sword. This construction was used for offering sacrifices, animal as well as human, to the god of war.

In the Siberian part of the Steppes, manmade sanctuaries were first erected by Sarmatians at the beginning of the Early Iron Age (about 2,300 years ago) to commemorate their heroes. Their ceremonial complexes featured stone statues of hero-ancestors, three to four metres tall, grouped around circular arrangements of stone slabs, which included large sacrificial altars. In Medieval times,

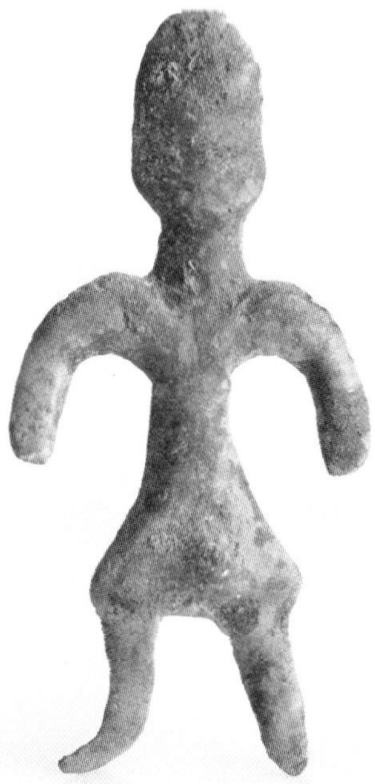

Bronze male figurine from a girl's burial (P. V. Alabin Museum of History and Regional Studies, Samara, KP-18783/1)

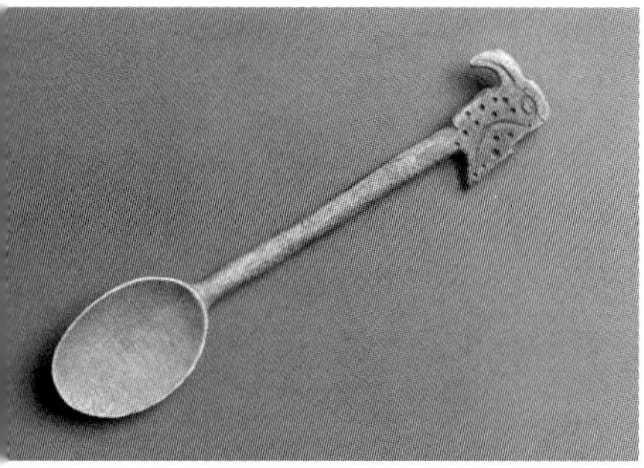

**Above** Ceremonial bone spoon, ca. 2,500 years old (Early Iron Age) (P. V. Alabin Museum of History and Regional Studies, Samara, KP-173/6)
**Below** Shamans (Peter Simon Pallas, *Reise durch verschiedene Provinzen des Russischen Reichs in den Jahren 1768-1773*, 1871)

stone and wood anthropomorphic statues set on the top of burial mounds served as shrines associated with an ancestor cult. Thousands of such sculptures survived until the 1600s.

**Ceremonies and Gatherings.** By at least 6,000 years ago, religious specialists were performing sacred ceremonies. These people were believed to be capable of restoring the world order that had been damaged by the death of an important leader. They could also appeal to the gods for help in the struggle with enemies, real or imagined. To achieve the desired result, certain rituals were carried out, often involving offerings or sacrifices. Depending on the types of sacral ceremonies they performed, specialists would be called shamans or sacrificers. Among the archaeological finds supporting special status for such people are burials, either of men or women, containing sacred objects such as bone spoons, incising tools, and portable altars for sacrificing liquids or burning incense. Ancient historians described sacrifices of water, blood and animal fat by the nomadic tribes of the Early Iron Age. The practice of human sacrifice appears in archaeological records by the end of the Bronze Age, in the Andronovo culture about 3,000 years ago, and continues into the Early Iron Age.

Images of shamans wearing masks and feathered headdresses while performing sacred rites were depicted in the rock art of Siberian nomads of the Okunev Culture, dating to about 3,000 years ago. The masks embodied the spirits that took part in these rites. Sacred ceremonies served many purposes, such as initiation, inspiration of warriors and commemoration of hero-ancestors. The rite of initiation is recorded archaeologically in children's burials through such finds as distinctive belts worn by boys who were older than 10 to 12 years of age, and needles and spindle whorls belonging to girls older than seven or eight. In Medieval burials of young girls, bronze male figurines are sometimes found, possibly symbolizing the post-mortem engagement of the girls.

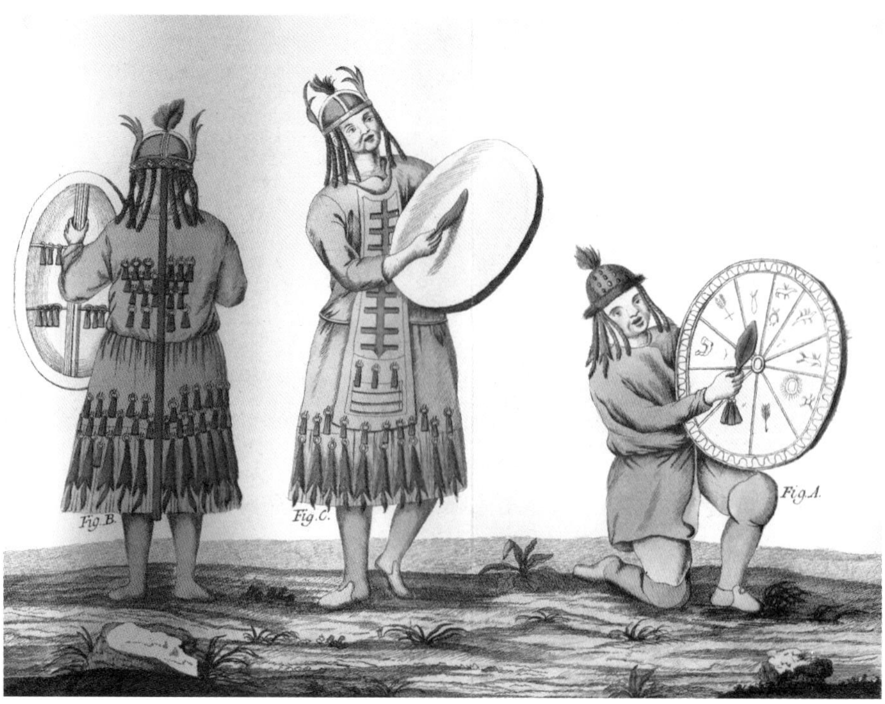

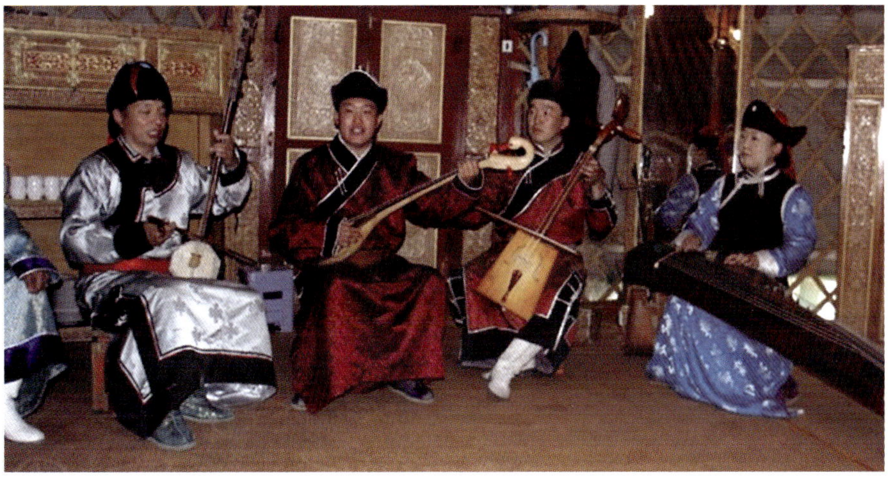

Ceremonies in which male warriors inhaled or drank cannabis-derived hallucinogens in special tents were described by Herodotus some 2,500 years ago. He asserted that cannabis was thrown on hot stones for inhaling, or burned in bronze vessels. Cannabis is native to the Steppes where it grows on very rich soils. For the production of hallucinogens, the female plants have to be grown separately from the male plants. This was an important ceremonial crop planted by the steppe nomads for their own use. It may have been one of the oldest trade items as well.

Funerals, marriages and seasonal festivities, such as sheep shearing and the New Year fertility festival, were accompanied by gatherings of people belonging to the same nomadic community or to even larger territorial units. Music and dancing were important components of such gatherings. Archaeological finds in burials show that steppe nomads used musical instruments such as the jew's harp, pan flute, and stringed instruments for at least 5,000 years. Simple flutes or whistles (hollow tubes made of bird bones) have also been found in Bronze Age burials, but it is not clear that they were used as musical instruments. The antiquity and popularity of stringed instruments among the steppe nomads is reflected by their diversity: over 20 types of stringed instruments are used in the folk music of modern Mongolian nomads. The bodies of such instruments were made of wood, while the strings were made of horsehair. The tambourine was an instrument used by shamans in special ceremonies—as described in historical sources and as depicted in rock art. Unlike instruments made of bone or wood, leather tambourines are not preserved in archaeological sites.

**Above** Mongolian musicians playing traditional string instruments in a yurt (courtesy of www.ulaantaij.com)
**Below** Cannabis plant and seeds were used by steppe warriors as hallucinogens. (courtesy of Missouri Botanical Garden, http://www.botanicus.org)

**Burial Rites.** Despite spending their lives on the move, nomads tended to select special places for the burial of their dead. These were used for hundreds and, in some cases, even thousands of years. Only a few of the deaths actually occurred at the burial places; most human remains were carried from elsewhere on the group's migrational route. According to ethnographic descriptions, some nomadic groups, such as the Kazaks, buried their dead only near winter pastures, whereas others buried their dead in convenient places along their migration routes.

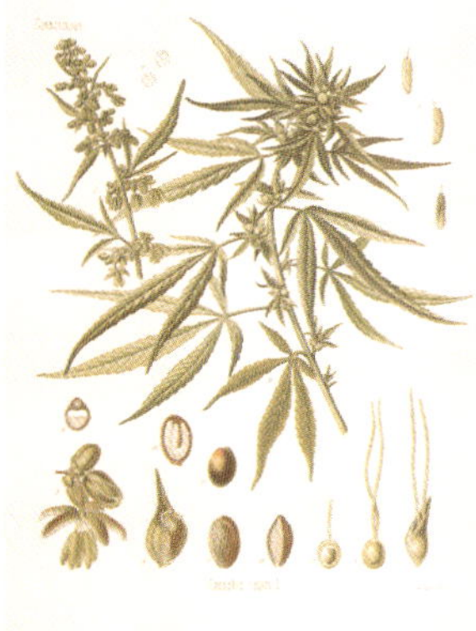

The religious beliefs and burial rites of steppe nomads changed over time. Among the types of burials practiced at various periods were pit inhumations in supine and flexed positions, inhumation under burial mounds, cremation, and secondary burials (re-burial of human remains after the soft tissue had disintegrated). All types might co-exist in a single cemetery, possibly marking differences in the origin, social status, or deeds of the dead. However, the proportion of various types of burials changed noticeably over time.

Secondary burials were of special importance, possibly reflecting winter mortality, or the need to transport human remains from the place of death to a remote burial ground.

Cremation in the Steppes is commonly associated with Zoroastrianism, which was the dominant religion of the Indo-Iranian tribes, being an official religion of the Persian Empire from 2,600 to 1,300 years ago. For Zoroastrians, cremation was preceded by leaving the dead on special above-ground structures (towers of silence) until the bones were free of flesh. In the Steppes, cremation was comparatively rare because of the lack of fuel; however, some signs of ritual burning are recorded for the Bronze and Early Iron ages. Burial mounds are the most noticeable type of burials, and symbolic of the nomadic lifestyle in the Steppes. Steppe nomads erected burial mounds from at least 5,000 years ago until 600 years ago. However, the peculiarities of mound burials and their proportion in the overall number of burials varied through time.

Some 5,000 years ago, at the beginning of the Bronze Age, types of burials differed for various social groups within the same society. People of high status were buried under burial mounds (kurgans) along with many mortuary goods. Ordinary people were buried in pit graves with little or no grave goods. The mounds were made of earth in a conical shape having an average height of 1-3 metres and diameter of 6-8 metres. Yet, the largest examples were gigantic—up to 100 metres in diameter. Kurgans were commonly found in groups situated on low river terraces adjacent to settlements. Two types of burial chambers have been recorded within mounds for this period. Most common is a log-covered subfloor burial pit; rarer is a subfloor burial pit with a wooden construction

Early Iron Age burial mounds, 3rd century B.C., Mangyrnyi Log, Khakassia (courtesy of Igor Kyzlasov)

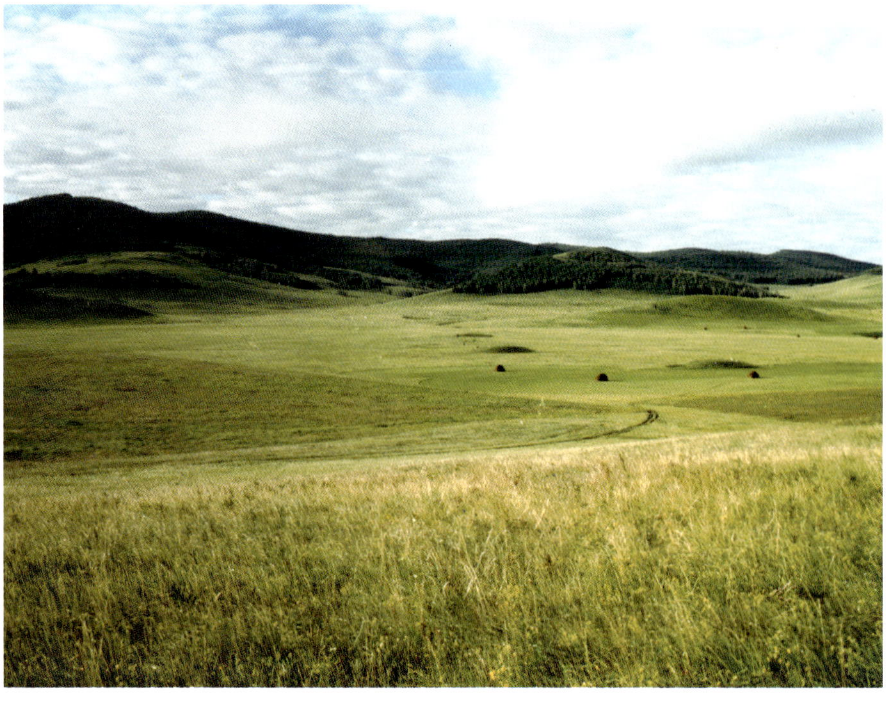

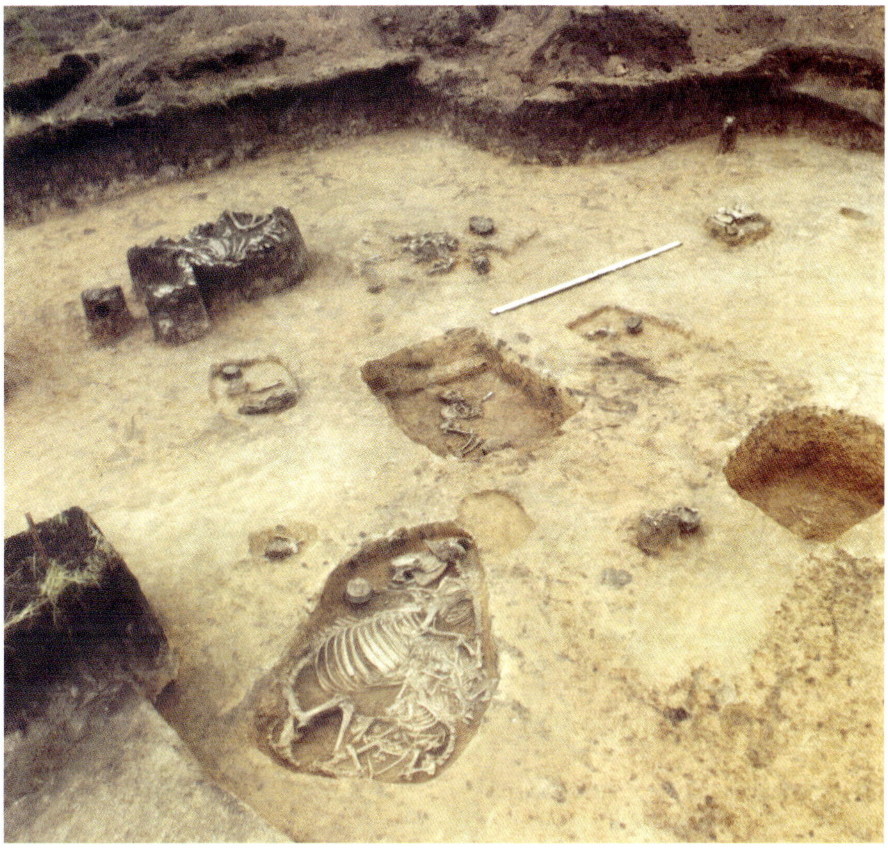

Nomad burial with oxen, ca. 3,500 years old, Samara Region, Russia (courtesy of Pavel Kuznetsov)

above it, imitating a house. The wooden constructions often show signs of having been burned before the mound was raised over the grave. Some mounds covered several inhumations, often buried over a long period of time before the erection of the mound. Cremation was practiced along with other inhumation under some mounds. Ochre was a required component of all burials.

Mound burials contain a wide range of objects that were meant to accompany the dead in the afterlife, from vessels containing food to cloth, jewellery and tools. Male warriors of high status might be buried with chariots, the means of transportation to the Other World, or with parts of chariots such as wheels and beams. In some burials, the chariot parts have traces of wear; in others, they are new. From the Bronze Age on, many items were made specially as mortuary goods: showy analogues of contemporary weaponry, tools, jewellery, pottery, and symbols of power, such as polished stone maces. Mortuary pottery was distinctive from utilitarian ware, usually being smaller and not as well fired. Among the utilitarian objects included in burials were pestles, mortars, hammerstones, knives, sickles, scrapers and axe/chisels. In addition, Bronze Age burials often contained antiquities such as Neolithic flint arrowheads.

During the Early Iron Age, burial mounds become more diverse in shape and size. In the European Steppes, conical mounds up to 12 metres in diameter prevailed. Siberian nomads constructed truncated, stepped, conical mounds along with regular conical mounds. Rectangular blocks of sod were used as construction material. In some areas a hierarchy of mounds can be found, possibly associated with rank. The largest were located on the highest points in the landscape, and were visually connected to other large burial mounds within five to ten kilometres. Smaller mounds might also be included in the arrangement. Single burial mounds were rare and found only at the beginning of the period. Constructions under the mounds varied greatly. Many mounds had wooden funeral chambers in pits below the original ground surface. This required a large amount of wood, which often had to be transported from a considerable distance.

The burials commonly contained weaponry, horse harness, and objects decorated in the animal style. Some burials contained bronze cauldrons, presumably designed for war parties. High-status people were accompanied by objects made of precious metals, such as gold bracelets, earrings and torques. Some burials contained mortuary pottery. Fragments of pottery or pots with broken bottoms were common components. From the Iron Age to Medieval times, warriors were often buried with harnessed horses. Herodotus observed that, in the case of Scythian kings, not only horses but also servants and warriors were sacrificed for inclusion in the king's burial to aid him in the afterlife. The burials of some nomadic groups also contained sacred materials, such as the chalk used by Sarmatians.

By the beginning of the Middle Ages, burial mounds had become smaller, averaging 10 to 15 metres in diameter. There was usually only one inhumation, and the mound itself was armoured with stone. The use of stone in burial ceremonialism was foreign to the loess-covered Steppes, but common in the Transurals and Siberian Steppes where stone is abundant. Burial goods declined in number, but inhumations with a horse or horse harness remained common. Sacred raw materials, such as powdered white minerals, chalk and limestone, were typical components of Medieval burials.

**Commemoration of the Dead.** Beginning in the Bronze Age, stone statues and bas-reliefs were used as gravestones to commemorate the high-status dead. These monuments evolved through time. During the Bronze Age (4,000 to 3,000 years ago), they were rock slabs shaped like humans, sometimes with eyes. During the transition to the Early Iron Age (about 2,500 years ago), "warrior" monuments appeared: similar anthropomorphic rock slabs, but with details of armament. In the Early Iron Age, people built a special type of burial mound without inhumation, the cenotaph. Presumably, this was made to honour dead warriors. At the beginning of the Middle Ages (1,400 to 1,300 years ago), a tradition of "stone *babas*" came into the European part of the Steppes from Siberia. Babas were three-dimensional statues featuring people with hair and costume, variously including a belt, dagger and goblet or bowl. Until 800 years ago, only male statues were erected, but after that, female statues became common as well. This tradition disappeared from the Steppes with the introduction of Islam about 700 to 600 years ago.

Stone statue of a hero-ancestor, Middle Ages (P. V. Alabin Museum of History and Regional Studies, Samara, KP-26050/2)

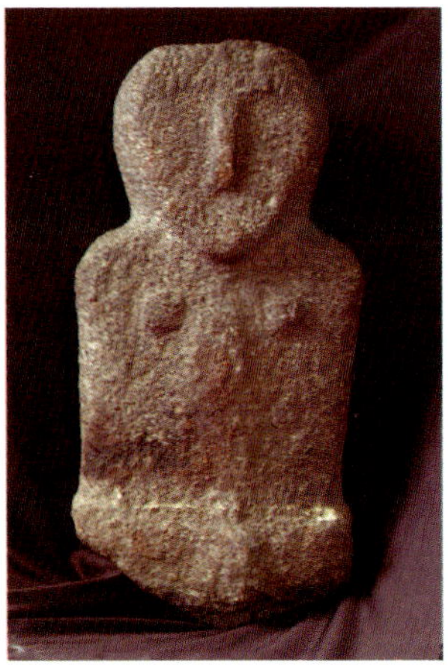

Monotheistic beliefs such as Judaism, Buddhism, Christianity and Islam spread among the nomadic groups of the Steppes, or were imposed on them, during the past 1,000 years. Buddhism was accepted voluntarily in the Late Middle Ages by some nomads; other religions were accepted by the rulers of Medieval nomadic empires—Judaism in the Khazarian State 1,200 years ago and Islam by the Golden Horde 700 years ago. In every case, the adoption of monotheistic beliefs was associated with attempts to centralize power.

# PRAIRIE NOMADS

**Systems of religious belief.** When Europeans arrived on the Prairies, the bison nomads they found there shared generally similar religious beliefs. The nomads believed that an all-powerful creator was responsible for everything in the universe. The creator was not personalized and did not occupy a particular locale. Every prayer acknowledged him, but he was too awesome to be asked directly for a blessing. Rather, he was represented by a legion of intermediary spirits. Plants, animals, inorganic objects and natural phenomena all had spirit powers. The sun, thunder and wind were among the mightiest. Stones were very important, being among the oldest and longest-lived spirits. Trees, bears, bison and humming birds all had spirits. There were also folkloric characters, such as tricksters, who had spirit powers. These many intermediaries resided in the things they were named for—bear spirits were in bears—but were not confined to them. They were omnipresent. In almost all things that people did, they consulted and propitiated the spirit powers in the hope of receiving guidance and protection.

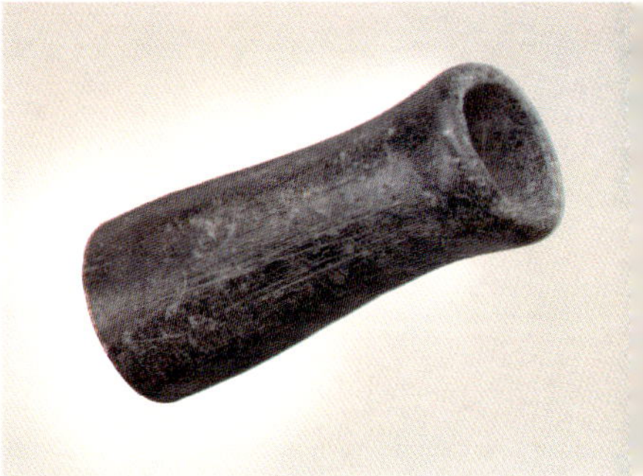

Shaman's sucking tube, ca. 900 years old (Canadian Museum of Civilization, X-A-328)

Some southern Plains tribes had totemic clans, but these were not present among the northern nomads. Instead, they were alert to a broad pantheon of spiritual forces. People sometimes appealed to these forces communally or as members of special societies, but tended to place much reliance on personal spirit helpers. When a spirit power revealed itself to an individual in a vision, it became that person's spirit helper. It did not provide protection against all dangers, but rather offered assistance in certain situations. At the time of revealing itself, the spirit listed the blessings it would confer and the kinds of feats it would aid. A person who had a spirit helper generally painted its image on important articles such as a tent or shield.

Although many people had spirit helpers, some individuals—shamans—were known to be favoured by especially strong supernatural powers. Shamans were asked to invoke their powers on behalf of distressed individuals or groups. One of their important capabilities was the power to cure illness, which usually involved elaborate rituals of prayer, song and magical acts aimed at removing a malevolent object believed to have lodged in the victim's body. Depending on the nature of their knowledge and powers, shamans also administered herbal remedies, dispensed love potions, foresaw important events and launched malevolent "objects" into unfortunate victims.

Apart from spirit powers, prairie nomads believed that there was a life force present in all living things. A person's life force could leave his body and travel with a spirit helper during a vision, but then returned again to the body. After death, the life force left the body and wandered aimlessly for a time before entering the land of the dead—a green grass world in which game was plentiful and men, women and children lived carefree lives. A life force could return to earth to haunt a place or habitation if, for example, the dead person had not been properly mourned or if relatives had not given a proper feast when visiting the grave.

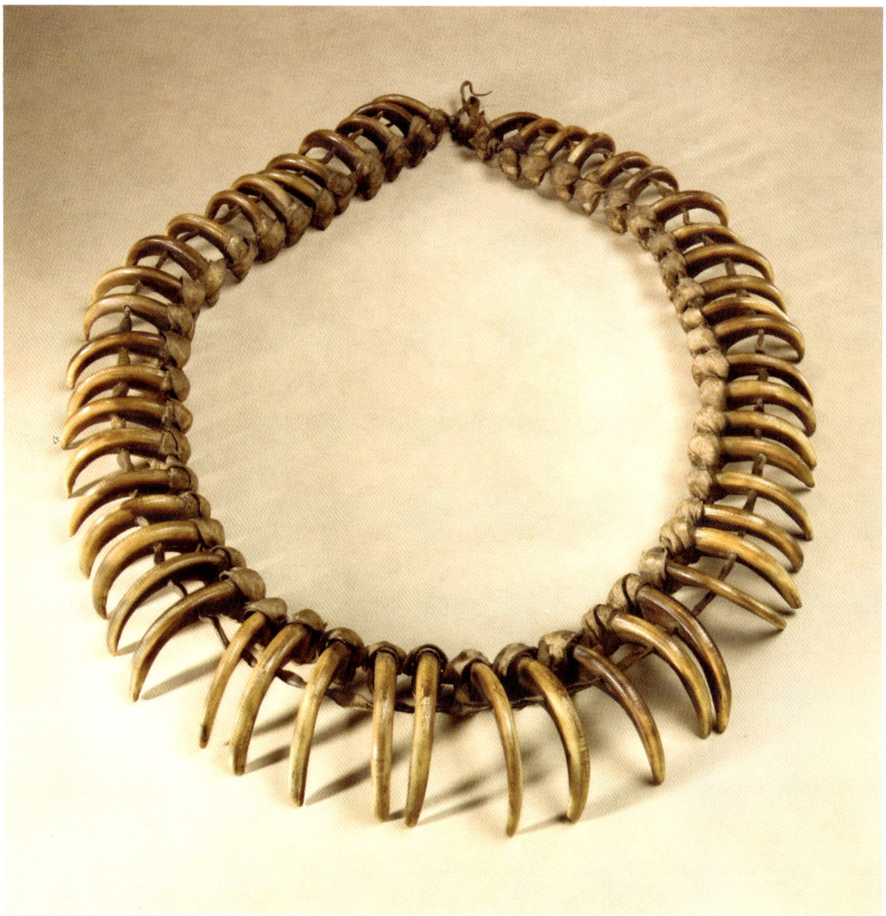

Grizzly bear claw necklace, ca. 150 years old (Canadian Museum of Civilization, V-X-396)

The religious beliefs of prairie nomads were formulated in numerous myths, some of which appear to have been reflected in burial rites. These can be recorded and, to some degree, interpreted archaeologically, allowing an estimation of the age of certain beliefs. For example, the Earth Diver myth seems to be reflected in a specific arrangement of sacred black mud or white sand in burials dating to at least 3,000 years ago.

**Imagery.** Most imagery was expressed by painting on skins or rock surfaces and by embroidery on skins. Incision and sculpting of wood, bone and stone did occur, but not frequently. Geometric designs and simple images of animals and humans prevailed until European contact, while images of plants were less common. In the decoration of clothing, bands of colour, rows of lines, zigzags, triangles, rectangles and circles were much used. Images of animals were common in men's robe art, shield art, rock art, occasionally in the decoration of ceremonial plates and spoons, and as figurines carved, pecked or incised on rock or bone. People made frequent use of images depicting the turtle, snake, beaver, grizzly bear, bison heads, and the mythical thunderbird. Wolves, dogs and fish are rare, and insects were not depicted. Interestingly, images of bison are not nearly as common as might be expected, given the important role of these animals in the lives of prairie nomads. However, an indirect depiction of bison in the form of hoofprints is a distinctive feature of some Northern Plains rock art. Images of shamans are common in rock art, usually distinguishable as a person holding a drum, a rattle or a sprig of tobacco. Boulders with an anthropomorphic face pecked or incised on one surface were often used by shamans in ceremonies designed to help them see great distances in order to find lost people, objects or game animals.

**Personal protection.** To ward off evil influences, most people wore amulets, consisting of a small object encased in a leather pouch. The nature of the amulet varied—a bear's claw, a small bone, a mixture of roots, and so forth. Some people wore the amulet they received when they were infants throughout their lives. Others made their own amulets according to instructions from their personal guardian spirits. To obtain a personal guardian, young males underwent certain sacred procedures, which usually were associated with fasting in secluded places (vision quests), or with self-torture. The latter was less common, practiced mainly by people who desired to become warriors or shamans. Through such initiation, young males obtained visions that informed them about the personal taboos they would have to observe and the objects they would need for personal protection. These sacred objects might be worn as amulets or carried in a medicine bundle.

The medicine bundle was a set of sacral objects, wrapped in a hide, and carried on one's back. A wrapping was made of the skin of specific animals. For example, the outer wrapping might be made of bearskin, and the inner one of elk skin. Typical components of a bundle might include pipes, tobacco, a bunch of sweet grass, skins of birds (e.g., swan, crane, owl), skins of animals (e.g., otter, fawn, prairie dog), and a rattle. The bundles were opened only for certain ceremonies; no serious endeavour could be undertaken without opening and consulting such bundles. Tribal bundles were kept by a trusted man, but carried

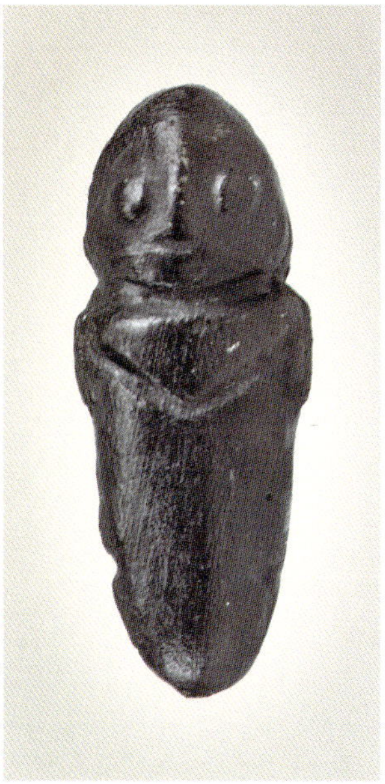

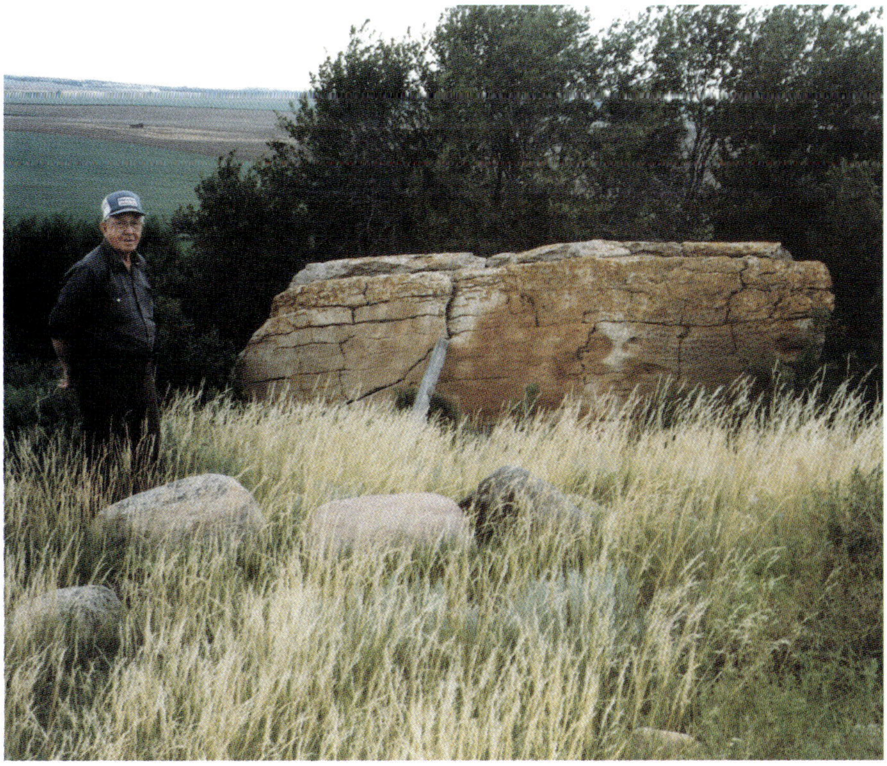

**Above** Miniature figurine (replica) (Canadian Museum of Civilization, X-B-277 ca)
**Left** Large glacial erratic near Outlook, Saskatchewan, revered by aboriginal people as a sacred site and used by bison as a rubbing stone to relieve the itch of parasites (I. Dyck)

during migrations by his wife. In camp, a medicine bundle hung on a tripod outside the owner's tipi, but in bad weather or at night, it was carried inside and kept at the rear of the tipi behind the altar.

Shields used in war served both magical and practical protection functions. Made of tough rawhide, the shield was decorated with feathers around the circumference and with a picture or collage on the front representing the warrior's spirit helper.

**Sanctuaries.** Nomads believed that certain unusual locations in the landscape either were the homes of spirit powers or had special power. These were regarded as sacred places. Among them were very large solitary boulders (glacial erratics, often used by bison as rubbing stones); prominences overlooking plains or valleys; waterfalls and rapids; large solitary trees; and soft rock deposits sculpted into arches, caves and hoodoos by water and wind erosion. In all these places, people made offerings to the spirits and held sacred ceremonies.

**Ceremonies and gatherings.** Nomads recognized some people as leaders or specialists in organizing sacred gatherings, performing sacred rites and interpreting unusual or threatening situations. Among prairie nomads, spiritual leadership was provided by elders, bundle keepers and shamans. Elders and bundle keepers were somewhat the equivalent of wise, benevolent priests whose services benefited the whole group. Shamans played more specialized roles, often aimed at resolving problems for individuals. Among the shaman's paraphernalia were rattles, drums and a headdress, feathered or horned, all used during sacral ceremonies.

There were many ceremonies aimed at ensuring success in hunting. An important example was bison ceremonialism—involving dancing and bison propitiation—aimed at attracting bison into close enough proximity to be killed. It was believed that the hunt would be successful only if the animal gave itself

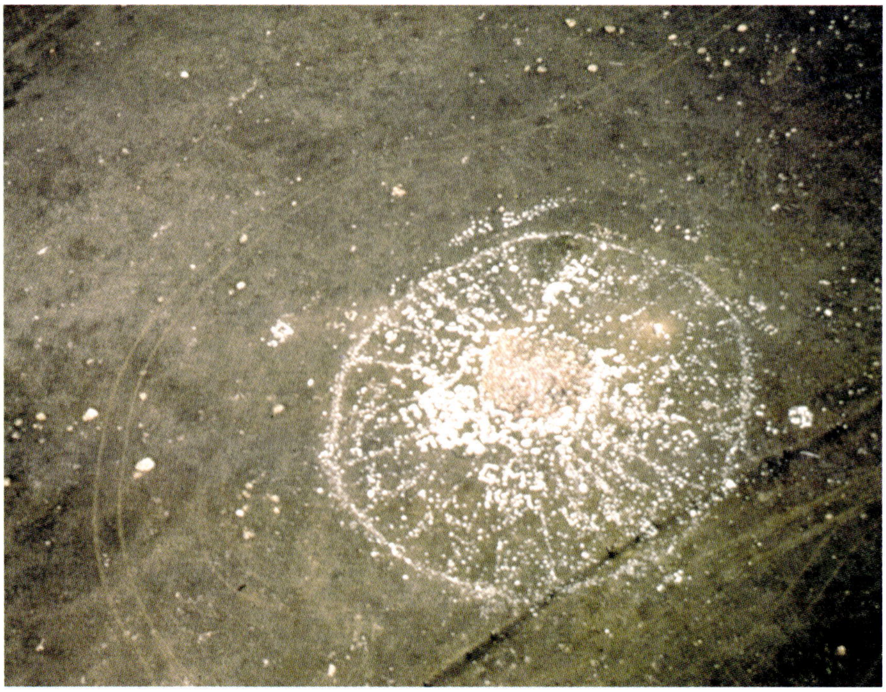

Aerial view of the Majorville cairn and medicine wheel, a 5,000-year-old stone monument in southern Alberta (Royal Alberta Museum, EdPc1-5)

to the hunter. To encourage this, the hunters gave offerings to the buffalo during these ceremonies—bison skulls painted red, feathers, new pots, red-painted leather, and so forth.

The Sun Dance (sun-gazing dance or thirsting dance) was a midsummer ceremony, preceded by fasting and purification and often accompanied by self-torture. There were many variations of this ceremony, ranging from mourning to world renewal, to securing supernatural help in hunting. Common features of the dance structure were a circular arrangement of poles, with the tallest set in the centre adjoining an altar. During the ceremony, people danced around the pole making offerings to the sun. Both men and women danced, wearing special feathered headdresses and having their faces and bodies painted. The ceremony was accompanied by singing and could continue day and night.

Sweatlodges were used for preliminary purification before ceremonies. Burning of incense (e.g., sweet grass, sage and cedar twigs) was also part of most ceremonies.

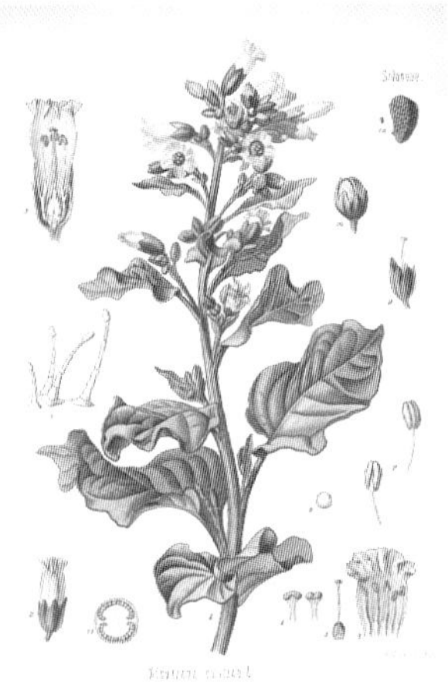

Aztec tobacco (*Nicotiana rustica L.*) (courtesy of Missouri Botanical Garden, http://www.botanicus.org)

Smoking tobacco was a ceremony itself. Tobacco has a mild narcotic effect when inhaled in small quantities and can cause hallucinations and trances in large doses. It was originally cultivated in South America 7,000 to 5,000 years ago, where it was chewed, made into a drink, or smoked—either as cigars or in a cane pipe. Tobacco was introduced to North America about 4,500 years ago where stone and eventually clay pipes were invented. By about 2,000 years ago, stone pipes were appearing in the Great Plains. The earliest examples in the Prairies had the form of stone tubes. Later, these were replaced by so-called elbow pipes, which had a bowl at right angles to a short stem. A long wooden stem was inserted into the stone stem to make a composite pipe, often referred to as a calumet. Various types of stone were used for pipes, but by about 500 years ago, a red Catlinite, acquired from a quarry in southern Minnesota, was the preferred pipestone throughout the Prairies. Tobacco was the only plant cultivated by the nomads.

Tobacco smoking was used in many rites, such as declaring war, making peace, or sealing an agreement. Shamans used tobacco in almost all aspects of their work. They smoked it in order to reach a trance in which they could obtain the guidance of spirits. The smoke was also used as a diagnostic tool for revealing illness, and as a medicine to cure it. Early in a ceremony, the smoker exhaled once in each of the four cardinal directions, "sending his prayers to their intended recipients." Over time, not only tobacco but also pipes became sacred ceremonial objects. For example, in a ceremony establishing kinship, a pair of calumet pipe stems was placed together and wrapped in a skin to create a ritual binding of participants into a brotherhood.

Music, dancing and singing were important parts of most gatherings. Human voices were of central importance, but were accompanied by musical instruments such as drums, rattles and flutes. Whistles found in archaeological sites, also known from ethnographic observations, seem to have been used more often as an aid to a person undergoing self-torture ceremonies than for conventional musical performance.

**Burial rites.** According to historic records, the preferred mode of burial among prairie nomads was on above-ground scaffolds. After the death of a warrior, for example, the body was straightened, dressed for battle with face painted red, and wrapped in an ochered skin. Next, the warrior's weapons and

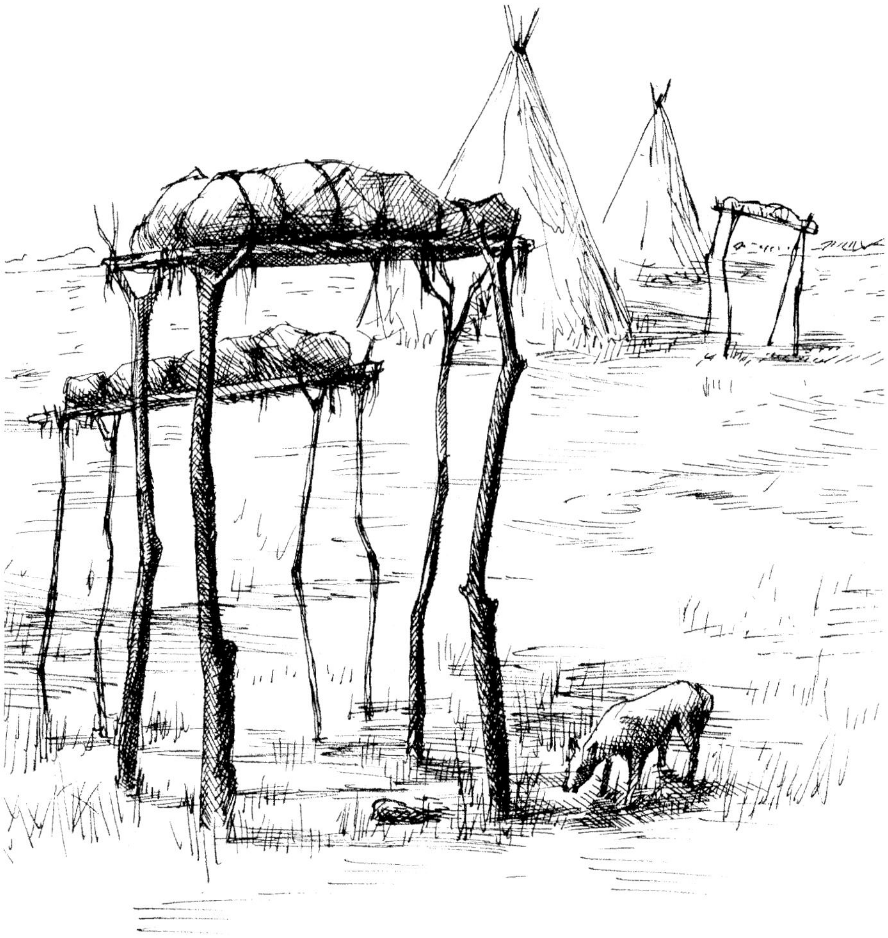

Scaffold burials near a nomads' camp (Larisa Nikolaeva, P. V. Alabin Museum of History and Regional Studies, Samara)

medicine charm were laid beside him and, together with the body, bundled into his robe. The last covering was a buffalo raw hide, hair inside, strapped tightly with strong cords. The next day the wrapped body was conveyed to the place selected for scaffolding. If there was a suitable tree, then the body bale was raised into the branches where it was firmly tied. If no suitable trees were available, then a scaffold was built of four stout poles, set upright in the ground, supporting a platform to receive the burial. After the body bale was securely tied to the branches of the tree or the platform, mourners cut themselves, sometimes severed finger joints as a sacrifice, sometimes sacrificed an animal, and howled their misery. This went on for several days until the mourners were exhausted and left the site. Over the next year or more, the corpse and its wrappings gradually disintegrated and the bones fell to the ground. Eventually, relatives and friends returned to the scaffold site where the friends gathered the bones into a bundle or into several bundles if there was more than one scaffold burial at the site. Later, these were interred in a pit in the ground. Historically, there were no repeatedly used cemeteries (as we will see below, this was not the case in more ancient times). Interment was simply at a convenient and often scenic place. After additional mourning, a feast to the dead was prepared and the spirit of the dead was propitiated with prayers and invocations. This being done, the relatives resumed their normal lives, returning to the grave whenever they happened to be in the vicinity to once again feast the dead.

Some individuals preferred to be interred in the ground immediately after death. In these cases a burial pit was dug on the top of a hill and the corpse was laid in it with the clothing, arms, tools and food it would need in the afterlife. The pit was filled with earth and often covered with a cairn of stones to prevent the ravages of foxes and wolves. The mourning rites were the same as for scaffold burials. A few renowned warriors sometimes requested that they not be buried in any way. They were placed inside their lodge, propped into a sitting posture, dressed and painted. The door was closed tight and the lodge was enclosed in a thick hedge of branches and dirt or stones to prevent the entry of wolves. Eventually the lodge rotted and the bones were scattered.

In general, archaeological evidence confirms that the burial practices of prairie nomads over the past 5,000 years conform to those observed in historic times. Human burials could be single, primary, pit inhumations in extended and flexed positions; single or multiple secondary burials, usually bundled. There was some variation in burial contents and context with different archaeological cultures. For example, those belonging to the Oxbow complex (about 5,100–3,000 years ago) tended to be situated well away from occupation sites and contained very few grave goods, but lots of red ochre. Those belonging to the McKean complex (about 4,800–3,200 years ago) were always in shallow pits within occupation sites and contained no red ochre. By the time of the Pelican Lake complex (about 2,800–2,100 years ago), grave goods had increased in quantity, quality and range, red ochre was being used again, and burial pits were often covered with stone cairns. Late prehistoric burials are not well known in the Prairies, but their predecessors' practices suggest many continuities with historic observations.

Beyond the confirmation of historic observations, archaeology has revealed at least one 3,200–year–old cremation; one cemetery containing at least 304 individuals spanning the period from 5,100 years ago to 2,900 years ago; and, on the eastern fringes of the region, a peripheral representation of the impressive North American burial mound complexes centred on the Mississippi River Valley between about 3,200 and 700 years ago. The cremation (of a bundle of weathered bones) belonged to the McKean complex and was situated in a river valley campsite. The cemetery belonged to the Oxbow complex, was unmarked on the ground surface, and was located on a hill slope separate from any known campsite. It contained individuals of both sexes and all ages in 99 burial units—primary extended and bundle burials for the most part—all in subsurface pits. Burial goods consisted of stone projectile points, knives, scrapers, worked flakes, bone tools, shell gorgets and pendants, rolled copper fragments, and various faunal remains, including sets of eagle talons. The bones and pits were abundantly covered in red ochre.

Prairie burial mounds date between about 1,900 and 600 years ago and are found only in the eastern parts of the Prairies. They appear to be grassland reflections or imitations of Adena/Hopewell and Mississippian burial mound complexes of the woodlands to the east and southeast of the Prairies. Indeed, the number of mounds declines quite noticeably as one moves westward into the grasslands away from the upper reaches of the Mississippi River. Nevertheless, several hundred mounds have been located on the Prairies, including a range of types. Most common are domed mounds made of earth or of earth and stone. These vary from 5–7 metres in diameter and 0.3 metres in height to 20–30 metres in diameter and 3–4 metres in height. Often they occur singly on a prominence overlooking a valley, but they can be found in groups of from two or three to fifty. Linear or elongated mounds are much less common. Some of these are simple low platforms 70 metres long, 7–10 metres wide and 0.6 metres high. Occasionally, linear mounds have rounded expansions at one or both ends, and sometimes they connect to other linear mounds at an angle. Mounds in the shape of animal effigies (e.g. beavers or salamanders) are present but rare in the Prairies.

The nature of these mounds was a matter of much curiosity during the late 1800s and early 1900s when the grasslands were being settled by European agriculturalists. That is also when most of the recorded excavations were carried out. In or under most of the excavated mounds were one or more circular, oblong or rectangular pits, these being 1–4 metres long by 0.5–1.3 metres deep. Each pit contained the remains of one or more humans. Some pits contained whole skeletons in proper anatomical relationship, indicating primary burials; most contained bundled mixtures of bones, indicating secondary burials. In some mounds, decayed pieces of wood were found over the pits, indicating that they were covered with poles or logs before the mound was built. A fair number of mounds contain intrusive burials showing later reuse, sometimes hundreds of years after original construction. A few mounds, mostly of the linear type, contain no burials at all.

Animal bones were usually part of the contents, bison bones being the most prominent. Often the bones were broken, suggesting that they were the remains of food offerings or feasts. In a few cases, however, large articulated portions of bison skeletons have been found on the original ground surface adjacent to the burial pit. One example included the partial remains of at least 18 bison, mostly calves and yearlings. Many other animals are also represented by bones—antelope, deer, elk, dogs, wolves, coyotes, foxes, prairie dogs, rabbits and various birds.

Mortuary vessel (replica), ca. 1,000–600 years old (Canadian Museum of Civilization, X-B-278 ca)

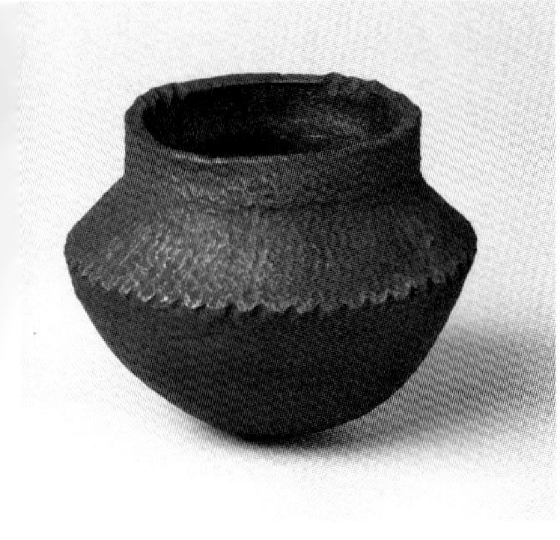

Grave goods comprised many kinds of artifacts, but none in great quantity. Ceramics were present in prairie mounds of all archaeological cultures dating from 1,900 to 600 years ago. Chipped stone grave goods included arrow points, spear points, end scrapers and knives. Ground and polished stone artifacts included pipes, tablets with incised designs (often animals) and disks. Bone tools were represented by fleshers, flakers, cancellous bones for hide-working, antler tines, beads, whistles, and polished armlets and headbands. Shell was chiefly in the form of ornamental objects—flat washer-like objects, tubular beads and pendants made from the columella of marine shells, pierced Marginella shells for necklaces and occasional gorgets. Native copper artifacts were present in some mounds—axe heads, pike heads, spear points and pieces of sheet copper, as well as sheet copper beads and tinkling cones. Pigments were present in the pits or pit fill of most mounds. They occurred both in powdery form and as lumps or balls. Hematite was the most common pigment, but greenstone, magnetite, yellow ochre and whitish clay was also used.

**Commemoration of the dead.** The prairie nomads commemorated their dead with feasts whenever they visited a burial site containing relatives or band members. If the grave was already covered with a stone cairn, the visitors would often add a few stones together with a small offering, such as an arrowhead or a bit of tobacco. Over time, the cairns grew into fairly large mounds of stone. Long lines of stones looking like spokes were added to some of these stone mounds together with an encircling line of stones creating a large boulder monument known to archaeologists as a medicine wheel.

In the Prairies, a shift toward monothesism occurred at the end of the nomadic era. European colonization during the 1800s was accompanied by strong missionary efforts to Christianize the Aboriginal populations. With the extinction of the bison, the nomadic lifestyle came to an end, and by the late 1800s, most nomadic groups had accepted the new power structure and its religion.

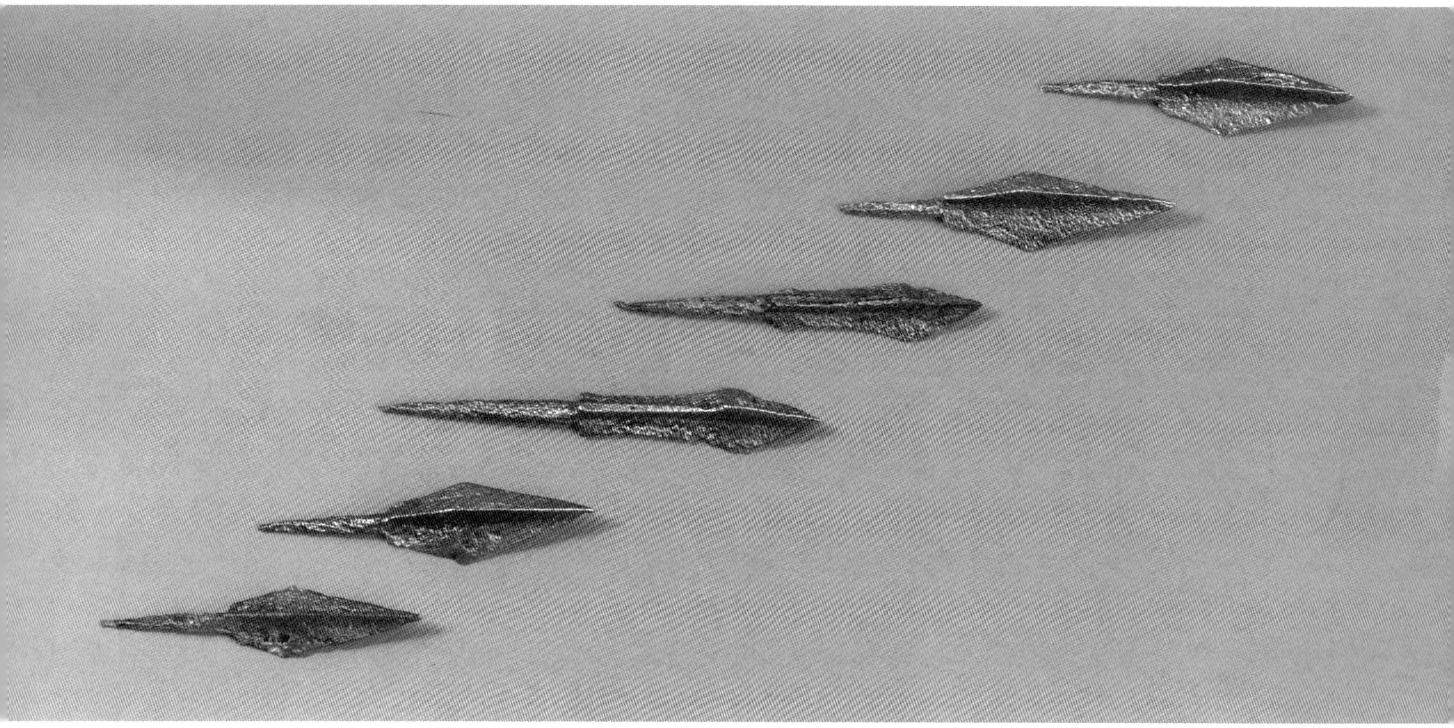

**Above** Iron arrowheads, 5th century A.D. (Hun) (P. V. Alabin Museum of History and Regional Studies, Samara, KP-211/4-9)
**Below** Dakota bow, arrows and quiver, ca. 100 years old (Canadian Museum of Civilization, V-E-273 a, c and V-E-274 a, b, i, j, m)

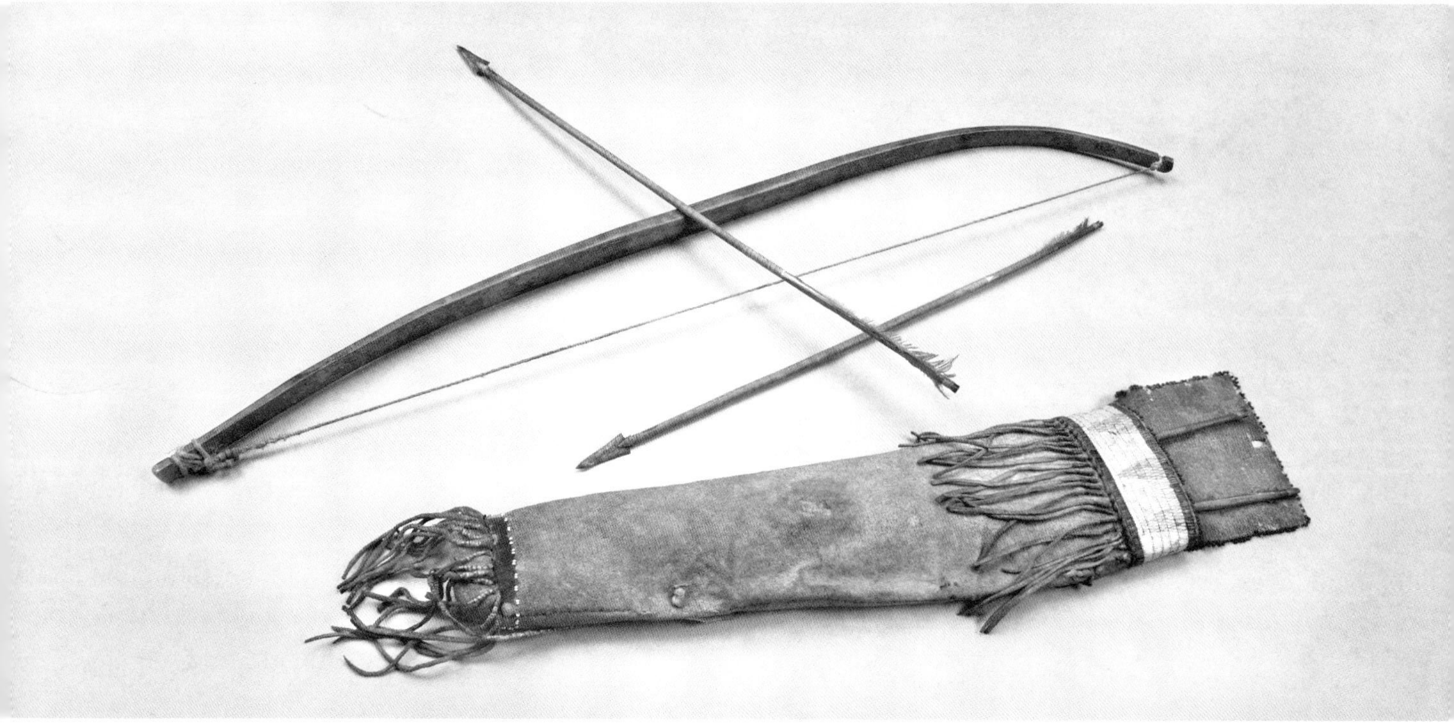

# INTERACTING WITH OTHERS

Contact between nomads and other groups, both nomadic and sedentary, led to cultural exchange through warfare, trade and migration.

In both regions, nomadic societies were warrior societies, often in conflict with surrounding groups over territories, resources and possessions. They developed and refined war techniques and paraphernalia designed for high mobility. In the Steppes, nomads on horseback had a military advantage over sedentary populations. With great mobility and unlimited capability for travel, they could attack settlements many hundreds of kilometres from their own camps. Pillage and extortion of gifts or tribute became an important part of the nomadic economy in the Steppes. In the Prairies, nomadic and sedentary populations had rather similar weaponry and military skills. Although booty was always of interest, it was seldom a significant part of their economy. War honours, however, were much sought after.

In the Steppes, the military orientation required constant modernization of weaponry. Weapons were developed specifically for warfare, and particularly for fighting at a distance. Even though nomads used bows and arrows for hunting, the main use of these weapons was for attacking enemies from horseback. Horse paraphernalia was constantly improved, becoming more and more convenient for the rider-warrior. The weaponry of the prairie nomads was not nearly as diverse and specialized. The same weapons were used in hunting and warfare. The only major technological developments in the Prairies during the last 5,000 years were the adoption of the bow and arrow and the development of protective leather armour.

In both regions, nomads formed alliances with other nomadic and sedentary groups. In the Steppes, some people became professional warriors, serving as soldiers of fortune for sedentary states. Steppe nomads formed some very large alliances, which initiated and participated in large-scale war actions. In the Prairies, most warfare was limited to small, individually organized war parties.

As a result of warfare, the size and location of nomadic territories changed through time, sometimes very dramatically. Several major resettlements were caused by the military campaigns of steppe nomads. One of them, the Hun invasion, caused what has been called the Great Resettlement of Peoples, a movement that generated the modern ethnic geography of Europe. Another, the Mongolian invasion, formed the world's largest empire during the Middle Ages. Invasions and reorganization of territories also occurred in the Prairies, for example, the Shoshone advance and retreat at the dawn of the historic (horse) era, and the expansion of the Sioux and Blackfoot confederacies.

Nomadic societies were also trading societies, negotiating the exchange of goods, services, people and ideas on a peaceful basis. Prime nomadic exports in the Steppes were livestock, horses, wool and slaves; while prime imports were craft and status objects, and agricultural products such as wine, spices, sweets and cereals. Prime exports in the Prairies were bison products, wild prairie turnip produce, pigments for paint, high quality stone tools and tool materials, and captives or slaves. Prime imports were shell jewellery from the west and south coasts of North America, agricultural products from the Mississippi and Missouri river regions, copper from the Great Lakes and ceramic technology from the east. Important imports included ceremonial and status objects and materials such as tobacco, pipe stone, shells, ochre and copper.

In the Steppes, nomadic and agricultural populations could offer drastically different sets of objects for trade, whereas in the Prairies, the difference between the material cultures of nomadic and sedentary populations was not quite so marked. In the Steppes, the volume of trade was limited only by the demand for certain products and the access to markets. As early as the first centuries B.C., nomadic products such as livestock and wool could be sold in wholesale as well as retail markets. The products were carried to trade centres on ox-drawn wagons and packed on camels, with herds of livestock trailing along. In the Prairies, the volume of trade seems to have been more limited, perhaps due to the more limited carrying capacity of people and dogs. In both regions, trade was carried out mostly by barter, but in the Steppes, coins were circulated periodically and, in Medieval times, even minted by nomadic states.

## Steppe Nomad Warfare

Evidence for increasing militarization began to appear in the Steppes during the Early Bronze Age. By about 4,000 years ago, severe traumas had become common features in male burials. In close battle, foot-warriors used stone and bronze war axes, bronze daggers, and spears with bronze spearheads—weapons which could cause great injury and which were buried with warriors. High-status burials of that period also contained two-wheeled chariots or parts of chariots. The invention of such vehicles likely occurred in the Near East where squadrons of charioteers complemented blocks of infantry in large-scale warfare. Contemporary Assyrian frescos show phalanxes of foot soldiers, with chariots protecting their flanks, their most vulnerable areas. On level ground against ordinary foot soldiers, chariot-supported phalanxes of infantry were almost invincible. Some authors suggest that chariots were used as battle vehicles

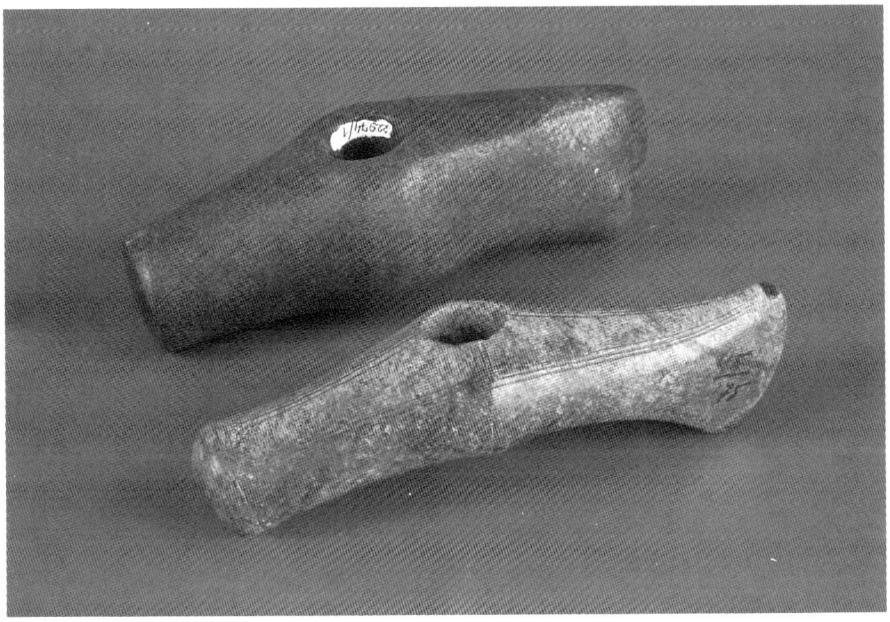

Drilled and polished stone axes, ca. 3,500 years old, (Bronze Age) (P. V. Alabin Museum of History and Regional Studies, Samara, KP-22974/1, KP-25407)

in the Steppes, but others argue that the rugged terrain limited their use to ceremonial racing and burial objects that symbolically transported the dead to the Other World (as described in the *Rigveda*).

By 3,500 years ago, horse-drawn chariots had come into use in Europe, Mesopotamia, Syria, Egypt and even China. However, chariots remained an aristocratic prerogative, as their manufacture required skills, materials and time that ordinary nomads were not likely to have. At this stage, horse paraphernalia was quite primitive, limited to reins with cheek pieces (psalia) and awls for spurring the horse.

About 3,200 years ago, steppe nomads began to use the horse as a riding animal. They also invented the short composite bow, which could be shot from horseback in all directions and which allowed the release of more arrows per minute than the old-fashioned long bow. With the development of a mobile cavalry and the composite bow, nomads became soldiers of fortune, pillaging and destroying the camps and towns of their enemies. The agricultural towns and states of that time could not afford to keep large groups of cavalry: all surpluses of grass were saved for cattle. Nomads had little difficulty keeping large herds of horses on the their vast steppe pastures.

By about the seventh century B.C., the names and origins of nomadic groups began to be recorded. Caucasoid nomads, presumably of Iranian origin, entered the Western Steppes from the south at this to time. During the fifth century B.C., Herodotus described the nomadic tribes occupying the steppes west of the Don River as Scythians, those between the Don River and Ural Mountains as Sarmatians, and the tribes on the steppes of the northern Caucasus as Maeotians. These Early Iron Age tribes dominated the Steppes between the fifth and first centuries B.C. and were in constant and often violent contact with such great ancient states as Assyria, Babylon, China, Urartu and Greece. Indeed, it was the Greeks who left the earliest historical descriptions of nomads. Even the Great

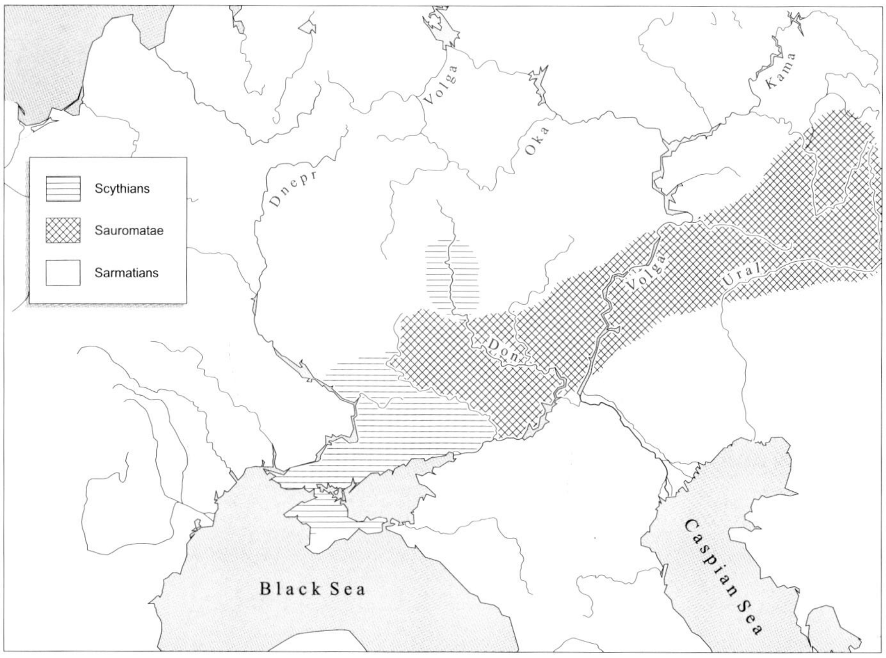


Location of Scythians, Sarmatians and Sauromatae, 2,500–2,000 years ago (Oleksiy Vasilenko, Canadian Museum of Civilization)

Wall of China, erected in the third century A.D., provided only partial protection against nomadic attacks.

In close fighting, the nomads used pikes, short iron swords and lassos made of hair. They wore helmets and body armour made of leather. By the second century B.C., their leaders were wearing metal-plated armour. According to finds in the Pazyryk burial mounds, Scythian horses were stocky and brown or black. For a saddle, warriors used brightly coloured, leather-covered cushions. The Scythians developed a new type of bridle, consisting of side-straps, nose bands with or without chinstraps, and bronze bits.

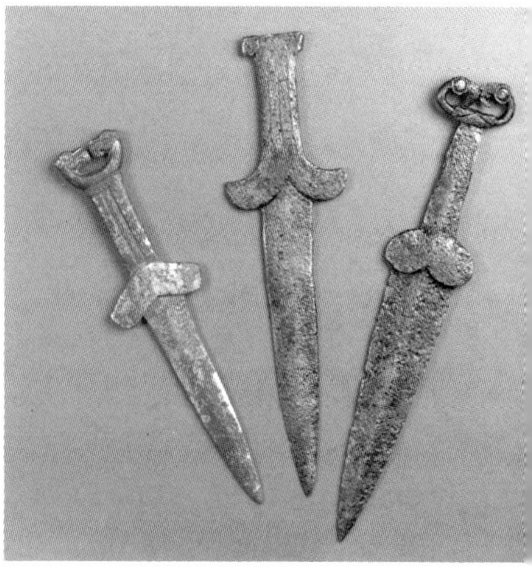

Iron short swords (Akinak), ca. 2,500 years old (Early Iron Age) (P. V. Alabin Museum of History and Regional Studies, Samara, KP-18486, 20729, 21983)

The nomads' military spirit became a war cult. They worshipped at mobile shrines—piles of brushwood surmounted by a platform. They set a short sword, symbolizing the god of war, on this platform and sacrificed animals and people to him, pouring the blood on the sword. The war cult was reflected in many other rites and customs described by Greek historians. Scalps of enemies were used to decorate the warrior's belt, and wine cups were made from enemy skulls. A warrior's share of loot depended on the number of people he killed, which had to be confirmed by the heads of his victims.

The main tactics were sudden attacks by comparatively small, mobile war parties, consisting of male warriors. These parties moved without food supplies, relying entirely on pillage. Each party did carry a supply of iron with which a smith replenished their arrowheads using small casting moulds. Quivers with up to 300 arrowheads are found in burials of this time, reflecting the persistent bombardment of enemies with arrows. Other elements of war equipment included clay flasks used to carry liquids and bronze cauldrons, presumably used for food preparation. Military raids necessitated some centralization of power, and by the fifth century B.C., nomadic groups were being governed by a military aristocracy (including both men and women) that claimed divine origin. By about the fourth century B.C., all nomadic groups inhabiting the steppes around the Black Sea were united under the rule of a Scythian king. A number of fortified settlements where such rulers lived and collected tribute from vassal tribes are known in the region west of the Dnepr River.

During the second century B.C., Parthians living south of the Steppes found a way to support horse breeding by introducing lucerne (alfalfa) as a green crop on fallowed fields. Their horses fed with alfalfa (supplemented with grain) grew larger than the stocky horses of the nomads, and were able to carry a heavily armoured man and horse armour. The Parthians could not sustain a large cavalry of this type, but what they had provided significantly improved protection of their border against nomadic incursions. By the first century B.C., the Chinese emperor (Han Dynasty) had learned about these large horses and had obtained a sufficient quantity to transform his cavalry and improve his ability to protect his empire.

As a result, the balance of power shifted, and steppe nomads began attacking to the west, leaving the sedentary empires to the south (modern Iran and China) in a comparatively peaceful state. By the second century B.C., the Scythians were dislodged from their dominance of the Western Steppes by a combination of Thracian and Celtic forces from the west and Sarmatians, nomadic tribes of Iranian origin, from the east. These nomadic invaders had heavy cavalry, equipped with protective armour and long swords.

While Scythian nomads dominated the Western Steppes, a group known as Huns, Turkish-speaking nomads of Mongolian origin, dominated the Eastern Steppes. The Huns cultivated some millet, but their main subsistence was based on pastoralism, supplemented by loot from regular attacks on sedentary Chinese settlements to the south. Eventually, the Huns formed a federation connected with the Han dynasty by intermarriage, and the two cultural regions entered a period of comparatively peaceful trade, which lasted from the first century B.C. to the second century A.D. During the third century A.D., the Huns were pushed west, out of their tribal territories, at first to the open steppes of Western Mongolia, then to the steppes of East Kazakhstan, and finally to the semi-deserts of the Aral Sea lowlands.

During the fourth century A.D., the Huns formed a powerful new union that swept even farther west into the Western Steppes. In less than 10 years (A.D. 370–376) they moved from the Aral Sea lowlands to the eastern borders of the Roman Empire. All along the path of their invasion, peoples were pushed out of their fields and pastures, settlements were destroyed and only the greatest state of the time, Byzantium, survived by paying large tributes. Some of the conquered tribes were incorporated into the horde; others fled or were killed. The Hun invasion produced what has been called the Great Resettlement of Peoples, ultimately shaping the modern ethnic geography of Europe. The invasion is also reflected by a radical change in archaeological cultures. No permanent settlements are known from this period. In contrast to previous periods, only solitary burials, rather than burial grounds, are found in the Steppes.

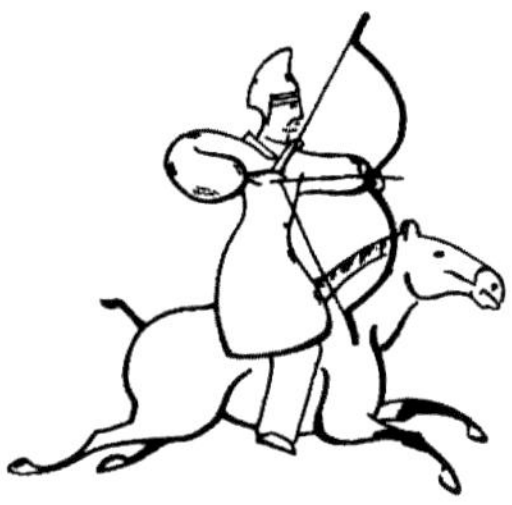

Hun warrior, 1st century A.D. (after Chinese chronicles)

The encounter with Hellenic states gave the Huns a taste for richly adorned outfits, including gilded and golden diadems and earrings looted from Rome and Iran. The Huns left numerous hoards, reflecting both the incredible wealth they had accumulated and the extreme instability of their political situation. By the seventh century A.D., nomadic society was led by an incredibly rich military elite. The Huns used a special bow with bone overlays and arrows that emitted a whizzing sound that horrified their enemies. They wore chain armour, helmets and shields and used short swords and daggers in close battle. They were the first nomads of Mongoloid origin to reach Europe, their very appearance contributing to their military success. An important part of the warrior's outfit was a heraldic belt with metal plaques symbolizing the warrior's bravery. Belts were usually custom-made by artisans following common styles. In A.D. 453, the leader of the Huns, Attila, died and his empire fell apart. Some Huns were assimilated by sedentary peoples of the Balkan Peninsula, but the majority retreated to the Black Sea lowlands.

A century later, nomads of the Altai formed a new confederation, a Turkish Kaganate (551–744 A.D.), which developed in close contact with Chinese civilization. Their nomadic lifestyle was supplemented by sedentary centres along the rivers Yenisei and Orkhon. Their towns hosted many crafts, such as weaving, leather working and woodworking (particularly noteworthy for carts). Here, iron was mined, bloomed, and forged into weapons, elements of horse harness and ceremonial dishes. There appears to have been some specialization in this society, with the formation of a richer guild of professional warriors and a poorer guild of shepherds. Part of the population even grew some millet.

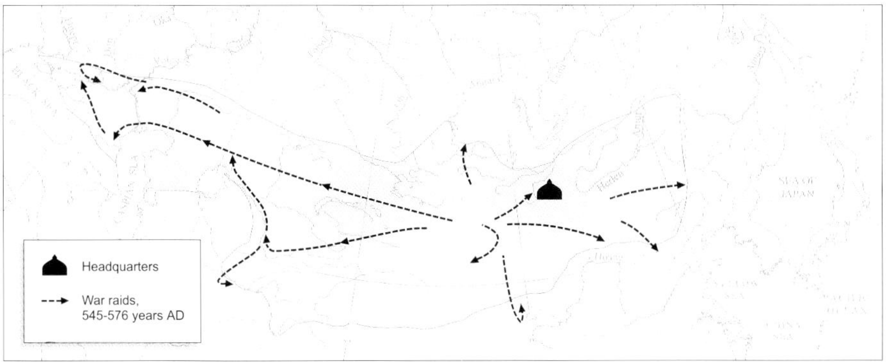


The Turks developed their own writing system, the so-called runic script, derived from the Aramaic alphabet. With this, they left chronicles of their deeds carved on rock faces in South Siberia. The Turkish Kaganate subjugated the peoples from the Yellow River to the Caspian Sea, including the northern part of China, and pushed a new array of tribes, such as Bulgars, Khazars, Magyars, Pechenegs and Polovetz, from the Caspian Sea lowlands into the open steppes. Their main weapon remained the bow and arrow, but the Turks were the first to use a rigid saddle with stirrups. This freed the rider's arms for shooting on the move. Turkic warriors wore helmets, mail-armour, and a leather belt with bronze or golden plaques.

During the seventh century A.D., the Turkish confederation fell apart and, on its ruins, two new nomadic states were formed. Khazars (a tribal union from the northern Transcaucasus) formed the Khazarian Kaganate with its capital on the lower Volga River. Bulgars formed a state in the lowlands of the Azov Sea, but soon were annexed by the Khazars. The Khazarian Kaganate established fortified towns at places strategic for trade and advantageous as wintering

**Above** Location of Turkic Kaganate, 588–630 A.D. (Oleksiy Vasilenko, Canadian Museum of Civilization)
**Below** Location of Khazarian Kaganate and Volga-Bulgaria, ca. 1,000 years ago (Oleksiy Vasilenko, Canadian Museum of Civilization)

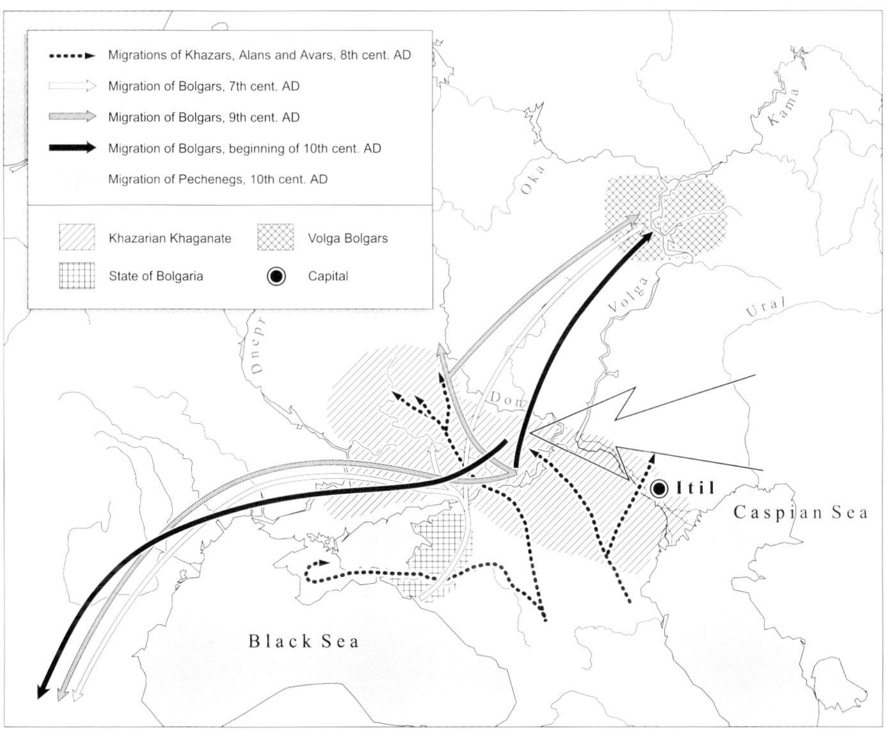

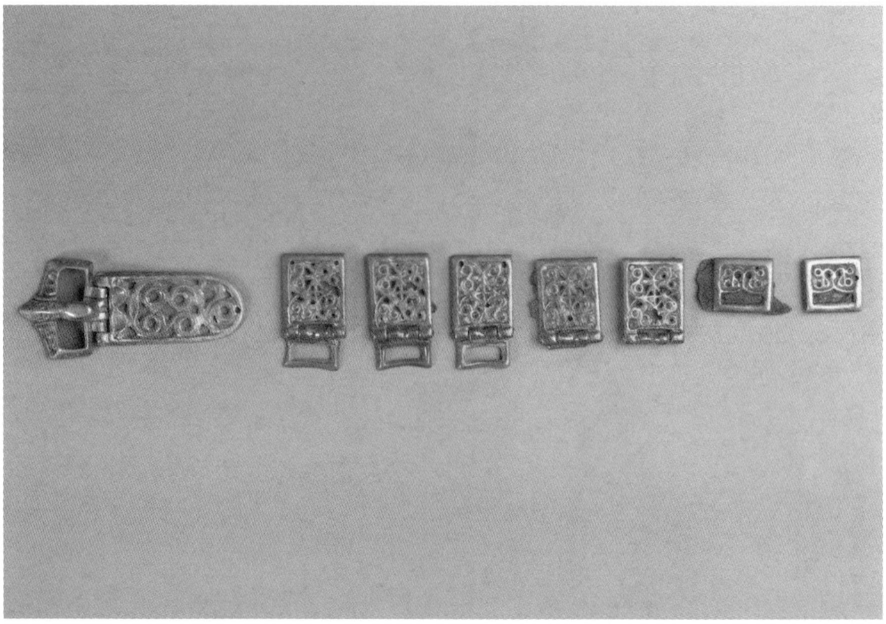

**Above** Elements of a belt, ca. 8th century A.D. (Early Middle Ages) (P. V. Alabin Museum of History and Regional Studies, Samara, KP-26045/8-16)
**Below** Male golden earrings, ca. 8th century A.D. (Early Middle Ages) (P. V. Alabin Museum of History and Regional Studies, Samara, KP-22976/34, 35)

grounds for people and herds. Several military inventions appeared during this period, such as sabres and backswords for use from horseback. Other new weaponry included clubs, jacks and throwing knives. The Khazarian Kagan accepted Judaism in the eighth century A.D. With the rise of Islam during the tenth century, the Kaganate was torn by religious discord and in A.D. 965 it was destroyed by Pechenegs under the command of the Russian Prince Svjatoslav.

About the same time, Volga Bulgaria accepted Islam as its state religion. After A.D. 965, Volga Bulgaria stopped paying tribute to the Khazars, and began expanding its domains in the mid-Volga River area, establishing fortified towns in the forest-steppe transition zone near large rivers such as the Volga, Kama, Zna, and Big Cheremshan. These towns thrived until being conquered and demolished by Genghis Khan in A.D. 1236.

Between the eighth and thirteenth centuries A.D., the Steppes were populated both by nomadic states and by other nomadic groups. In the Russian Chronicles, these other peoples were referred to as Pechenegs, Torks (Guzs), and Polovetzs. The Pechenegs formed mobile military parties, which pillaged and extorted tributes from sedentary populations. Muscovite Russia paid tributes to the Pechenegs until Prince Yaroslav was able to defeat them in A.D. 1036. After the defeat, some Pechenegs moved to the Byzantine state, while the rest remained in the Steppes serving as soldiers of fortune for Russia. During the eleventh century, the Polovetzs moved into the Steppes from the Azov Sea lowlands. Other tribes already inhabiting the Steppes joined the Polovetzs, forming a union called the Black Klobuks, which also served as vassals of Muscovite Russia until the Mongolian invasion of the thirteenth century.

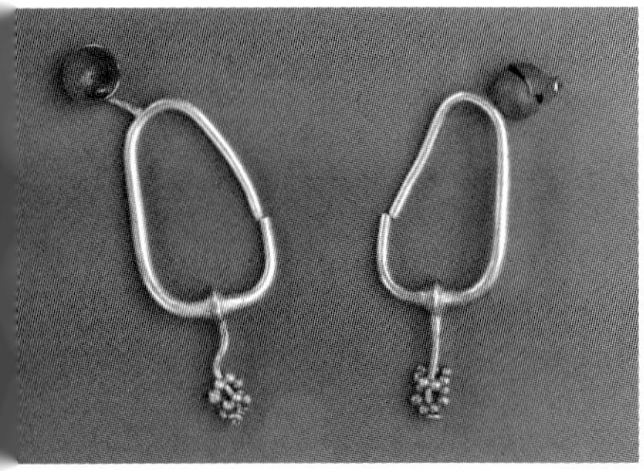

Changes in nomads' military equipment from the eighth to the thirteenth century reflected the needs and high status of an increasingly mobile cavalry. Stirrups became arch-shaped with a wider footrest (as wide as 7 centimetres by the thirteenth century). Darts became longer and more curved, approaching the form of a sabre. Bows had long, thin central overlays made of bone; by the thirteenth century, additional end-overlays further increased the shooting range. The Polovetzs used the same protective armour as Russian warriors of the period: chain mail or, less commonly, scale-armour and helmets made either of iron or of leather over an iron frame. Iron masks or visors are found in some nomadic burials. By the twelfth century, nomads' saddles had a high front pommel and a low rear pommel, both trimmed with bone overlays. Decoration was applied more lavishly to horse harness than to warriors' costumes: the overlays and buckles on the warriors' belts became less elaborate, and jewellery became less common and diverse than in previous periods. Common parts of the warrior's accoutrement were simple cooking utensils—a small bowl and kettle made of copper foil by the nomads themselves. In rich burials, large hammered copper caldrons with an iron holder are found.

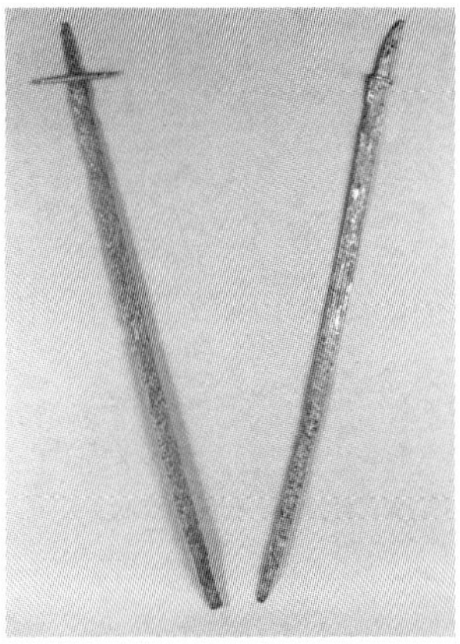

**Above** Iron sabres, ca. 8th century A.D. (Early Middle Ages) (P. V. Alabin Museum of History and Regional Studies, Samara, KP-22976/17)
**Below** Extent of Mongolian Empire, ca. 700 years ago (Oleksiy Vasilenko, Canadian Museum of Civilization)

At the eastern frontier of the Steppes, centralized power in China had declined after the collapse of the Tang dynasty in the tenth century A.D. That allowed autonomy for several nomadic peoples in the northern part of China, who formed states combining Chinese principles of bureaucratic management with a nomadic lifestyle. After several centuries of development, the most successful of these states was the one founded by the Mongolian nomad, Genghis Khan, at the beginning of the thirteenth century. Genghis Khan created a militarized nomadic society in which promotions were based solely on warrior skill, in contrast to the old system based on kinship. His army was divided into tens, hundreds, and thousands of warriors, each commanded by an appointed officer. The army was very inclusive: no limitations were put on faith and ethnicity. Even defeated enemies could be incorporated under Mongol commanders. As a result, Genghis Khan's army was capable of unlimited expansion. Moreover, it assumed a process of constant modernization, using the artisans obtained from conquered territories to make the best weapons of the time, and former enemy commanders to develop new military tactics.

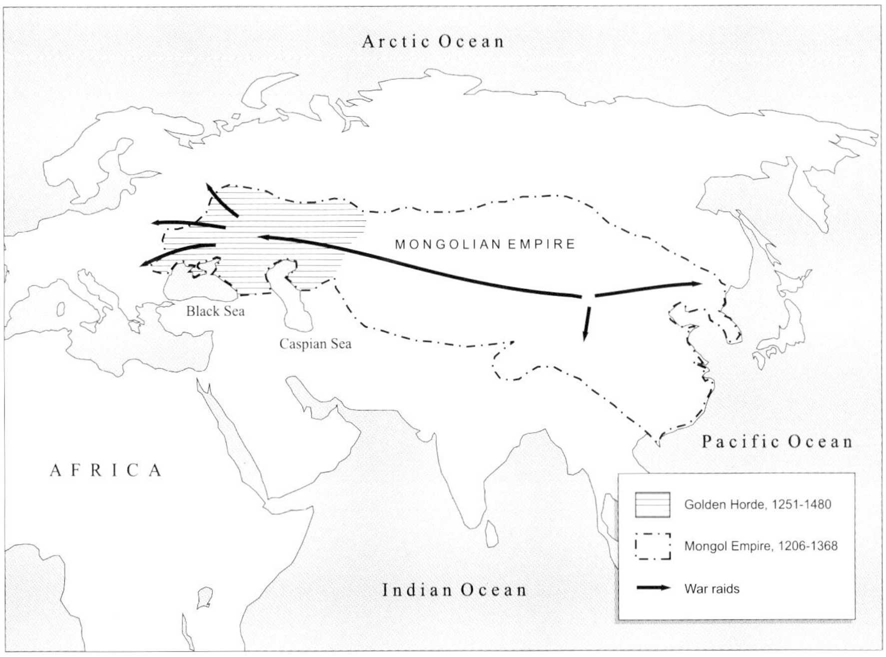

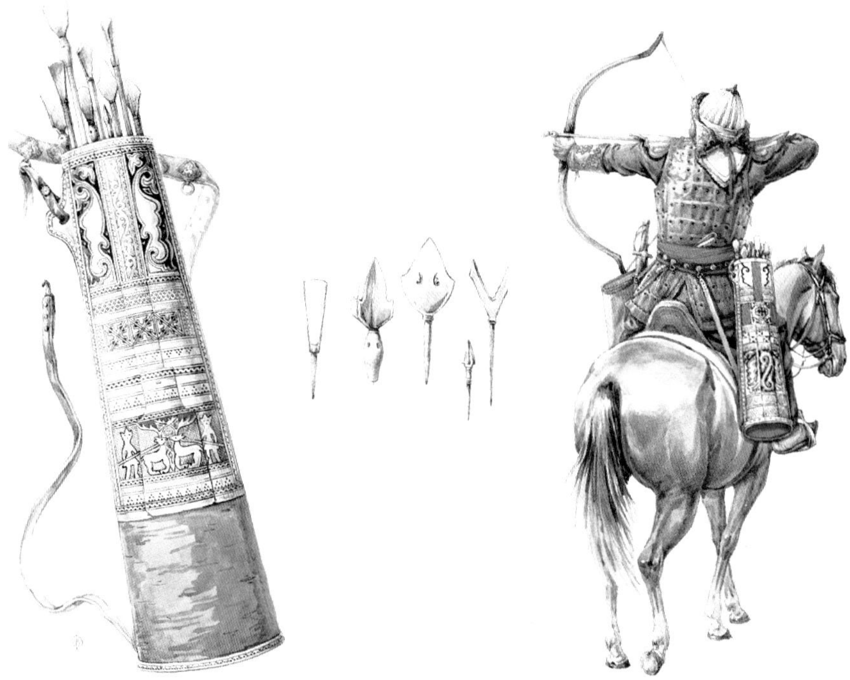

Outfit of a Golden Horde archer, 14th century A.D. (courtesy of Oleg Fedorov)

The Mongols used all known techniques of warfare. They mastered the siege, using catapults that could break walls. Their armies were the first to use gunpowder, invented by the Chinese, to blow up city gates during attacks on East European cities in 1241. Their cavalry was complemented by foot soldiers. The Mongols also used the Chinese crossbow. Because of their organization, hardware and tactics, Mongol military success was unparalleled in world history: territories from Manchuria to the Ukraine were united under a single nomadic empire in less than 50 years.

After the death of Genghis Khan in A.D. 1227, his empire was divided into four parts, governed by his immediate heirs. The modern territory of Russia, including the Steppes, went to his oldest son, Jochi, whose lineage became known as the Golden Horde. The Golden Horde established a network of regional headquarters along the Volga River with a capital at Sarai Batu. In 1345, Mongol soldiers returning from European raids brought bubonic plague, the Black Death, with them. The plague decimated the Steppes population. During the following decades, the region was afflicted with civil war, rulers replacing each other almost annually. In the late 1300s, a military leader from Samarkand, Timur Tamerlane, invaded the Steppes with an army of 100,000 men, defeated the Golden Horde and destroyed Sarai Batu and other towns on the lower Volga. By the mid-1400s, the territory had been divided into small Khanates.

Meanwhile, European countries of that time were maintaining regular armies with heavy cavalry, and developing techniques of gunfire not available to the nomads. By the 1400s, they were using cannons for defense of their own fortresses and for breeching the castle walls of their enemies. Invention of the blast furnace allowed production of lighter, cheaper cannons, as well as cast iron cannon balls. The technology advanced further and, by the 1600s, their field armies were using light portable cannons. By the mid-seventeenth century, European gunfire had become more effective than nomad bows; and by the beginning of the eighteenth century, guns had become the decisive weaponry.

During the 1550s, Muscovite Russia annexed the Kazan and Astrakhan Khanates on the Lower Volga, and began slowly but steadily to encroach upon the Steppes. By 1783, the last remnant of the Golden Horde, the Crimean Khanate, had been annexed by the Russian Empire, ending the long dominance of nomadic peoples.

## Steppe Nomad Trade

The trade systems of steppe nomads changed through time, depending on connections with their great neighbours, the sedentary civilizations to the south, east or west. As sedentary states rose and fell, the flow of goods to and from the Steppes was redirected toward one or another market. Along with goods, religious beliefs were absorbed and disseminated among the nomads, often increasing the demand for ceremonial objects from sedentary areas. At different times, Persia, Greece, Rome, Byzantium, the Caucasus and China each took the lead in trade with the nomads. Crafted metal objects, fine pottery, fabrics and jewellery, as well as cereal grains, were imported into the Steppes in exchange for livestock, wool and slaves.

From archaeological evidence, it is hard to distinguish between trade and pillage. Beginning at least 3,200 years ago, pillage seems to have been central to obtaining desired goods, especially cattle, from sedentary and nomadic neighbours. During periods of peace, however, goods could flow in both directions through trade or through the exchange of tribute and gifts between rulers of sedentary and nomadic unions.

The earliest evidence of exchange between pastoralist communities of the Steppes and artisans from sedentary areas coincides with the increasing demand for copper and bronze objects during the Early Bronze Age. The Bronze Age of Europe was a time of extensive trade, with copper ingots and tin travelling long distances in exchange for finished copper and bronze objects, slaves, cattle and incense. Throughout most of this period, high-status interments under burial mounds contained copper and bronze mortuary goods produced and obtained specifically for burial. The relative uniformity of burial ceremonialism, particularly in respect to mortuary goods, over vast areas from Western Europe to the Ural Mountains, implies the presence of a continental-scale trade network.

The eastern part of the Steppes was at the periphery of this exchange, several large metallurgical centres being established in the Transural region. Presumably, ore was traded at least partially to areas south of the mines, since local wood supplies would have been insufficient for the long-term maintenance of a metallurgical industry.

Clay amphora, 7th–8th century A.D. (Early Middle Ages) (P. V. Alabin Museum of History and Regional Studies, Samara, KP-25963/1)

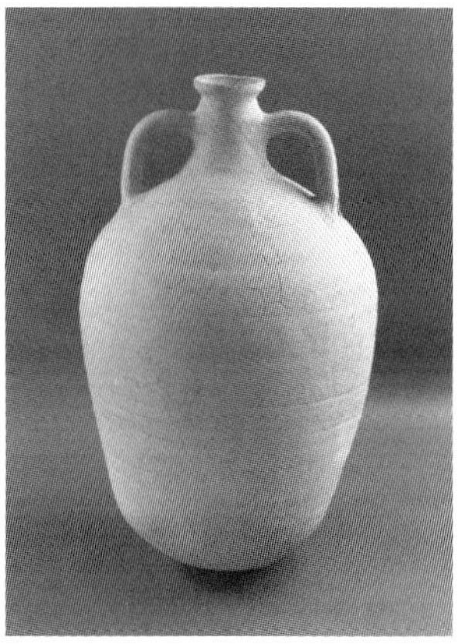

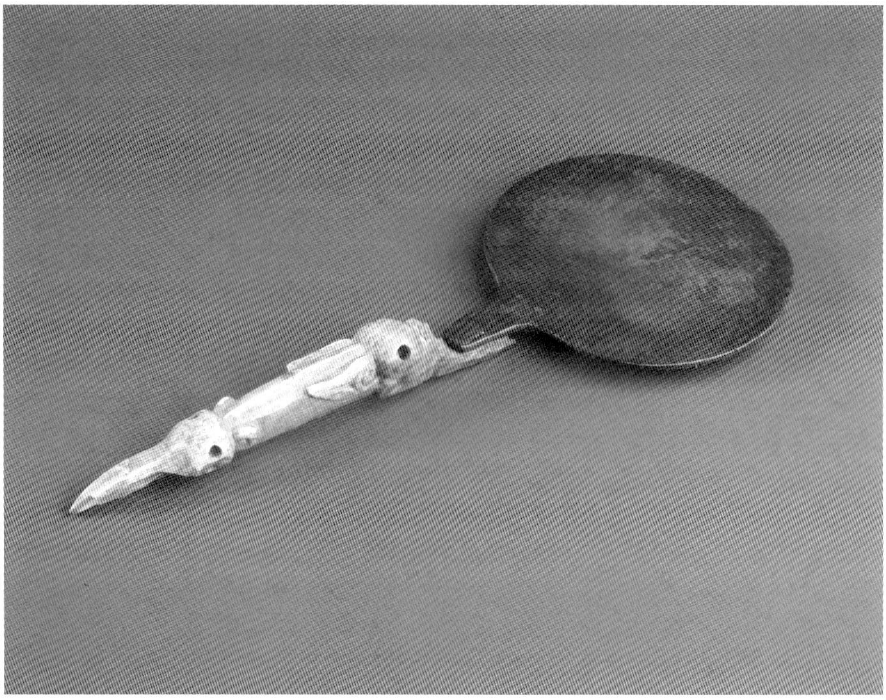

Bronze mirror, ca. 2,500 years old (Early Iron Age) (P. V. Alabin Museum of History and Regional Studies, Samara, KP-173/4, 5)

**Scythians and Sarmatians.** In Greece, the beginning of the Iron Age (3,200 years ago) was marked by growth in urban populations and decline in agricultural production. At this time, the Greeks began to establish colonies on the north shore of the Black Sea in order to trade with steppe populations. According to Greek historians of the first centuries B.C., trade with the Scythians involved wine, olive oil, fine pottery, metal weaponry, mirrors, bronze "Q-tips" and jewellery in exchange for steppe livestock, wool and slaves. The Scythians also established cereal production in the western-most part of the Steppes (modern Ukraine) and exported grain to Greece. The trade was based on barter. Even though Greek coins have been found in Scythian burials, they reflect the influence of Greek mythology—a small coin (*obolon*) being placed in the mouth of a corpse for Kharon, the ferryman, who rowed the souls of the dead across the River of Woe. On the eastern Steppes, the Sarmatians traded with Eastern and Near Eastern civilizations: Pazyryk burials contain Persian rugs and vases, silk and fine pottery from China.

**The Silk Road at the time of the Sarmatians.** About 330 B.C., Alexander the Great of Macedonia conquered the Iranian empire and opened opportunities for long-distance trade from the Mediterranean to the Transcaucasus. Greek coins were widely adopted as currency. Two centuries later (138–125 B.C.), the Chinese emperor sent exploratory expeditions to the west, which opened trade routes with Parthia. This trade was enlarged during the first century B.C. as a result of Roman campaigns against Parthia. In consequence, the Romans learned about Chinese silk and Parthia acted as a middleman in trading silk with the West. Continent-wide trade was established, stretching from China to Rome along routes known now as the Silk Road. Caravans carried gold and other precious metals, ivory, precious stones and glass to China and returned with ceramics, bronze and iron objects, jade and lacquered pottery.

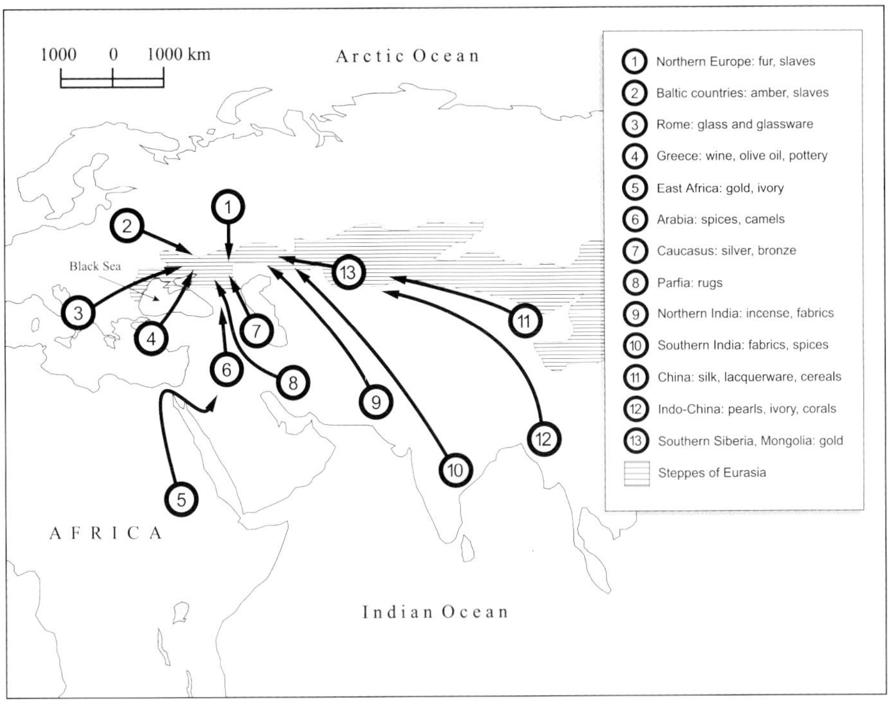


**Above** Trade connections of the steppe nomads from the 1st century B.C. to the 3rd century A.D. (Oleksiy Vasilenko, Canadian Museum of Civilization)

**Below** Crystal and carnelian bead necklace, ca. 2,000 years old (P. V. Alabin Museum of History and Regional Studies, Samara, KP-18548/23)

Until the first century B.C., Chinese emperors did not allow trade with nomads. Chinese borders were closed and goods could be obtained only by looting or as gifts or tribute. After an effective war against the Chinese, the Huns were able to force the Emperor to establish markets at the border where Chinese millet, rice vodka, wadding, and silk fabrics could be exchanged for nomads' livestock.

During the fifth and sixth centuries A.D., when the Huns invaded the western Steppes, no evidence for trade is found. Trade remained meagre in the following period as well, the time of the Turkish Kaganate (sixth–seventh centuries A.D.). Some jewellery made in the Bosporus Kingdom is recorded in steppe burials of this time, but it was likely there as a result of marriage or captivity.

**Khazar Kaganate.** Trade emerged again with the establishment of nomadic states during the seventh–ninth centuries. In the Khazar Kaganate, fortified towns hosted artisans while farmers produced grain on fields adjacent to the towns. During the ninth century their production even included grapes. In the Steppes, both artisans and farmers were actually forced labour drawn from sedentary states. In nomad towns, the aristocracy lived in "winter yurts" alongside the wood and daub dwellings or semi-subterranean dwellings of the poor. Khazars used Byzantine and Arabic coins in their trade.

**Volga-Bulgaria.** In the ninth and tenth centuries A.D., during the climatic episode called the Medieval Warm Period, when average temperatures were about 2° C higher than they are now, the population of Volga-Bulgaria turned to an even more sedentary lifestyle. Permanent fortified settlements were established along the middle stretches and tributaries of the Volga River. These towns were not much different from modern eastern towns, with Mosques and Turkish baths, houses made of wood, wood and daub or bricks, with a sophisticated under-floor system of heating, and sofas as part of the furniture. Subsistence was based on the cultivation of wheat, millet and barley, using diverse iron

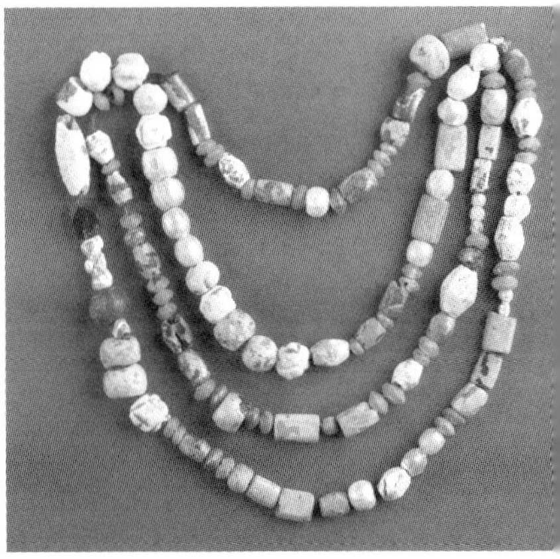

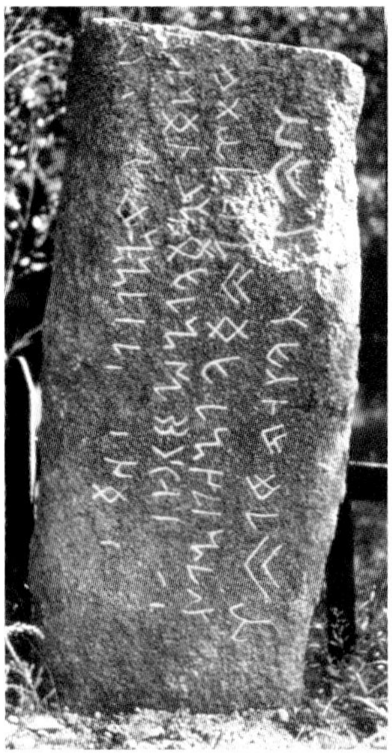

**Above** Runic scripts on a stone monolith, ca. 7th century A.D., Altai Republic, Russia (courtesy of Sergei Klyashtornyi)
**Below** Coin of Bosporian Tsar, Rescuporid V, 264–265 A.D. (top) and Golden Horde coins, 14th century A.D. (Middle Ages) (P. V. Alabin Museum of History and Regional Studies, Samara, KP- 9944/2, KP-26049/1, 2)

implements such as the ard, plow, spuds, scythes, and sickles. Pastoralism was no longer a significant element of most people's lives, but agriculture was supplemented by stockbreeding.

A wide spectrum of craftsmanship was practised in the towns, including blacksmithing and production of wheeled pottery. Craft products were traded to rural populations in adjacent areas. Towns functioned as trade centres as well. Glazed (lacquered) pottery from Central Asia and the Caucasus, Iranian ornamented faience, glass vessels and jewellery from Byzantium, amber from the Baltic Sea coast, and slate spindle whorls from Russia are common in archaeological sites of that time on the Steppes. While Europe was experiencing its dark ages, the towns of Volga-Bulgaria were thriving on trade with eastern and southern sedentary states. During the tenth century, Volga-Bulgaria minted its own silver coins (*dirkhems*), but in subsequent centuries they resorted to trade through barter or by the use of metal nuggets as currency.

**The Golden Horde.** Beside their mission of conquest, the Mongols were experienced traders and effective transmitters of inventions. They brought the compass, gunpowder, porcelain, silk and printing to Europe from China. Having conquered the Steppes, they developed their own trade network, establishing about 100 towns along the Volga River, and turning them into craft and trade centres. The centralized power of the Golden Horde provided protection for trade caravans. Their way stations along the Silk Road hosted wholesale markets, where travelling caravans rested, traded and obtained food and fresh animals. The khans of the Golden Horde minted their own silver and copper coins—about twenty of the steppe towns had mints. However, most of the steppe population maintained a migratory lifestyle: it was only impoverished nomads and the nomadic aristocracy that settled in towns. Some agricultural production was maintained by slaves on fields around the towns, but the majority of plant produce consumed by the Golden Horde came as paid tribute from conquered sedentary populations, such as the Russians, Crimean Greeks, Georgians and Armenians.

During the late 1300s, Timur Tamerlane looted all the major trade centres in the Steppes and deported all the best artisans to Samarkand (modern Uzbekistan). The region became dangerous and trade routes shifted south of the Caspian Sea. The Golden Horde's economy declined rapidly and, only a century later, no sign of urban life remained in the Steppes.

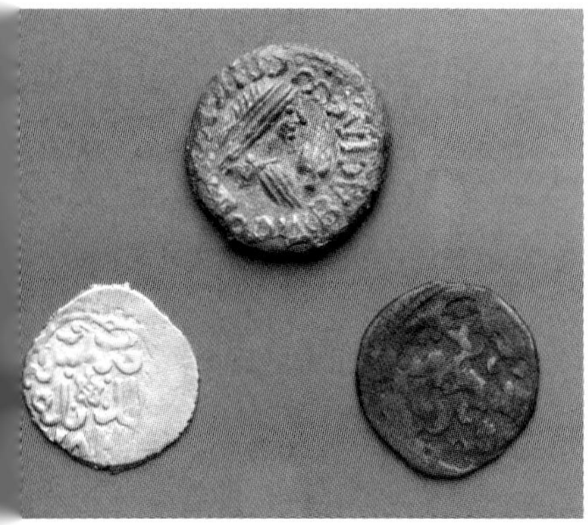

# PRAIRIE NOMAD WARFARE

Ancient prairie warfare is not well known, but some aspects of it can be glimpsed archaeologically through the types of weapons used, rock art showing warriors bearing shields, the remains of trenches and palisades built as fortifications around some sites, distinctive bone damage on some human remains and occasional evidence for large-scale massacres. The weaponry used by prairie nomads for warfare was basically the same as for hunting. Their arsenal consisted of stone-pointed projectiles, stone knives hafted in wood or bone handles, and stone clubs hafted in wood with leather bindings. For personal protection, warriors resorted to leather body armour and/or large leather shields.

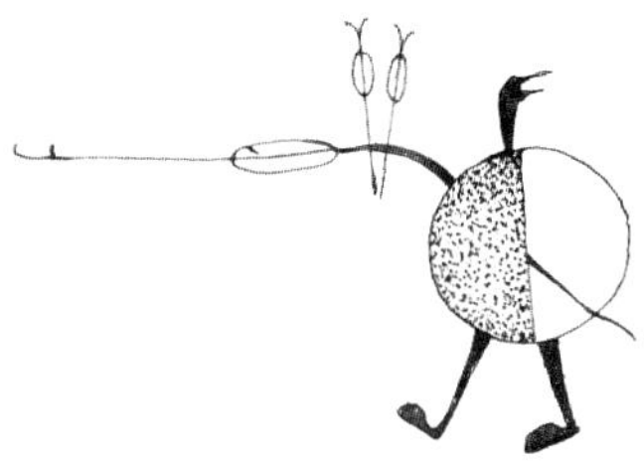

Stone projectile points are abundant in the archaeological record and indicate that projectiles were principal weapons throughout the nomadic era. From at least 5,000 years ago until about 1,600 years ago, stone-tipped darts propelled by hand-held throwing devices (*atlatls*) and, to a lesser extent, hand-thrown spears, were the principal types of weaponry. During the early part of this period, the Oxbow archaeological complex, apparently derived from a previous culture in the area, dominated the Northern Great Plains. Almost contemporaneously, the McKean archaeological complex spread into the Northern Plains, possibly from the Great Basin to the southwest. Westernmost examples of the McKean complex perpetuated the intensive use of wild plants common in the Great Basin, but as the complex spread northeastward into the prairies, it adapted to bison hunting.

About 3,000 years ago, the Pelican Lake complex replaced the Oxbow and McKean complexes and lasted until about 2,000 years ago. The Pelican Lake complex appears to represent an infusion of new people with different burial

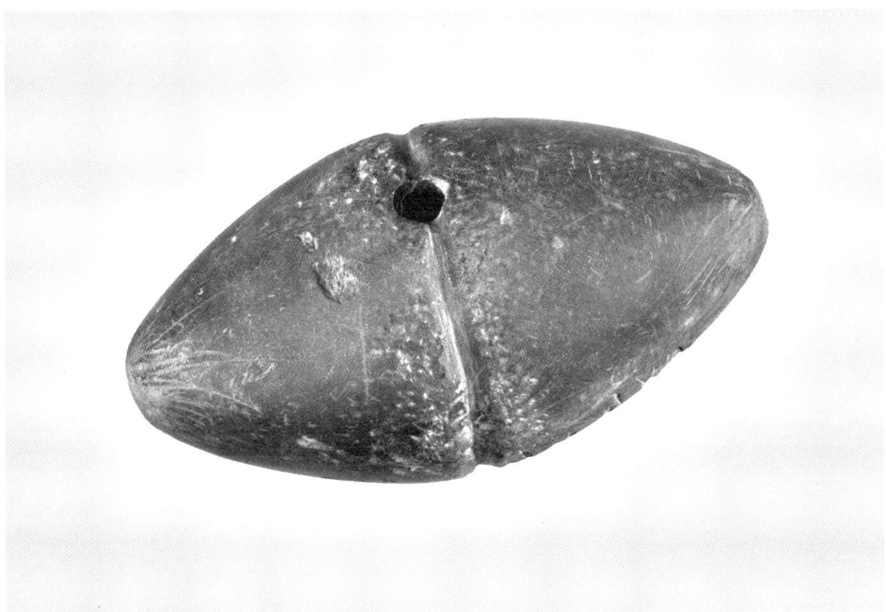

**Above** Shield-bearing warrior carrying an atlatl and darts, before 5th century A.D. (after Keyser and Klassen, *Plains Indian Rock Art*, 2001)
**Left** Stone club head (Canadian Museum of Civilization, X-B-116)

traits and projectile points, but their origin is unknown. During Pelican Lake times, bison hunting became almost an industrial activity as mass bison kill sites began to appear throughout the prairie region. Some archaeologists speculate that these hunters developed a market for bison products in the great Hopewellian chiefdoms to the southeast. Beginning perhaps 2,500 years ago, but certainly by 2,000 years ago, a group of people, recorded archaeologically as the Besant complex, entered the Northern Plains from the southeast. These people also focused on large-scale communal bison hunting and gradually became dominant in the area.

By the first centuries A.D., bow and arrow technology had been introduced to prairie peoples, having arrived in northwestern North America about 350 B.C. from the Eurasian Arctic. The first prairie people to make it their principal weapon were those of the Avonlea archaeological complex. It appears, however, that bows and arrows were not overwhelmingly superior to atlatls as military weapons since Avonlea peoples did not displace the Besant peoples, but co-existed with them during several centuries. By about A.D. 750–850, bow and arrow warfare was used by all prairie nomads and was accompanied by the use of protective shields and probably also body armour. Pedestrian warriors hiding behind large, body-sized shields are depicted in prehistoric rock art dating to this time.

Chipped stone spear point, ca. 3,000–2,000 years old (Canadian Museum of Civilization, X-B-4)

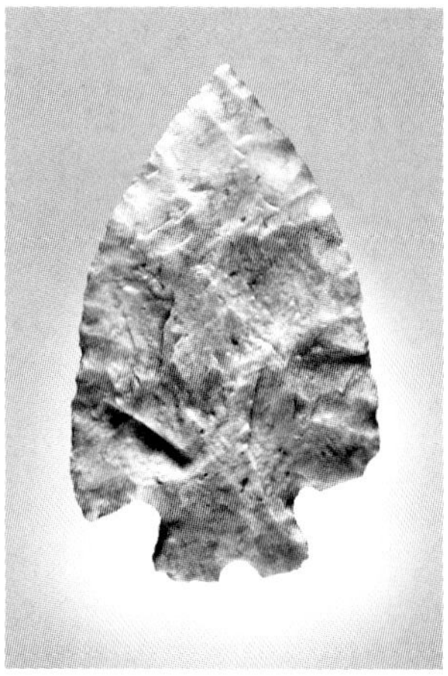

Prairie-wide adoption of bows and arrows coincided with, or slightly preceded, the encroachment of semi-sedentary horticultural villages from the eastern Woodlands into the eastern Prairies along the Mississippi and Missouri rivers. Strongly influenced by Mississippian chiefdoms to the south and east, these horticulturists pushed north to the limits of maize agriculture along the Missouri River. As the horticultural populations grew, they experienced hostility from other horticultural communities and from bison nomads whose lands they were occupying. Horticulturists built trenches and wooden palisades around their villages to protect themselves. Yet, even these defenses sometimes failed—as in the case of the Crow Creek site which dates to about A.D. 1325. At Crow Creek, at least 486 people, representing roughly 60% of the inhabitants, were massacred, mutilated, scalped and buried in the fortification trench surrounding the village. Young females, under-represented among the dead, were likely taken away among the captives.

In A.D. 1691, Henry Kelsey, travelling in the company of Cree and Assiniboine from Hudson Bay, was the first European to enter the Northern Great Plains. The region was rife with intertribal warfare and Kelsey had difficulty persuading his companions to enter enemy territory. His observations included the fact that warriors used a feathered bonnet during battle and carried a sacred pipe stem, indications of the importance they placed on war medicines.

Prairie warfare was enveloped in ceremonialism. Preliminaries to departure might include a combination of debate, ceremonial dances and ceremonial parades. Once on its way, the war party often established a special camp at the edge of their territory. This contained an unusual tipi built of poles and stout branches, which was surrounded with a wicker-like fence. Provisions for the return trip were stored in this tipi, which could also serve as a defensive retreat if the warriors were pursued by the enemy. At such camps, the first war songs were sung and special rules governing the relations among members of the warrior group came into effect. Subsequent camps inside enemy territory were

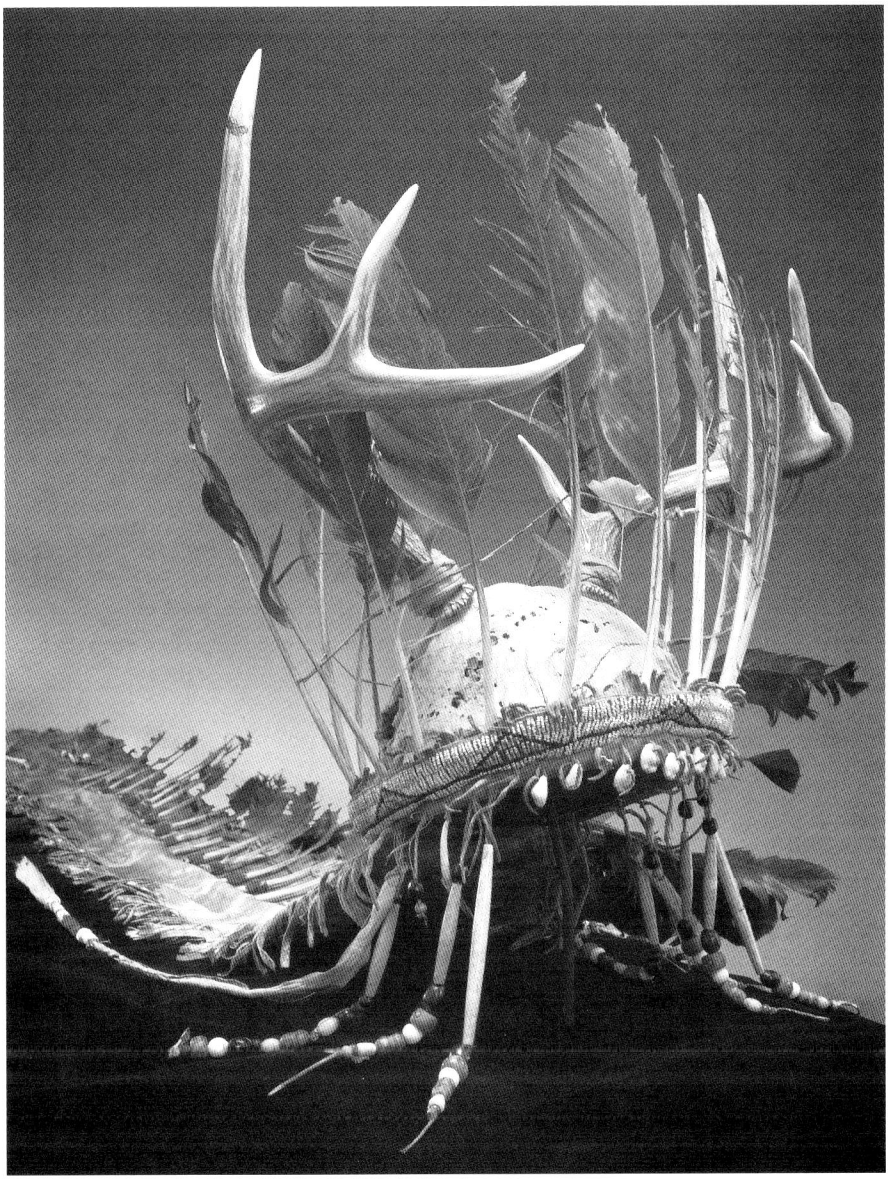

Man's war headdress used at the Battle of the Little Big Horn, ca. 150 years old (Canadian Museum of Civilization, V-E-257)

much less obtrusive, and in the last camps before reaching the enemy, the war party paused to seek spiritual guidance and assistance—war bundles were opened and consulted. Finally, in the last camp before the attack, weapons and amulets were put in order, war paint was applied and special paraphernalia, such as feathered bonnets, were donned.

War honours included not only the killing of enemies and the taking of trophies such as scalps, fingers and heads, but also acts of bravery such as simply touching an enemy ("counting coup") or taking his weapons and personal amulets. These war honours were confirmed by the warrior societies and commemorated by many different means. The warrior narrated stories of his successful war experiences, and depicted them in a pictographic form on his robe, shield and tipi cover. Only distinguished warriors could wear certain decorations, such as leggings with horizontal black stripes and fringes made of human hair (among Blackfoot), or a war bonnet adorned with the feathers of flesh-eating birds.

As later European explorers discovered, the prairie atmosphere was charged with concern about strangers. Warfare was wide-ranging and complex—motivated by revenge, competition for choice hunting grounds, capture of women or inanimate property, and the desire to win individual war honours. Armaments consisted of stone-headed war clubs, lances, knives, wooden bows up to 1.4 metres in length and stone tipped arrows. Warriors carried shields up to a metre in breadth and sometimes wore body armour consisting of several thicknesses of rawhide. Tactics varied from major standoffs to devastating ambushes. When two forces of approximately equal size met for battle, they arranged themselves in well-separated opposing lines and showered each other with arrows and insults. Darkness generally brought an end to the battle, few casualties having been suffered on either side. In ambushes, the intention was either to harass or to completely overwhelm the other side. One gains some idea of the high end of such hostilities from an ambush that took place in 1742 between a combined force of Assiniboines and Crees and a large hunting band of Prairie Sioux. During a four-day battle, the Assiniboines and Crees killed more than 70 Sioux warriors and took more than 200 captives. Most ambushes, however, involved small war parties and the killing of one or two unwary persons near the edge of an enemy camp.

Warfare was not limited to engagements between bands or individual tribes. Although autonomy was highly prized, in order to survive, people formed alliances with one or more neighbouring tribes against common enemies. At the time of earliest European contact (seventeenth–eighteenth centuries), Shoshonis were part of a Numic-speaking alliance that had pushed out of the Great Basin and Rocky Mountains and was dominating the northwestern Plains. At the same time, Crees and Assiniboines were in an alliance that controlled the northeastern periphery. Bloods, Blackfeet, Piegans, Sarcis and sometimes the Atsina were in a confederacy that held the west-central part of the Northern Prairies. Two horticultural tribes, the Mandans and Hidatsa, were allied with the nomadic Crows in defending a slice of territory centred on the Upper Missouri River Valley. Another horticultural tribe, the Arikaras, lived in the next section of the Missouri Valley to the south; they were sometimes opposed to the Mandan-Hidatsa-Crow confederacy, sometimes allied to them, and often at war with the Dakota. The fearsome Dakota alliance, including many Siouan-speaking tribes, occupied the southeastern portion of the Northern Prairies and gradually expanded into the centre. These alliances waged almost relentless war on one another. By the end of the buffalo era, the Dakota, Blackfoot and Cree-Assiniboine confederacies were in ascendance while the others were in severe decline.

Between about A.D. 1700 and 1770, the introduction of European horses and guns revolutionized warfare in the Northern Plains. Horses arrived from the south and were at first used to enhance hunting and transportation. For a short time, the use of armoured cavalry had a tremendous impact on warfare. Traditional pedestrian war parties were simply no match and fled before the mounted warriors. Fortunes were somewhat reversed, however, as guns arriving from the northeast gave the advantage to tribes in the northeastern Prairies. Leather armour provided no protection against musket balls. Yet, while supplies of guns and ammunition needed constant replacement from outside sources, supplies of horses could be more easily maintained by raiding, trading and self-replacement. Thus, horses became measures of wealth and prized objects of capture. While supplies of new weaponry remained uncertain, traditional weapons remained in use with modifications to suit the changed circumstances. Warriors abandoned body armour for themselves and their horses, and reduced the size of their shields to a little more than a half metre in diameter. Bows were shortened for more effective use from horseback and the composite bow, adopted from tribes west of the Rocky Mountains, gave arrows greater range and impact. Open lines of confrontation were forgotten as ambush became the primary tactic. Warfare remained endemic in the Prairies until the disappearance of the bison ended the nomadic lifestyle.

## PRAIRIE NOMAD TRADE

Evidence for trade during the Paleoindian period (13,000 to 8,000 years ago) consists chiefly of the long-distance exchange of high quality tool stone. For example, obsidian from the Yellowstone River and Knife River Flint from the Missouri River was being quarried and widely distributed as early as 10,000 years ago. During the long-term drought that affected the Plains from about 10,000 to 6,000 years ago (Paleoindian and Early Archaic periods), the evidence of trade and exchange is very sparse.

**3,000 B.C.– 300 B.C.** Evidence for trade emerges again about 6,000 years ago (Middle Archaic) following the great mid-Holocene drought. Knife River

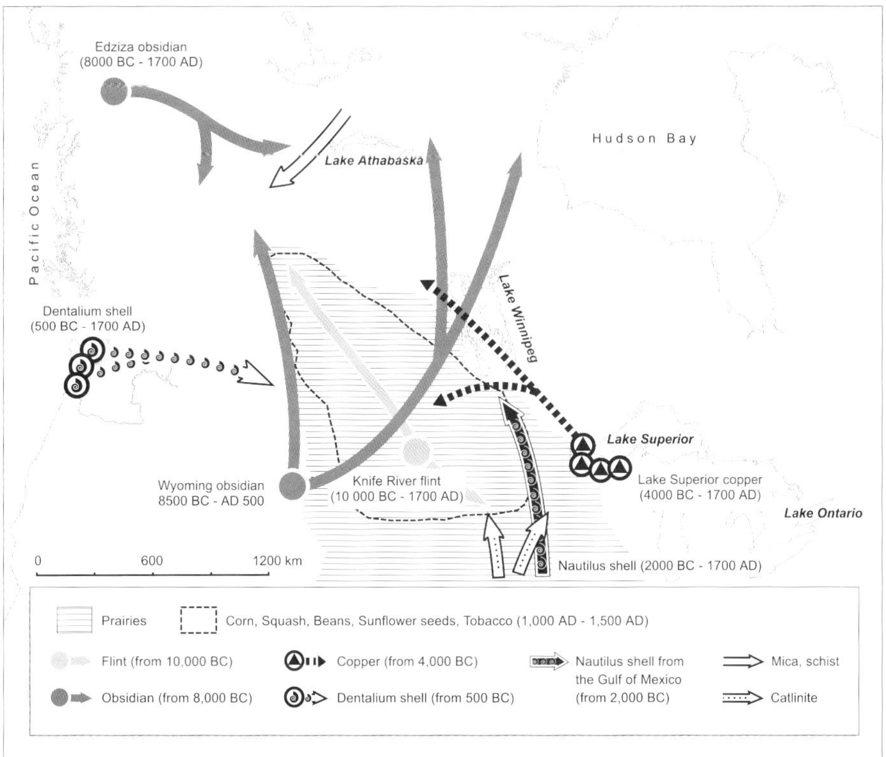


Trade connections of the prairie nomads from 8,000 years ago to the time of European contact (Oleksiy Vasilenko, Canadian Museum of Civilization)

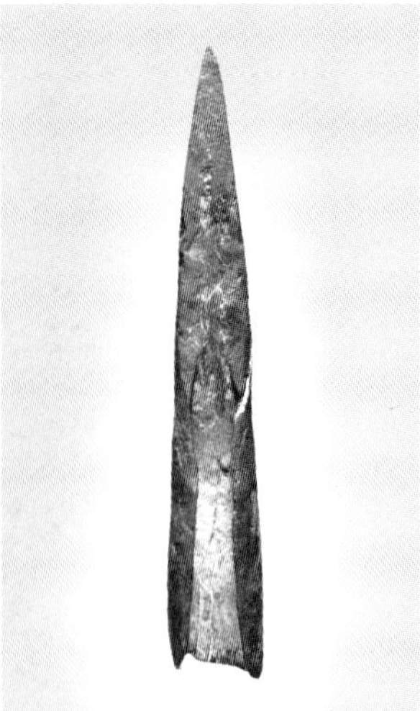

**Above** Socketed copper spear point, ca. 3,500 years old (Canadian Museum of Civilization, X-A-439)
**Below** Columella shell pendant, ca. 700–300 years old (Canadian Museum of Civilization X-A-356 ca)

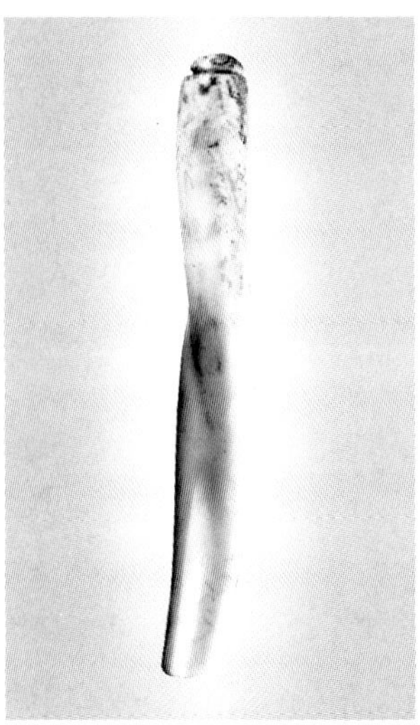

Flint procured at quarries in North Dakota has been recorded in sites of this period hundreds of kilometres north, south, east and west of the source area. Copper artifacts from the Great Lakes region, marine shells from the Pacific Coast and the Gulf of Mexico, and argillite and obsidian from British Columbia are other exotic materials found in prairie sites of these times. Materials acquired from the most distant regions are found mostly in mortuary complexes among burial goods, whereas materials from closer sources are often utilitarian objects found in everyday sites.

**300 B.C.– 850 A.D.** At the beginning of this period, the Hopewell culture came to prominence in the woodlands southeast of the Northern Prairies. Hopewellian people practiced a sedentary or semi-sedentary lifestyle: for part of the year, they lived in villages with permanent houses, surrounded by stockades. They experimented with horticulture, growing local domesticates such as sunflower, squash/gourds, marsh elder, goosefoot, maygrass, little barley, erect knotweed and, toward the end of this period, beans and maize. Their attempts at agricultural were complemented by hunting and gathering. The Hopewellian people were skilled artisans. They fired pottery and clay figurines of animals, produced cloth woven of local plant fibres, and worked copper into a variety of objects. The Hopewellian period is characterized by mortuary ceremonialism involving the construction of earthen burial mounds and by the establishment of a continental trade network (the Hopewellian Interaction Sphere) spanning the area from the Rockies to the Atlantic and Gulf Coasts.

In the Northern Prairies, the old trade networks, established long before the rise of the Hopewellian Interaction Sphere, were maintained during Hopewellian time. This continuity is reflected by imported materials which were the same as those imported during the previous period (copper, obsidian, seashells, Kootenai argillite, Montana cherts). However, as a result of distant Hopewellian influence, pottery first appeared along the eastern edge of the Northern Plains during this period. Burial mound construction and its accompanying mortuary ceremonialism were also adopted by Besant peoples on the eastern fringes of the Northern Prairies but did not become popular elsewhere on the Plains region. Some archaeologists suggest that bow and arrow technology entered the Northern Plains from the northeastern woodlands during these times. We can only speculate about what commodities were exported from the prairies, as most were probably perishables: pemmican, hides, and crafts made of hide. Knife River Flint continued to be used throughout the Northern Plains and was traded outside the Plains as well.

**A.D. 850–1700.** The archaeology of this period is complex. The eastern peripheries of the central and southern Plains were occupied by populous horticultural societies while the major river valleys of the central and northeastern Prairies contained scattered horticultural towns and villages and the balance of the northern and central Prairies was controlled by nomadic bison hunters. Nomads in the northwestern part of the Prairies (Old Women's culture) maintained strong trade connections with peoples in the Rocky Mountains (Montana and British Columbia), obtaining obsidian, Montana cherts, and Kootenai argillite and steatite (green pipestone) in return for prairie products. Nomads in the northeastern Prairies continued to trade with woodland peoples south and west of Lake Superior, obtaining copper objects and horticultural produce such as wild rice.

About A.D. 1050, as part of a florescence throughout eastern North America, a group of horticultural chiefdoms, known by archaeologists as Mississippians, surged up the Mississippi River to the outlet of the Missouri River, only a few hundred kilometres east of the central Plains. There, they established the first city in North America at a place called Cahokia (opposite present-day St. Louis). Although Mississippians built other large regional sites in the Eastern Woodlands (presumably each the centre of a chiefdom), Cahokia was the grandest of their large ceremonial/administrative sites. It covered about 13 square kilometres and was part of three monumental precincts in close proximity to one another. Cahokia contained 120 truncated earthen pyramids, which were associated with numerous large public plazas. Most people lived in rectangular thatched-roof houses either within the city or in outlying horticultural hamlets; the rulers appear to have resided toward the centre of the complex on top of the pyramidal mounds. Cahokia, itself, contained 10,000 to 15,000 people, but the local administrative complex, of which it was part, is estimated to have sustained a population of 40,000 to 50,000.

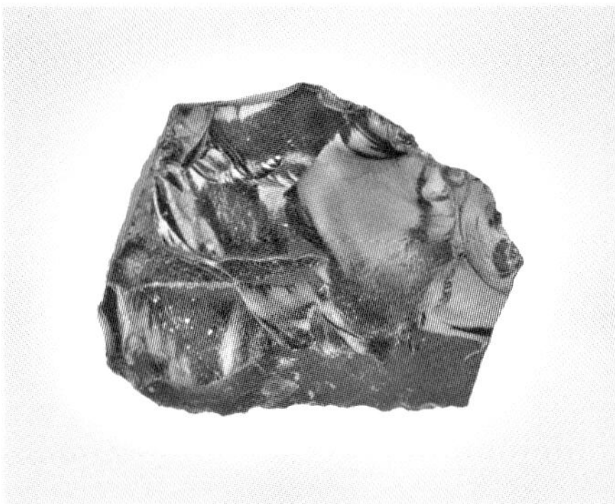

**Above** Obsidian traded from the Rocky Mountains (Canadian Museum of Civilization, X-C-1)
**Below** Dried maize, beans and squash—important trade goods in the Northern Prairies (Canadian Museum of Civilization)

Mississippian people farmed maize, beans and squash in fields around the city. Craft specialists made fine shell-tempered pottery, exquisite chipped stone tools and distinctive ornamental objects. They carved human statues out of calcareous rocks for mortuary/commemorative purposes, sculpted clay effigies, and made clothing from fabrics of woven plant fibres. Mississippian influence was far-reaching and appears to have touched the nomads of the northeastern Prairies, who imitated some aspects of their mortuary ceremonialism in what has been called the Devil's Lake-Sourisford Burial Complex. In Eastern North Dakota and adjacent areas of Saskatchewan and Manitoba, objects such as whelk shells, dentalium and columella shell beads, Illinois cherts, and tubular pipes of red pipestone indicate Mississippian influence. It is unlikely, however, that northern Prairies nomads traded directly with Cahokia. Rather, the exchange of goods and ideas was probably achieved indirectly through intermediate peoples. By A.D. 1150 Cahokia began to collapse and by 1200, it was abandoned.

While Mississippian cultures were occupying the Mississippi Valley and its major woodland tributaries, pre-existing horticultural societies that had already

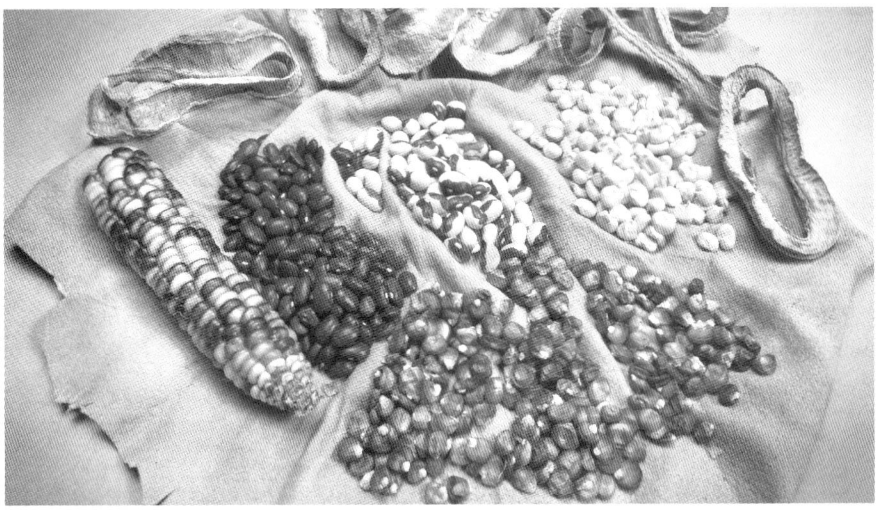

begun to spread into the central Plains turned their attention northward. Between about A.D. 900–1000, peoples of the Middle Missouri Tradition introduced a distinctive new mixed economy of horticulture and bison hunting into the river floodplains of the northeastern Plains. Taking advantage of the warm climatic episode (the "Medieval warming" from A.D. 850–1250) and possibly pushed by expanding horticultural populations on the western peripheries of the woodlands, Middle Missouri peoples moved northwest up the Missouri River trench to the northern limits of native agriculture (about $48^{o}$ north latitude). Living in semi-permanent fortified villages situated on high terraces overlooking the river floodplain, these people grew cultigens such as sunflowers, marsh elder, goosefoot and tobacco, and eventually corn, beans and squash. They also hunted bison in the surrounding countryside. Middle Missouri villagers developed an extensive trade network with surrounding prairie nomads, trading corn and exotic luxury goods such as Great Lakes copper, Gulf and Atlantic coast shells such as whelk, marginellas and olivella in return, presumably, for bison products such as dried meat and hides, plant products such as dried prairie turnip, and exotic shells and stone tools obtained by the nomads from more westerly peoples. With the beginning of the Little Ice Age about A.D. 1300, the area occupied by Middle Missouri villages was reduced first to two regions in present North and South Dakota and finally to one region in North Dakota. However, the villages retained their importance as trade centres for prairie nomads into the historic period.

**After A.D. 1700.** Historical descriptions dating to the 1700s and 1800s enlarge our picture of trade between nomads and villagers in the Northern Prairies. For this era, we know the names of the village tribes—Mandan, Hidatsa and Arikara—and of the nomadic tribes who traded with them and with each other—Assiniboine (Nakota), Sioux (Dakota, Lakota), Cheyenne, Cree, Atsina, Blackfeet, Arapaho, Crow, Comanche, Plains Ojibwa and others. Trade might take place within villages or at unoccupied locations between tribes, and at any season of the year, although it was most common during spring, summer and fall. It might occur between groups or individuals—many people had special friends in other tribes with whom they would trade.

Exchanges included foodstuffs, medicinal plants, raw materials, manufactured products, exotic goods, horses (introduced during the 1700s), slaves, ceremonies, and craft knowledge. Many kinds and great volumes of food were traded—maize, beans, squash and sunflower seeds produced by the villagers; dried meat, fat, berries, and prairie-turnip flour produced by the nomads. In addition to food, many kinds of medicinal plants were exchanged; some nomadic tribes, for example, were dependent on villagers for the tobacco that they used in ceremonies. Raw materials included different kinds of wood for tipi poles and bows, stone for tool and pipe making, feathers for decoration and so forth. Manufactured goods were also important including large amounts of clothing—plain and decorated bison robes, dressed skins, shirts, leggings, headbands, moccasins, etc.—and personal ornaments such as shell and turquoise beads and otter skins for dressing braids. Transactions also involved the transfer of ceremonial property ranging from songs and dances to personal ceremonial items to medicine shields and war bonnets. Sale of craft knowledge, such as pottery making and flint working, also occurred in trade fairs, which may account for the uniformity of such products over wide areas of the northern Prairies. Slaves were commodities of exchange during the early historic period, probably an enlargement on traditional captive taking.

Among the means of communication associated with trade were calumet ceremonialism and sign language. The calumet ceremony, featuring tobacco smoking with a large wooden-stemmed pipe, symbolized agreement for peaceful association among the participants. This convention was universally recognized in the North American grasslands and did much to reduce hostility among tribes during formal meetings. A sign language, which presumably grew out of the inter-tribal trade system, was known and used by every group in the grasslands.

Trade was by barter. No monetary exchange existed in North America prior to the arrival of Europeans. According to early descriptions, one common unit of value in the prairie trade was a robe: one good bison robe was generally worth one abalone shell or ten dentalium shells. Another measure was the volume of a common burden basket (about one bushel). For the Arikara and their customers, one basket of shelled corn was worth one robe or two packs of dried meat.

After A.D. 1700, the arrival of European goods in the Northern Prairies, particularly the horse and the gun, had a huge influence on prairie societies, but the details of those developments are beyond the scope of the present study.

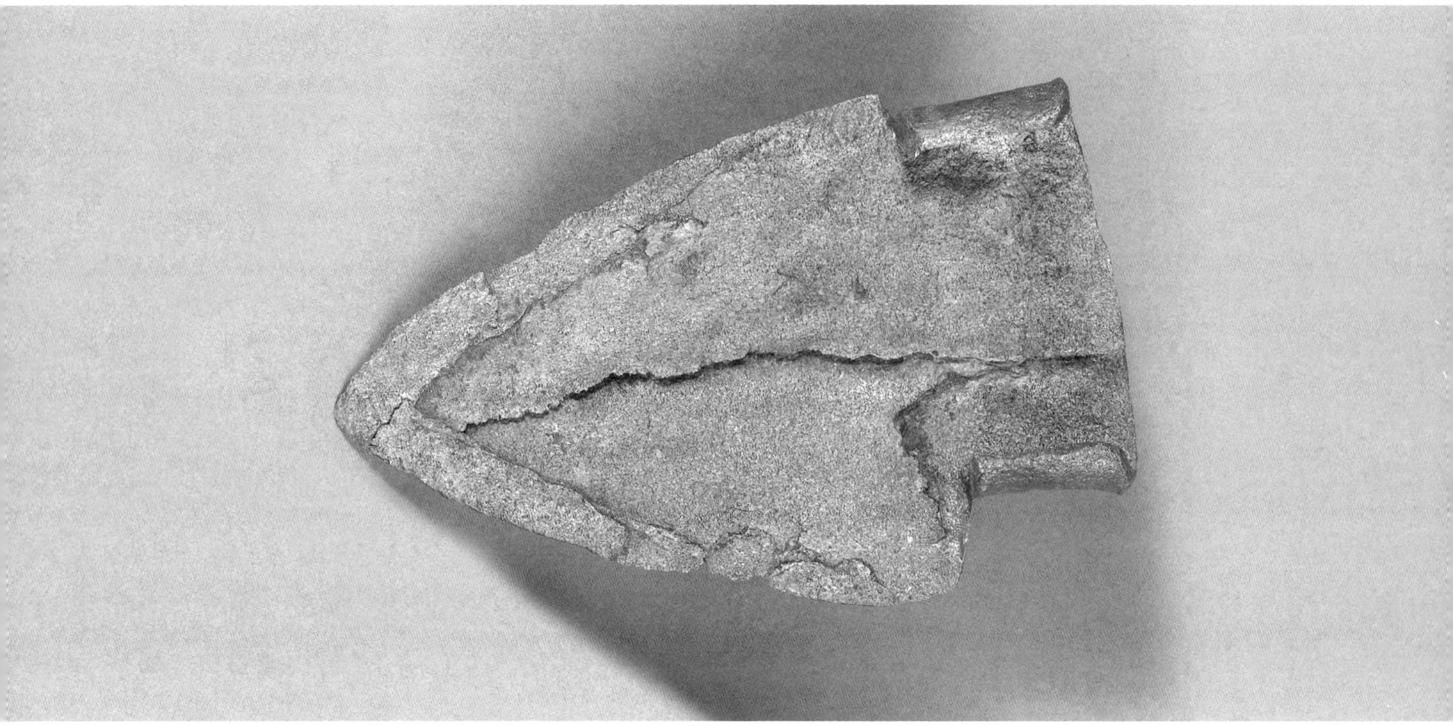

**Above** Plough blade, 14th century A.D. (P. V. Alabin Museum of History and Regional Studies, Samara, KP-18454/1616)
**Below** Bison vertebra with embedded lead musket ball, 19th century A.D., reflects the rapid demise of the wild bison herds (Canadian Museum of Civilization X-B-16)

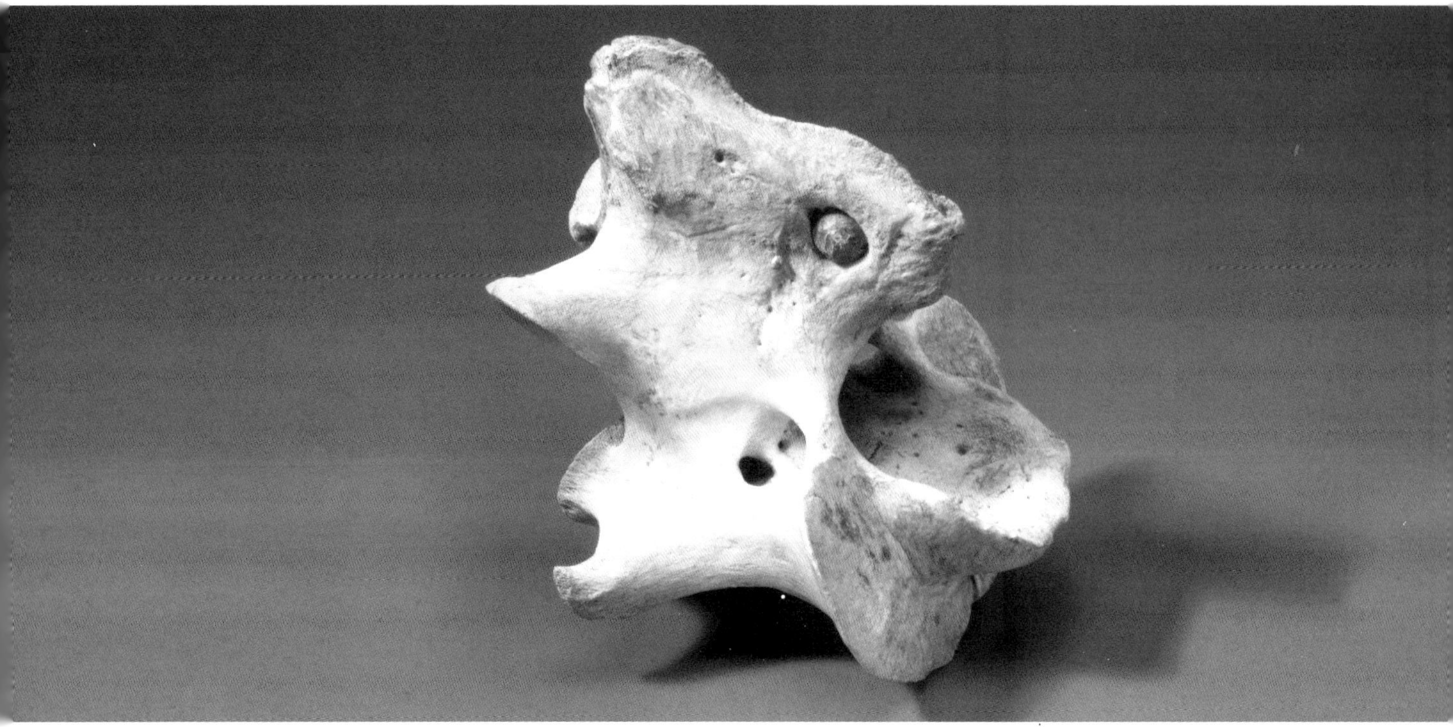

# CONCLUSION

About 5,000 years ago, the Eurasian Steppes and the North American Prairies assumed approximately their historic forms. About the same time, the peoples of these regions, who had been through a number of adjustments since the end of the last ice age, adopted lifestyles that they were able to sustain until modern times.

These lifestyles were two distinct forms of nomadism—one in the Steppes based on the management of domestic grass-eating animals, the other in the Prairies based on the hunting of wild grass-eating bison. Major prerequisites for these lifestyles were the availability of suitable herd animals, the development of portable dwellings, beasts of burden capable of transporting essential goods, and technologies for food preservation. In both areas, these prerequisites appeared about 5,000 years ago.

Between natural extinctions at the end of the Ice Age, a post-glacial drought that lasted thousands of years, and over-hunting, the European Steppes, with long-established populations of human hunters and gatherers, were gradually deprived of most big game animals. By 5,000 years ago, that gap had been filled by the importation of domestic herd animals such as sheep, goats and cattle from sedentary societies of the Near East. Gradually, instead of growing or bringing food to the animals, steppe peoples began to move their animals to ever more distant pastures, the composition of their herds being attuned to the nature of available grasses. Experiments led to the development of new beasts of burden that were much more effective in an arid environment (oxen and later, horses), as well as new food preserves (various cheeses), and new materials for making portable dwellings (felt).

The Prairies experienced similar post-glacial extinctions of large game and prolonged post-glacial drought, but the recently arrived peoples who occupied the newly exposed landscape never became so populous as to denude the area of its remaining large game. Human populations remained low and dependent on the hunting of wild animals, particularly bison. Had that failed, they did not have access to large domestic animals in any neighbouring societies. They continued to rely on an essentially Palaeolithic tool kit of stone, bone and wooden tools, and lived in circular hide and wood-pole dwellings that could be transported by their dogs. When the Prairies became more hospitable about 5,000 years ago, human populations slowly began to rise as the old hunting technologies were perfected and adapted for use on a new, more migratory and gregarious form of bison. The invention of meat/grease preservation techniques provided highly nutritious food reserves for periods of scarcity. Yet, prairie cultures never became so populous as to threaten the bison populations, which, prior to the 1800s, grew to be the most numerous of the planet's ungulates.

A crucial resource in both regions was grass. Steppe nomads guided their herds to the best available pastures; prairie nomads followed the bison in their search for better grass. Thus, people migrated for much of the year, either guiding or following the seasonal migrations of ungulates. Migrations in the two grasslands presented different challenges and opportunities. During the last glaciation, the Prairies were covered with ice while the Steppes were south of the continental glaciers. As a result, the Prairies are richer in surface water, workable stone and wood, and berry plants. The Steppes, buried during the glacial period with wind-blown loess, have little workable stone and little surface water, except in deeply incised river valleys and gullies. The Steppes are also considerably less forested than the prairies, except along the edges of major rivers. Such differences allowed for much more freedom in choosing migration routes on the Prairies than on the Steppes. It also made the prairie populations less dependant on imported materials for tool making.

The number and diversity of objects used in both nomadic societies was kept to the minimum needed to satisfy bodily and spiritual needs. Moreover, the nomadic technologies themselves were minimalist in terms of materials and time spent or needed for the fabrication of certain products. Crafted objects whose manufacture required specialized knowledge or materials were traded from sedentary neighbours. The most striking difference between the two regions was in the use of metal. In the Prairies, metal was used mainly for sacred objects, metal itself being a sacred material. In the Steppes, after a stage of sacral use, metal was used for a wide range of objects, but first of all for weapons. The use of metal made the greatest difference in warfare, allowing steppe nomads to develop new forms of weaponry. The every-day objects created with metal tools in the Steppes were amazingly similar to those made using stone tools in the Prairies. Metal tools (axes, knives, chisels) reduced the amount of time, energy and skill required for the production of the basic components of the nomadic household, but the functionality of the products did not differ drastically—compare, for example, the tipi and the yurt.

Steppe nomads were much more involved in trade and large-scale warfare with their sedentary neighbours (and with the great civilizations living to the south) than were prairie nomads. Domestication of the horse gave steppe nomads a huge advantage over sedentary peoples, making robbery and extortion a practical profession. Thousands of nomad-riders served as soldiers of fortune for temporary allies. In trade, nomads could offer mainly food to their partners—meat and meat products in the Prairies, livestock in the Steppes. Overall, the distance, speed, and mass of goods transported was greater in the Steppes. In the Prairies, transportation was limited by the carrying capacity of dogs, the absence of large draft animals making development of wheeled transport impossible.

Population size in the Prairies was constrained by the uncertainty of the food supply. Even though people, at times, experienced enormous plenty, which they shared and preserved for later use or trade, at other times they starved. Starvation was unfortunately a fairly frequent fact of life on the Prairies, because people could not adequately control, keep up with or predict the movements of their principal prey, the bison. Regular periods of starvation are particularly hard on the old, the ill and the young, keeping populations vigorous but small. Although steppe nomads also experienced periods of privation, their food supply, being always at hand, was considerably more reliable. As a result, the nomads of the Steppes were able to sustain an overall population at least ten times larger than that of the Prairies, which partly accounts for their periodic development of empires. Centralized power, however, always remained ephemeral.

Although they were peerless in their mobile lifestyles, the nomads were no match for later European empires. Europeans brought their powerful organizations, tools and appetites to the Steppes and Prairies during the 1700s and 1800s. The nomads, and the ancient grasslands themselves, were gradually humbled by the five-fold threat of disease, firearms, immigration, the plough and formidable administration. The impact of agriculture alone was massive. In less than 200 years, distinctive habitats that had thrived for thousands of years were changed beyond recognition. More than 98% of the native grasslands on the Prairies and the Steppes were destroyed and replaced with cultivated cereals such as wheat. Where newcomers and governments claimed the land, nomads could no longer fight. After 4,700 years of dominance, they finally succumbed to a new way of life.

# Selected References

**Binnema, Theodore**
2001 *Common and Contested Ground: A Human and Environmental History of the Northwestern Plains.* University of Oklahoma Press, Norman.

**Blakeslee, Donald J.**
1975 "The Plains Interband Trade System: An Ethnohistoric and Archaeological Investigation." Unpublished Ph.D. dissertation, The University of Wisconsin-Milwaukee.

**Boyle, Katie, Colin Renfrew and Marsha Levine (eds.)**
2002 *Ancient Interactions: East and West in Eurasia.* McDonald Institute for Archaeological Research, Cambridge.

**Davis-Kimball, Jeannine, Eileen M. Murphy, Ludmila Koryakova and Leonid T. Yablonsky (eds.)**
2000 *Kurgans, Ritual Sites, and Settlements: Eurasian Bronze and Iron Age.* BAR International Series 890, Archeopress, Oxford.

**DeMallie, Raymond J. (ed.)**
2001 *Handbook of North American Indians, Volume 13, Plains.* Smithsonian Institution, Washington.

**Ewers, John C.**
1968 "The Indian Trade of the Upper Missouri before Lewis and Clark." In *Indian Life on the Upper Missouri*, pp. 14–33. University of Oklahoma Press, Norman.
1997 "Intertribal Warfare as the Precursor of Indian-White Warfare on the Northern Great Plains." In *Plains Indian History and Culture: Essays on Continuity and Change*, by J.C. Ewers, pp. 166–179. University of Oklahoma Press, Norman and London.

**Geist, Valerius**
1996 *Buffalo Nation: History and Legend of the North American Bison.* Fifth House Press, Saskatoon, and Voyageur Press, Stillwater.

**Hall, Robert L.**
1997 *An Archaeology of the Soul: North American Indian Belief and Ritual.* University of Illinois Press, Urbana.

**Khazanov, A. M.**

1984 *Nomads and the Outside World*. Translated by Julia Crookenden with a foreword by Ernest Gellner. Cambridge University Press, Cambridge and New York.

**Laubin, R.**

1977 *The Indian Tipi: Its History, Construction, and Use*. University of Oklahoma Press, Norman.

**Levine, Marsha, Yuri Rassamakin, Aleksandr Kislenko and Natalia Tatarintseva**

1999 *Late Prehistoric Exploitation of the Eurasian Steppe*. MacDonald Institute for Archaeological Research, Cambridge.

**Levine, Marsha, Colin Renfrew and Katie Boyle (eds.)**

2003 *Prehistoric Steppe Adaptation and the Horse*. MacDonald Institute for Archaeological Research, Cambridge.

**Martin, Susan R.**

1999 *Wonderful Power: The Story of Ancient Copper Working in the Lake Superior Basin*. Wayne University Press, Detroit.

**McHugh, Tom, with the assistance of Victoria Hobson**

1972 *The Time of the Buffalo*. Alfred A. Knopf, New York.

**Milner, George R.**

2005 *The Moundbuilders: Ancient Peoples of Eastern North America*. Thames & Hudson, London.

**Pletneva, S. (ed.)**

1981 "Steppes of Eurasia in the Middle Ages." A volume in the series on the *Archaeology of the USSR*. Nauka, Moscow (in Russian).

**Secoy, Frank Raymond**

1953 *Changing Military Patterns on the Great Plains (17th Century through Early 19th Century)*. J.J. Augustin Publisher, Locust Valley, New York.

**Vehik, Susan C., and Timothy G. Baugh**

1994 "Prehistoric Plains Trade." In *Prehistoric Exchange Systems in North America*, ed. by T. G. Baugh and J. E. Ericson, pp. 249–274. Plenum Press, New York and London.

**Winham, R. Peter, and F. A. Calabrese**

1998 "The Middle Missouri Tradition." In *Archaeology of the Great Plains*, ed. by W. R. Wood, pp. 269–307. University Press of Kansas, Lawrence.

**Wright, J. V.**

1999 *A History of the Native People of Canada, Volume II (1,000 B.C. – A.D. 500)*. Canadian Museum of Civilization Mercury Series, Archaeological Survey of Canada Paper 152, Hull (now Gatineau).

# Acknowledgements

The Canadian Museum of Civilization (CMC) funded research and writing by Elena Ponomarenko and Ian Dyck, plus book design and preparations for publication in three languages. The Samara Museum of History and Regional Studies (SMHRS) funded contributions by Anna Kochkina, Dmitry Stashenkov and Ludmila Kuznetsova, and translation of the Russian version by Tatiana Istomina; while the printing costs were funded by the Samara Regional Government. At the CMC, David Morrison, Stephen Inglis, Diane Lalande and Sylvie Ledoux provided administrative assistance; Deborah Brownrigg, Rachel Locatelli, Ginette L. Côté, Victoria Barkoff and Mike Teixeira were instrumental in preparations for printing and book design; Marie-Louise Deruaz, Harry Foster, Chris Uhlig, Steven Darby and Ann Rae were involved in the photography of prairie artifacts; Oleksiy Vasilenko drafted the maps; Roger Marois translated the French version; Dominique Fortier edited the French version; and Sam Morgulis, Brigitte Lafond and other librarians helped with needed reference material. At the SMHRS, Pavel Vorob'ev was responsible for photography of steppe artifacts, Larisa Nikolaeva drew a number of the illustrations and Ilya Smeljanski assisted in selecting and providing other illustrations. We are sincerely grateful for the assistance of these individuals and institutions. In addition, the senior authors express appreciation to their spouses, Serguei Ponomarenko and Sherry Dyck, for unwavering family reinforcement throughout the project.

# The Authors

**Elena Ponomarenko** (Ph.D., Moscow University, 1987) is a consulting soil scientist, Ottawa, Canada and co-director of the Ancient Nomads project, Canadian Museum of Civilization, Gatineau, Canada.

**Ian Dyck** (Ph.D., University of Alberta, 1976) is Curator of Plains Archaeology and co-director of the Ancient Nomads project, Canadian Museum of Civilization, Gatineau, Canada.

**Anna Kochkina** (M.Sc., Kazan State University, 1977) is Senior Archaeologist at the Samara Museum of History and Regional Studies, Samara, Russia and a collaborator in the Ancient Nomads project.

**Ludmila Kuznetsova** (Ph.D., Leningrad Branch of the Institute of Archaeology of the USSR Academy of Science, 1985) is Director of the Samara Museum of History and Regional Studies, Samara, Russia and a collaborator in the Ancient Nomads project.

**Dmitry Stashenkov** (Ph.D., Institute of History of the Tatarstan Academy of Science, 2007) is Assistant Director of the Samara Museum of History and Regional Studies, Samara, Russia and a collaborator in the Ancient Nomads project.

**Mikhael Turetzky** (Ph.D., Institute of Archaeology of the Russian Academy of Science, 1992) is Senior Archaeologist at the archaeological laboratory of the Samara Pedagogical Institute, Samara, Russia.

**Edward Dubman** (Doctor of History, Saratov State University, 2000) is Professor at the Department of Russian History of Samara State University, Samara, Russia.

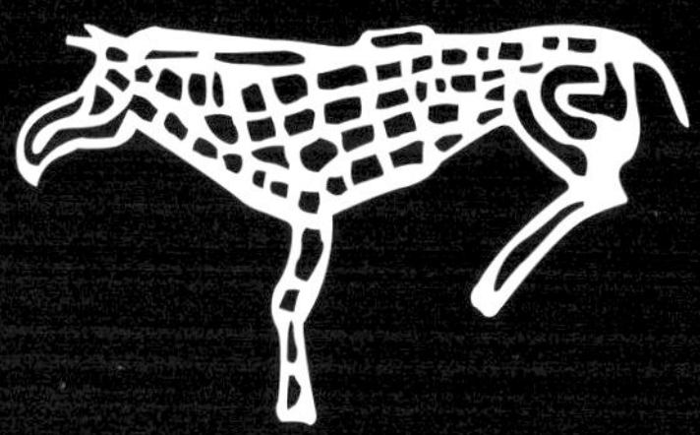

**Iconic horse pictograph**

*Numerous horse pictographs made in the Eastern Steppes (Boyarskaya Pisanitza, Khakassia) between approximately 2700 and 2100 years ago reflected the increasing importance of horse in the life of the steppes nomads following the invention of horseback riding (after Devlet, Rock Engravings in the Middle Enisey Basin, 1976).*

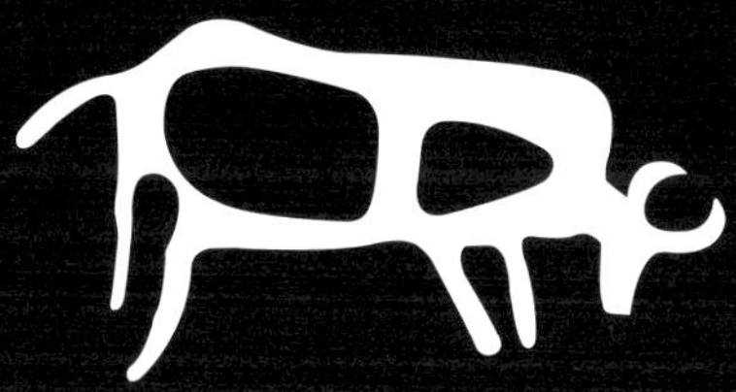

**Iconic bison pictograph**

*Bison pictograph made in the Northwestern Plains Hoofprint style–believed to reflect ideas about fertility and fecundity, and to date between approximately 3000 and 300 years ago (after Keyser and Klassen, Plains Indian Rock Art, 2001, p.177)*

**Co-published by the**
Canadian Museum of Civilization Corporation (CMCC)
100 Laurier Street, Gatineau, Quebec K1A 0M8
**And**
Samara Museum of History and Regional Studies (SMHRS)
443041 Russia, Samara, ul. Leninskaja, 142

Acting Manager, Publishing: Rosemary Nugent
Coordinator, Publishing: Rachel Locatelli
English Editor: Victoria Barkoff
Graphic Design: Teixeira Design
Printer: Ofort (Samara)

**Library and Archives Canada Cataloguing in Publication**
Ponomarenko, Elena, 1959-
Ancient nomads of the Eurasian and North American Grasslands/
Elena Ponomarenko and Ian Dyck; with contributions by Anna Kochkina, Ludmila Kuznetsova, Dmitry Stashenkov, Mikhael Turetzky and Edward Dubman.

"This book is a companion piece for an exhibition entitled "Masters of the Plains: Ancient Nomads of Russia and Canada." Both book and exhibition are products of a comparative project, undertaken by the Canadian Museum of Civilization (Canada) and the Samara Museum of History and Regional Studies (Russia)"— Introd. Issued also in French under title: Les anciens nomades des steppes de l'Eurasie et des plaines de l'Amérique du Nord. Issued also in Russian under title: Drevnie kochevniki stepeĭ Evrazii i Severnoĭ Ameriki.

**ISBN 978-0-660-19771-5   CAT. NO.: NM24-19/2007E**

1. Nomads—Eurasia—Social life and customs—Exhibitions.
2. Nomads—Prairie Provinces—Social life and customs—Exhibitions.
3. Grassland people—Eurasia—Social life and customs—Exhibitions.
4. Grassland people—Prairie Provinces—Social life and customs—Exhibitions.
5. Indians of North America—Prairie Provinces—Antiquities—Exhibitions.
6. Russia—Antiquities—Exhibitions.
7. Prairie Provinces—Antiquities—Exhibitions. I. Dyck, Ian G. II. Kochkina, Anna III. Canadian Museum of Civilization IV. Title.

**DJK37.P66 2007   305.9'069180947   C2007-980239-7**